LONDON 2012

HOW WAS IT FOR US?

For Vera Caslavska, Mexico 1968 Gymnast Gold Medalist. A proud Czech defying with her artistic agility the Soviet Tanks at that moment crushing the Prague Spring. My first sighting of resistance as the true spirit of sport. An inspiration then, now and for ever.

LONDON 2012

HOW WAS IT FOR US?

Mark Perryman (editor)

London Lawrence & Wishart 2013

Lawrence and Wishart Limited
99a Wallis Road
London
E9 5LN

Cover: Liz Millner
Typesetting: Etype
Printed by ImprintDigital, Devon

ISBN 9781 907103797

British Library Cataloguing in Publication Data.
A catalogue record for this book is available from the British Library

CONTENTS

Acknowledgements

This book would of course have been impossible without the glorious summer of sport that London 2012 became. It was the Games that provided me with the impetus to expand my critical sporting horizon beyond the sphere of football and national identity that has been the main focus of my thinking, writing and activism since 1996.

Many thanks to Becky Gardiner and Philip Olterman at *Comment is Free*, Luke McGee at *Huffington Post*, Jamie McKay at Open Democracy, Greg Needham at the *Morning Star*, Louise Potter at *Red Pepper*, Andy Newman at *Socialist Unity*, David Renton at *LivesRunning* and Conrad Landin at *Left Futures* for providing me with the space during the Olympics to develop my critique in articles as the events took place. Since London 2012 the new Left Unity website has become another space for me to write about the politics of sport – thanks to Kate Hudson for that opportunity – as has the *Inside Left* blog, so thanks to Gareth Edwards too.

BBC local radio was a regular outlet for my views throughout London 2012. Thanks in particular to BBC Sussex, BBC Northampton, BBC Derby, BBC West Midlands, BBC Cumbria, BBC Merseyside, and not forgetting BBC Radio 5.

James Graham organised an excellent roundtable for the journal *Soundings* to review the Games and was kind enough to invite me to take part. The University of Brighton, where I am a Research Fellow in Sport and Leisure Culture, continues to provide an intellectually stimulating and supportive environment for my writing. Both the Third Year sports journalism students and the Hastings campus sociology lunch group provided invaluable feedback, and occasionally laughed in the right places too. The same goes for sports journalism students at the London College of Communications, University of the Arts London, who were sufficiently interested in what I had to say about London 2012 to convince me there was a collection to edit.

On the night of the Opening Ceremony the company I co-founded with Hugh Tisdale, Philosophy Football, organised an alternative event at East London's Rich Mix Arts Centre. Again this was a useful stimulus towards the decision to put this collection together. For their varied contributions many thanks to Martyn Routledge, Paul Sinha, David Goldblatt, Alan Tomlinson, Martin Polley, Jude Bloomfield, Bob Gilbert, David Renton, Rod Laver, Mel Gomes, Isy Suttie, Tricity Vogue, Sharon Sukhram and Owen Tudor.

Sally Davison at Lawrence & Wishart didn't take too much persuading to publish the collection. Always a joy and a pleasure to work with, a publisher that appreciates that the point is to change it. Colin Robinson at OR Books persuaded me I was a fit and proper author to write about London 2012 and published my *Why The Olympics Aren't Good For Us And How They Can Be*, to which this book is a kind of sequel.

Assembling a collection of this sort is a bit like managing Team GB. I needed a variety of viewpoints, backgrounds, areas of expertise and styles of writing, and when writers dropped out a pair of impact substitutes as well. Thanks to all the contributors for agreeing to write and being such a nice bunch to edit.

One of my oldest friends Paul Jonson was kind enough to read my essay for the collection. He described it as 'spiky and contemporary'. I blame him entirely if other readers fail to agree.

A key argument of this book is that all sport is socially constructed. So it is only right that I acknowledge the ways in which my own sports have framed my writing. My daily eight mile running route to Mount Caburn and back is rounded off by a Sunday morning sixteen-mile long run via Kingston near Lewes along the South Downs Way to Beddingham Hill before heading home to Lewes through Glynde. Neither route ever fails to inspire my thinking about sport. The swimming pool at Waves Leisure Centre adds an aquatic dimension, the community-owned Lewes FC a spectating perspective, and taking my son Edgar to Little Kickers for his football training provokes thoughts on children's coaching. Thanks to you all.

None of this would have been possible without the Games themselves of course. I spent four unforgettable days there with my partner Anne and Edgar – and filling my head with ideas to turn into a book at no time stopped me from enjoying myself immensely. This was the experience that left me wondering how was it for us.

INTRODUCTION

Fifty years ago CLR James wrote *Beyond a Boundary* – probably the best book ever written about any sport, not just cricket. On the first page he asks 'what do they know of cricket, who only cricket know?' This maxim guides much of the thinking behind this book – 'what do they know of the Olympics, who only the Olympics know?' Or, if you prefer – 'politics can't be kept out of sport because sport is political' – just as it is indivisible from economics and culture.

London's bid to host the 2012 Olympic and Paralympic Games was a bipartisan affair, however. All the main party leaders backed it, and in London successive mayors – Ken and Boris, who disagreed on just about everything else – each accepted that the Games would be a great thing for their city. The sporting establishment also united behind the bid, and the cheerleading involved most of the mainstream media, especially the BBC, which eventually became 'the Olympic broadcaster'. All of this meant that there was very little serious discussion about the principal non-sporting claims of the worth of hosting the Olympics – whether back in 2005, during the years of preparation, during the Games themselves or afterwards. But this discussion matters – not in order to decry the very obvious joy that London 2012 ignited in so many of us, but so that we can interrogate the surrounding rhetoric and politics of the Games, particularly its claim to be a tool of economic regeneration and a means of increasing physical participation. The Olympics matter precisely because of the huge claims made – by the IOC, the London Games organisers and all the politicians – about its ability to make a difference way beyond the spectacular action in pool, velodrome and track.

Most of us revelled in that Super Saturday of Jess, Mo and – not least – Greg. Wiggo in the time trial. Laura, Victoria and Chris heading up Team GB's absolute dominance of track cycling. Nicola making history in the boxing ring. Katherine winning Gold at last in the rowing. The Brownlee twins battling it out for Triathlon

Gold. Jade punching and kicking her way to Taekwondo glory. The victorious elegance of our Dressage riders. Andy becoming the darling of the Centre Court at last. Louis doing so well on the pommel horse (before, just in time for Christmas, going one better in *Strictly*). The WeirWolf, Jonnie, Sarah and Ellie helping to make the Paralympics a sporting mega-event. And that's just Team GB.

As always with the Olympics, it was the spread of human excellence from sport to sport, contributed to by nation after nation, that helped make 2012 so memorable. Usain on the track. Marianne on her bike. Michael and Missy in the pool. Hope Solo keeping goal for Team USA. The interest and the excitement was hardly affected by our national loyalties. Maybe Team GB victories tasted that much better for many of us in Britain, but that was not, for the most part, at the expense of enjoying what the Olympics should be about – the fastest, highest and strongest of the best that sport can offer, whatever the team colours worn.

* * *

The contributors to this book do not by and large argue that the summer of sport was in any way a disappointment in sporting terms. Instead they ask a series of important questions about the Games and offer some initial answers. Could the Games have been even better? Will we see any significant impact in terms of regeneration and participation? What remains of the Olympic effect one year on? How will we feel about what we've experienced by the time the Rio Games open in 2016?

This book isn't a manifesto based on a single point of view. Contributors vary in their degree of enthusiasm for the Games; they have differing opinions, make points that sometimes overlap – and more than occasionally contradict – each other. For most of us our own experience of London 2012 wasn't unitary: there were bits we liked and bits we didn't. The contributors also write in a variety of styles, drawing on a range of backgrounds and experiences. But what they all agree on is that the Olympic Games mattered.

Some have contributed pieces originally written during the Games, giving a sense of the instant impact of 2012 on their emotions, their feelings about GB and their expectations of what sport can mean. Singer-songwriter Billy Bragg, journalists Suzanne Moore and Yasmin

Alibhai-Brown and comedian Mark Steel provide these Olympic snapshots.

Alan Tomlinson opens the first section with a historical overview of claims made about mega sporting events and their legacies, discussing how the Olympics manages to enchant so many. Eliane Glaser then looks at the empty rhetoric of much of the discourse around London 2012; while Kate Hughes adds an essential philosophical dimension, unpicking the mythology that surrounds Olympism.

In the second section contributors discuss whether the Games delivered on its promise. Andrew Simms explores the precise nature of the Olympic feel-good factor, weighing up what the Games did right and wrong, and offering an analysis of what sport can do to help create a more contented and happier Britain. Ben Carrington connects 2012's summer of sport to the previous August's inner city riots, some of which were less than a javelin's throw away from the Olympic Park. What kind of nation did Team GB represent? How does the popularity of a multicultural Team GB engage with more racist versions of the popular? Is the idea of a sporting internationalism incompatible with the frantic flag-waving so many of us found ourselves indulging in? And, in an attempt to look back from the future, Gavin Poynter writes a Rio 2016 postcard, speculating on what change will have been made in the East End's housing, employment, social services and life chances by the time of the eve of the next Games.

The third section focuses on sport itself. Zoe Williams remembers Wiggins's time-trial win and wonders what it might mean for us ordinary cyclists. David Renton places Mo Farah's incredible gold medal double in the context of the state of British middle and long-distance running. P. David Howe offers a powerfully argued critique of Paralympic sport, documenting the inequalities between Paralympians that are scarcely commented upon by a media that is often eager to praise but not to engage critically.

One core claim of London 2012 was that it would increase participation. The final group of articles discusses whether the event lived up to the official Games slogan to 'Inspire a Generation'. Barbara Bell discusses participation targets and the reasons for the widespread failure reach them. Gareth Edwards suggests that one reason for this failure is neglect of the idea of play – of any recognition that this is part of the essence of most recreational sport. Anne Coddington looks at our consumption of sport, comparing what it means to be an Olympic enthusiast with the experience of football fans.

And the park where we watched all this sport? Environmentalist Bob Gilbert provides a London 2013 snapshot – an assessment of what was lost when the Olympic facilities concreted over what was once there, and the habitat that will remain long after the Games are over.

THE GOOD, THE BAD AND THE ORBIT

Mark Perryman

I was not alive in 1966. The last 17 days are comfortably the greatest achievements of British sport in my lifetime. I have screamed, roared, wept, jumped up and down, punched the air with joy, and I have loved every moment. I know many people who have refused to engage with these Games for their own reasons. That is of course their own choice. But instead of feeling smug, they should perhaps reflect on the fact that they have sleepwalked their way through the most astonishingly dramatic sport this nation has ever known.

Paul Sinha, 12 August 2012[1]

The London 2012 Olympics and Paralympics were absolutely impossible to ignore. Love them or loathe them, there is precious little that can compare with them. Even the 1966 World Cup cannot compete – for those of us that can still remember it – for that took place during an era when colour TV was still a faraway technological dream for most, and even a black and white set was more than some could afford; while its global reach was frankly parochial compared to that of the London Olympics.

It is likely that a fair few of us will never again experience another sporting event on the scale of London 2012. Even for teenagers and twenty-somethings, the biggest single sporting event on this island in their lifetimes may have already taken place. In the next few years England will host the first three days of the Tour de France, the Rugby World Cup and the World Athletics Championship, but even the most enthusiastic fan of these events would not seriously suggest that popular interest and enthusiasm for them, at home or abroad, will match what was experienced in and around the 2012 Olympics.

But the measure of London 2012 deserves to go beyond sport. Perhaps only peak experience royal occasions or the memory of war can come near to having the same emotional impact across the whole nation. Those of us who are over twenty will remember Princess Diana's funeral – the death of the People's Princess, Tony Blair's soundbite for every occasion, the floral revolution that engulfed the nation. And the funeral of the Queen herself will be a state occasion of similar magnitude. But that will be about looking back not cheering on, and it will be over within a few days – and a decent chunk of the world will be entirely uninterested in it.

For George Orwell, sport was 'bound up with hatred, jealousy, boastfulness, disregard of all rules and sadistic pleasure in witnessing violence ... it is war minus the shooting'.[2] And whether or not one accepts this premise, it is certainly true that remembering past conflicts remains a major source of national ceremonial and ritual – as will no doubt be evident in 2014's commemoration of the outbreak of the First World War. None of that war's generation now remains alive to tell their tale. And in a few years time the last few of those who fought in the Second World War will also have died. So let us hope that there will be no more global conflict to commemorate, and that the London 2012 of Orwell's 'war minus the shooting' will prove to be the single biggest cultural moment on these shores of most of our lifetimes. This is the scale of what we now have to look back upon – whether longing for more, or wishing for never again.

SPORT MATTERS

Of course how fast an individual can run, how far they can chuck an object, how high they can jump, hardly matters at all in the greater scheme of global justice and human rights. But that isn't what is being claimed on behalf of sport here. Its significance, rather, is in the grand emotional narrative that sport can help construct, arguably more effectively, and more internationally, than any other cultural pursuit. (Web 2.0 is a possible exception in terms of reach. But who, apart from the geekiest of the Geeks, is going to cheer on Apple vs Microsoft in the way millions cheered on London 2012's Super Saturday of grandstanding athletics.)

Some varieties of one-dimensional Marxism deny that there is anything meaningful to be derived from the masses' enjoyment of sport. It's as if those of us who do the cheering have deposited any consciousness we might have at the turnstiles, and those of us who do the training leave the same at the bottom of the changing room locker. Thus, writing before the Games were even over, the Socialist Workers Party in their Party Notes for members declared:

> Whatever brief effect the Olympics have, it won't last. Team GB medals won't be much of a consolation when news of crisis, cuts, job losses and pay curbs return to the front of people's consciousness. And the 'we are now all multiculturalists' line peddled by the Sun (!) etc will soon look ridiculous as scapegoating and whipping up of division returns.
>
> Meanwhile, struggle continues. See below for this week's strikes and protests.[3]

In a more sophisticated variation on this theme, Marc Perelman writes, in his treatise *Barbaric Sport: A Global Plague*:

> In the pestilential environment oozing out of sport, the question arises: what can critical theory come up with today against sport now it has become the visible face of every society? The only possible critical response is a firm assertion: there should be no sport.[4]

This is a pseudo radicalism of do-nothingness, of disengagement with the popular for fear of getting ideological hands dirty. It creates a vacuum, which others of a reactionary bent will fill with greedy readiness. Keeping politics out of sport means that its politics will remain unchanged and unchallenged.

Back in the 1980s the Bennite left was a potentially transformative force within Labour; and there was also a new version of municipal socialism. In Ken Livingstone's Greater London Council in particular, a politics began to take shape on Labour's fringes that sought to take popular culture seriously, including sport. Garry Whannel was one of those who set out the reasons for this. In his pioneering book, *Blowing the Whistle*, Garry set out a five point manifesto.[5] First, there was the need to take all aspects of social life seriously, especially popular cultural forms like sport. Second, it was important to recognise that sport contributed to the way people saw the world, and to engage and offer alternatives. Third, physical well-being, health and fitness were important to human development: socialism should be a way of making a healthier life possible for all. Fourth, play in some form would be an important element of a more fulfilling society. And, fifth, leisure was likely to become an increasingly politicised issue. Battles would be fought over who had leisure time, how it was spent and how it was provided for. Yet, as Garry commented, 'Sport is marked down as a natural, taken-for-granted activity. You don't need to talk or write about it. You just do it'.[6] This was a position that needed to be taken on then, and still does now.

The pressure from within the left to take popular culture seriously can be traced back to the First New Left. One of the figures most closely identified with this period, Stuart Hall, set out in an autobiographical essay why such a focus was so important:

> First, because it was in the cultural and ideological domain that social change appeared to be making itself most dramatically visible. Second, because the cultural dimension seemed to us not a secondary, but a constitutive dimension of society. Third, because the discourse of culture seemed to us fundamentally necessary to any language in which socialism could be redescribed.[7]

Stuart offered this position as representing a fundamental challenge to how politics was traditionally defined, by left and right alike:

> In these different ways the New Left launched an assault on the narrow definition of 'politics' and tried to project in its place an 'expanded definition of the political'. The logic implied by our position was that these 'hidden dimensions' had to be represented within the discourses of 'the political' and that ordinary people could and should organise where they were, around issues of immediate experience; begin to articulate their dissatisfactions in an existential language and build an agitation from that point.[8]

A programme of political action needed therefore to be governed by 'a recognition of the proliferation of the potential sites of social conflict and the constituencies for change'. In the mid- to late-1950s this was truly groundbreaking stuff, and it led directly to the emergence of Cultural Studies as an academic discipline. And by the mid-1980s the kind of politics Stuart was proposing were being pursued in a wide variety of ways, one of which was via the kind of writing on sport that Garry Whannel and others were beginning to develop and popularise.

Thus in 1984, in collaboration with Alan Tomlinson, Garry co-edited the collection *Five Ring Circus*, a critique by a diverse group of left-wing writers and activists of the forthcoming Los Angeles Olympics, now widely recognised as the Games which accelerated the processes of commercialisation into all that the Olympics have become today.[9]

Today, a re-reading of these analyses serves to make very clear the modern disconnect in left politics. The remaking of the political that, in their different ways, Garry and Stuart each advocated has now become almost entirely marginalised. The radical modernisation of the left that their position began to influence was replaced from the mid-1990s by the conservative modernisation of Blairite Labour. Neoliberalism ruled: free-market globalisation was treated as if it was a force of nature; the managerial and the technocratic were the only way things could be run; focus groups replaced any kind of model of change from below. What this amounted to was the privatisation of idealism – arguably New Labour's most profound achievement – a politics that sought to end any hope that things could be different. And it inevitably brought with it a rising popular disengagement with all that the Westminster bubble represents.

THE RIGHT TO BE CRITICAL

As the Games opened on Friday 27 July, in a front page article for the *Guardian*, Jonathan Freedland described the emotional turmoil many were feeling:

> Maybe, like some of the most successful host nations, we should just relax and invite the world to have a fortnight of fun, rather than fret about legacy and meaning. But it's hard to relax when so much is at stake. Seven years ago we told the world that we could come together to state a spectacular Olympic Games and that we were a kinder, gentler, more inclusive country, open to the rest of humanity. The world believed it. The question is, can we believe it too?[10]

And as the Olympics came to an end Jonathan returned, refreshed by the preceding fortnight of glorious sport, to this theme.

> A glimpse of another Britain. A place which succeeds brilliantly, not least by drawing equally on all its talents, black and white, male and

female. A place where money and profit are not the only values. A place that reveres not achievement-free celebrity but astonishing skill, granite determination and good grace. A place where patriotism is heartfelt, but of the soft and civic rather than naked and aggressive variety.[11]

This is the kind of window of opportunity that London 2012 represented. And in the midst of the Games it therefore seemed the worst kind of leftist miserablism to declare from an ideological high ground that nothing much would come of it. Not only does this kind of stance project a sour-faced version of socialism; it also legitimises a politics of abstention, and chokes off any ability to re-imagine and remake.

So how to share in the joy yet be prepared to shape something better? The American critic Stephen Duncombe describes our era, in which mega-events like the Olympics are dominant, as an 'age of fantasy'. In response he calls for, not the simple oppositionalism of old, but:

A politics that embraces the dreams of people and fashions spectacles which give these fantasies form – a politics that understands desire and speaks to the irrational; a politics that employs symbols and associations; a politics that tells good stories. We should have learned to manufacture *dissent*.[12]

An effective dissenting view of what the Olympics have become requires a vision and strategy for what they could be. My own position is that the problem is not the scale of ambition of the Games: it is, rather, their chronic lack of ambition. As the Games approached I therefore outlined some alternatives, in *Why The Olympics Aren't Good For Us And How They Can Be*.[13] My 'Five New Rings' were purposely simple yet enormously radical.

First, the Games had to be decentralised. Britain has a large number of huge stadiums; these are mainly football grounds, but with a small amount of investment they are capable of being reconfigured for all manner of sports. Many of these stadiums are located in and around major conurbations – Greater Manchester, West and East Midlands, Yorkshire, Scotland's Central Belt and South Wales. By utilising the entire nation's existing sports facilities not only would the Olympics have been accessible to infinitely more people as spectators, but costs too could have been considerably reduced.

Second, participation should be maximised. Surely the central objective of hosting a 'home games' must be to maximise the numbers who can watch it and be part of it – to experience the Olympics for probably the first and last time. Anything else means the Games might as well be somewhere else, with us watching it all from our sofas. Decentralisation could have meant using Old Trafford, Cardiff's Millennium Stadium, Glasgow's Celtic Park and plenty more across Britain. Not just for the odd Olympic football match disconnected from the rest of the Games. But with the aim of multiplying the numbers who could join in, enabled via a civic Olympism that could involve a region or nation hosting an entire Olympic discipline across their stadiums and other facilities.

Third, we need a relocation of the Games – to move as much as possible of the programme outside of the stadiums entirely. Historically the Olympic Marathon has proved enormously popular, an epic distance and free to watch. So why are so few Olympic events organised on this basis? Couldn't a half-marathon and road-relays be included in the programme? Add a multi-stage cycling road race, an Olympic Tour of Britain, and imagine the crowds that would turn out for that. A canoe marathon with crowds lining the riverbanks, and a Round Britain yachting race to pack the quaysides around coastal Britain. All of these would be low cost events, with no new facilities needed; their legacy would be focused on boosting the numbers able to see the Games.

Fourth, Olympic sport must be universalised. There remain huge parts of the Games programme where no medal has been won by anyone from entire continents, and there is not much sign of this changing. The most obvious examples of this are the Equestrian, Yachting and Rowing events, but the same narrow medal-winning chances apply also to sports such as fencing and the modern pentathlon, as well as one of the newer Olympic disciplines, the triathlon.

Fifth, the symbolism of the Olympic rings should be protected, and projected as a symbol of all that is good about sport. The Five Rings should not be flogged off to the highest bidder as a logo to sell fast food that makes you fat, fizzy drinks that rot your teeth and credit cards that lead to a lifetime of high interest-rate debt.

Is another Olympics possible? Not without fundamental reform – or perhaps even revolution. But this should not have stopped us from imagining the better Games that London 2012 might have been.

A RING OF STEEL

John Sugden makes the neat point: 'Perhaps it is time we got used to the fact that rather than watching the Games, for the foreseeable future, it is more a case of the Games watching us'.[14] He was alluding to a process that dates back at least to the hostage-taking of Israeli Athletes by the Palestinian Black September group at the 1972 Munich Olympics, and has been accelerated in the more recent period by all matters post 9/11. This has produced what John describes as 'the climate of fear that surrounds contemporary sporting events', which 'encourages vast expenditure on an intrusive security apparatus that violates principles of civil liberty and human rights and blurs the distinction between political and civil society'.[15]

Fear, a security apparatus (intrusive or otherwise), civil liberties abandoned, the politicisation of civil society: this is not quite the 'moment of utopia' of future memories of London 2012. Yet all of these were an integral part of the Games, not least the infamous East End missile launchers on the roof of local residents' blocks of flats. Stephen Graham, author of *Cities under Siege*, had a smart way of summing up the securitisation of the Games – 'society on steroids'. Here he was pointing to the way in which the scale and status of the Games legitimises pre-existing law and order agendas, in particular 'the rise of the homeland security complex, and the shift toward much more authoritarian styles of governance utterly obsessed by the global gaze and prestige of media spectacles'.[16]

While Los Angeles '84 shaped the commercialisation of the Olympics, it was the human tragedy of Munich '72 that determined the securitisation of the Olympics. In Gaza and the West Bank immense problems remain, the lethal consequences of Israel's war on the Palestinians. Yet in all the commentary on the security threat to London 2012, scarcely anyone managed to notice that at these Olympics – unlike at Munich – Palestine competed as a nation-state, its athletes marching into the Opening Ceremony behind their own national flag. This would have been almost impossible to imagine forty years ago. The lesson here should be that the threat of terror can never be defeated by military means; the root causes can only ever be addressed through a political solution.

Of course the Games organisers could not afford to wait for a political settlement for the problems that framed the main terror threat they identified as facing London 2012 – namely the fallout from the Iraq war and the continuing occupation of Afghanistan. But a recognition that there is a context for these acts of violence could at least be a starting point for an understanding of the securitisation of the Olympics. This point was almost entirely absent from all the frantic reporting on London 2012 security; there was no questioning about why all these tens of thousands of security staff were required in the first place.

It would be reckless to dismiss the bloody horrors that could result from a terror attack on the Games. But security is also a question of where you choose to draw the line between crowd safety and human liberty. Three examples here perhaps suffice to show how badly London got it wrong.

First, the closing of the Lea Valley Towpath, which runs alongside the edge of the Olympic Park. Already the park was enclosed by a sky-high fence, topped by razor wires and electronic sensors, with CCTV every few metres, and security patrols inside the perimeter – all to protect the Park from intruders. But it was still felt necessary to close the towpath to public access 23 days before the Olympics even began. And all across London similar catch-all restrictions were imposed around the edges of Olympic venues.

Second, the banning of 'the flag of any country not competing in the Games' as part of the list of objects that could not be taken into the Olympic Park. This was aimed specifically at Free Tibet demonstrators. Tibet is a country not represented at 2012, but what possible harm would there be if anyone waved Tibet's flag as a peaceful protest? Isn't that what's called free speech? This was just one more example of numerous other instances where the line was crossed between acceptable safety concerns and over-zealous policing of the right to protest.

Third, the failure to draw on the experience of similar events. I have been lucky enough to have been to the last four football World Cups, and in none of the host countries has there ever been the same level of very public mobilisation of armed forces; and nor has there been an obvious presence of missiles, warships, aircraft on standby or troops on the streets. There is something about the martial and imperial tradition that seems to insist that in GB we must parade our military hardware for all to see, in the belief that this will somehow act as reassurance.

While the security risk could not be entirely discounted, the overwhelming effort of all those employed to guard the Games had nothing to do with terrorism. They were there to prevent any sort of protest and to defend the interests of the sponsors. Another item on the banned list of products to be to taken into any Olympic venue was an 'excessive amount of food'. If fans were peckish, the organisers didn't want them tucking into an extra round of cheese and pickle sandwiches but into a Big Mac, or any other of the officially approved food and drink products.

And when the private sector provider couldn't manage to supply ever-escalating numbers of staff in order to frisk fans for their home-made sarnies or the wrong brand of fizzy drink, the public sector came to the rescue in the shape of the armed services. Many had only recently returned from Afghanistan. Instead of Help for Heroes it was Cheap Labour from Heroes – and not in order to protect you and me, but to safeguard the interests of McDonald's, Coca Cola, Heineken and the rest.

In recent years football and rugby internationals have seen members of the armed services carrying the flag of England round the pitch, where before this was done by young fans. And at the FA Cup Final the trophy is now brought on to the pitch by servicemen and women. Then there's the annual hoo-hah of embroidering the poppy onto every football club's shirt, another innovation since the Afghanistan mission began. At Wembley and Twickenham the stands are filled with servicemen given free 'Tickets for Heroes'. Richard Williams has been one of the few sportswriters to raise any kind of concern about what all this means:

> There is something disquieting about this gradual blending of sporting and military culture, with its underlying assumption that all the spectators at any given event involving an England interna-tional team necessarily share the government's view of the rightness of what our forces are doing overseas (as opposed to simply honouring their courage in doing it). My thoughts on that matter – which may involve perfectly legitimate reservations – are my own affair. And I resent the way such concerns are being dragged into sport, linked with it, somehow equated with it.[17]

Doreen Lawrence, Shami Chakrabarti and other national figures carried the Olympic flag on its final lap before it was hoisted high above the stadium. But who did they pass the flag to? Medalled and uniformed members of the four armed services. This increasing convergence of the military and public sporting events is described by Richard Williams as 'quasi-propaganda'.

Of course the Opening Ceremony will be best remembered for the sheer scale, audacity and imagination of Danny Boyle's extravaganza. And the volunteers who ushered us around the Olympic venues, all kitted out in purple and a weird shade of orange, are quite rightly given the credit for their selfless and unpaid efforts to help. And once the Gold Medal rush began, the performance of Team GB is what for most of us will be the grandest memory of all. But none of this should be allowed to undermine the significance of the less welcome ways in which the Games impacted. Olympic Legacy? – be careful what you wish for. Let us hope the Games will not be remembered as a step along the way to a surveillance society, and as heralding the seeping militarisation of our national culture.

HOME GAMES, BUT FOR WHOM?

Many believe that London's bid to host the Olympics was given the edge over earlier favourite Paris by Seb Coe's passionate promotion of London as a multicultural city, a home to the world. As the bid presentation ended in Singapore, Seb introduced thirty youngsters on stage, 'each from East London, from the communities who will be touched most directly by our Games': 'thanks to London's multicultural mix of 200 nations, they also represent the youth of the world. Their families have come from every continent. They practise every religion and faith.' (This was on 6 July 2005. The very next day London was rocked by the explosions on the underground and bus system – 7/7. The juxtaposition couldn't have been more dramatic, and many – too many – blamed the atrocities on the very multiculturalism that Seb had been celebrating as London's virtue.)

Very soon it began to feel that this apparent cornerstone of the winning bid was more a case of PR than real commitment, certainly from the host government. And by 2011 David Cameron – who just like Seb has a habit of coming over all touchy-feely when on stage with a bunch of black kids – was declaring: 'We have allowed the weakening of our collective identity. Under the doctrine of state multiculturalism, we have encouraged different cultures to live separate lives, apart from each other and apart from the mainstream'.[18] He might as well have added 'it's political correctness gone mad' or 'you couldn't make it up'. State multiculturalism? Has Cameron looked around Parliament's green benches, or the boardrooms he frequents, or the clubs of the newspaper owners and editors he spends so much time listening to? Or has he perchance glanced round his own Cabinet table and the legion of Downing Street special advisers who carry out his every command? If he could find there any evidence of state multiculturalism affecting the ranks of the powerful, the influential and the rich, he might well be on to something. As to the suggestion that somehow the state has been fomenting separatism? Rather than pointing to differences as framed by faith or dress, it would be salutary to look at some of the more noteworthy indices of difference in the multicultural Olympic boroughs of Tower Hamlets, Newham and Hackney – disproportionate unemployment, poverty, poor health and a wide variety of other social problems.

Addressing these kind of issues is surely what should have shaped a Games rooted in London's East End. It was Seb's claim in Singapore that London 2012 could achieve something for a part of the city that was scarred by discrimination and deindustrialisation. But, though there were indeed plenty of black and brown faces in the Olympic Park – just as there are at many modern sports venues – most were there as service workers. As writer on race and sport Dan Burdsey has memorably put it, apart from the athletes themselves:

> You will often see a significant presence of minority ethnic people in the stadium; they will be directing you to your seat or serving your refreshments. The racialised historical antecedents and continuing legacy of these roles – entertaining or serving the white folk – should not be lost within the contemporary clamour of positivity.[19]

The low-paid, mainly unskilled and temporary jobs London 2012 generated were disproportionately filled by the young people of ethnic minority origin. At the same time those with tickets – in an Olympic Park at the epicentre of three of London's most multicultural boroughs, Newham, Tower Hamlets and Hackney – were disproportionately white, entirely unrepresentative of modern East London. This was the Home Counties Games, not London's, white flight in reverse. Multicultural Britain on the track, maybe, but in the stands and the park the social divisions of modern Britain were as apparent as ever. Rushanara Ali, MP for the Bethnal Green and Bow constituency on the edge of the Olympic Park, described the post-Olympic mood amongst her constituents as one of 'betrayal'. In place of employment and career opportunities created by the Olympics, they were still enduring amongst the highest jobless rates in the entire country; long-term adult unemployment rose by 26 per cent in 2012, and long-term youth unemployment rose by a staggering 55 per cent.

Rushanara contrasted this to the Olympic mission: 'London 2012 made us believe there is no limit to what we can achieve'.[20] Of course this is the magical appeal of the Games, its compelling narrative of everyone's chance for success on the track, in the pool and elsewhere. But too many people from across the political spectrum and the sporting and media establishment help perpetuate the cruel deception that the success of Team GB and London 2012 will have an impact on the career and life chances for the majority. And if the Olympic Park isn't benefiting those on its doorstep, what chance the rest of the country?

In many ways Team GB was a better symbol of modern Britain than the groups that sit on the benches of Parliament, the seats of company boardrooms, or at the editorial desks of the nation's newspapers. That is something we can all recognise, and it is a version of Team GB that most feel at ease with; many see it as representative of the Britain we want to become. But many were at best only temporarily diverted from their defensive stance against difference. Multiculturalism is OK if it adds some finishing speed, fighting muscle and flair on the ball to Team GB. But not if it means more immigration – from Rumania and Bulgaria this time, and who knows where next?

The racialisation of Britishness is a complex matter, and to note that Britishness remains racialised is entirely different from claiming it is intrinsically racist. Sport can help unpick that complexity, offering moments of great hope and profound change, but it cannot effect that change on its own. A year on from London 2012, UKIP were riding high in the polls, scoring 23 per cent share of the vote in England's May local elections. Though it is not the same as the tinpot Nazis of the British National Party, this is nevertheless a party of the populist right, draped in that self-same Team GB Union Jack. Will Self describes UKIP (writing specifically in this case about England) as appealing to 'a sector of our society that still believes parliamentary democracy to be a sham; still thinks that black and brown people are inferior (while Jews are worrisomely and magically superior); remains powerfully xenophobic and looks to a nationalist renaissance; and of course, still reads the *Daily Mail*'.[21] Team GB and London 2012 did offer the possibility of a different version of Anglo-Britishness. But that was it – a possibility not the actuality.

GENDER'S SCORE DRAW

For quite some time now national sports teams have acquired a responsibility as symbols of acceptable multiculturalism. But when it comes to symbolising gender equality? Excuse the mixed-up metaphor, but sport isn't even at the races.

But within the Olympics women have a much higher profile. The final Thursday of London 2012 was by no means untypical. A world record crowd for a Women's Football match. Three more Team GB Golds, all won by women athletes. The first ever Women's boxing Gold, again won by a Team GB athlete. Indeed these Games perhaps represented the single biggest challenge to the traditional masculine hegemony that to date has gripped British sporting culture.

And it wasn't just in the ring, on the pitch or round the track. In the BBC TV studio Clare Balding was for most the stand-out presenter, putting to shame the more than occasional hapless amateurism of Gary Lineker when outside his football comfort zone. In the *Guardian*, usually no better than the rest when it comes to the number of women writers featured on the sports pages, the coverage was transformed, with unprecedented space given to Marina Hyde, Anna Kessel and Emma John. And elsewhere in the paper prominent feminist columnists Zoe Williams and Suzanne Moore contributed pieces that joined in the approval of what the Games had come to represent.

Inequalities do of course still exist. No Olympic woman star will ever earn even a fraction of what their male counterparts are paid – while, conversely, they are far more likely to receive comments on their appearance. But the Olympics does broadly treat women's versions of the medal sports on an equal basis with the male versions. Few but the most embittered chauvinist would treat Laura Trott and Victoria Pendleton's achievements in the velodrome as somehow inferior to those of Jason Kenny and Chris Hoy. Rower Katherine

Grainger was celebrated every bit as much as her male medal-winning counterparts – in fact, arguably, with even greater prominence. It is impossible and unhelpful to even try to weigh up the magnitude of Jess Ennis's Heptathlon Gold versus Mo Farah's 10,000m, both won on that same magical night. And while the most puerile sections of the media continue to sexualise the female athletes' bodies in a degrading manner that few male athletes will have to endure, this is no longer the norm.

On that last Thursday of the Games the Women's Gold Medal Football match at Wembley was a sparkling occasion, and I was lucky enough to be part of the crowd. The previous world record attendance for a women's match was 76,000, but this match topped 80,000. The standard of play was for the most part superb, perhaps a tad less physical, a fraction slower, but this makes for a more skilful, passing game. The goals were of the highest quality. Hope Solo, the US goalkeeper, put on a world class performance to keep the Japanese women at bay. It is true that it wasn't the same as 'men's football' – but then why should it be? These superbly gifted footballers aren't trying to play the men at the game blokes like to call their own, they're playing something different. With next to no dissent, one solitary dive, and a single yellow card, in many ways the game was better. In the stands the passion was different too, a much more joyful atmosphere than the one I've become too used to when watching England. No one standing up to block my view and refusing to budge, no foul and abusive language wrapped in hate for others in the name of passion, and, most of all, none of the drunken, threatening misogyny that too many have excused over the years as just what lads at football get up to.

That night at Wembley forced me to rethink the ways in which we romanticise the so-called authenticity of football's fandom. I shared Mark Steel's sentiment, though I just couldn't put it as well: 'the fans were so gleeful they'd be evicted from the ground at an England men's match for being too amicable'.[22] Since 1996 I've seen almost every England international, home and away. Fan? I'm more of a travelling fanatic. And although I reject the lazy stereotype – from left and right – that all who follow England are hooligans, racists or both, and I'm proud of having played a role in helping to change the image of England fans, at the same time I knew Mark was right in this. The way football fan culture trades on authenticity – 'where were you when you were shit', mixed with 'if you know your history', and 'only singing when you're winning' – masks an unyielding masculinity. From *When Saturday Comes* and the football writing quarterly *The Blizzard* via the national press sports desks, Radio 5 and Talksport phone-in callers and presenters, this is blokedom, and it has scarcely changed over the past twenty years. The presence of women either in the stands or on the pitch has been only grudgingly tolerated, rarely celebrated, and, most particularly, never allowed to transform. The hegemony of football alongside the even more male-dominated rugby, cricket and Formula One means that this impacts on and infects our entire sporting culture.

The Olympics only comes along once every four years, a home Games once in a lifetime. Football is there week after week, with scarcely any summer break to speak of now, when there's a Euro or a World Cup every other June and July. The Olympics couldn't break this grip, but the undoubted success of Team GB at least offered a glimpse of what an alternative might look like – and that meant, for the large part, women athletes being treated on a par with their male counterparts. At the Olympics the GB men's and women's football teams were given near equal prominence – something of a first.

Yet the English FA still, quite disgracefully, won't 'allow' the England Women's Football team to play a game at Wembley. And the advances in media balance were reversed almost as soon as the football season restarted after the Games. But many of us will never forget what the beginnings of equality in sport looked like. Woman athlete after woman athlete in Team GB are world record-holders and world champions, while most of our male footballers are middling also-rans. And making this point is nothing to do with class, as some have tried to suggest. It is everything to do with gender, and the ways in which we award the mantle of sporting greatness. London 2012 did at least for that glorious moment equal the scores between a masculine sports culture as defined by men's football, rugby and cricket, and a more equitable sports culture, shaped by the rest.

GOING TO THE GAMES – AN EXPERIENCE OF TWO HALVES

In my visits to the Olympic Park I relaxed in enjoyment of its magnificent ensemble of world-class sporting facilities, in a setting where there was plenty of well tended open space between them. World-class sporting stadiums are often awesome buildings, but they are usually hemmed in by their host city, and defined as much by their surroundings as their architectural features. The Olympic Park was quite different – with walkways and waterways, wide expanses of grass and flowerbeds connecting stadiums, a water sports centre, the velodrome, hockey centre, and more buildings for volleyball, handball, water polo and other sports. The crowds would criss-cross from one location and sport to another. As one lot headed off home overflowing with excitement, another lot would arrive full of expectation.

This is what the Olympic Park offered – an entire sporting city in one location. And, despite all our worst fears, the queues were manageable, while the tube trains taking us in and out were no more packed than a normal London rush-hour. Quite what it will look like in a few years time, who knows? But in the summer of 2012 the Olympic Park was like something Britain had never seen before and was to be hugely enjoyed.

As for the sport, like many we were last-minute applicants, picking up any tickets we could get our hands on; and so we were there to watch Australia vs Italy in a Women's Water Polo group-stage match. The temporary stands surrounding the temporary pool were packed to near capacity – quite something for a sport which in Britain at any other time would have attracted next to zero spectators, and with no Team GB to watch. I would guess that, like me, most had never paid to watch this sport before, let alone knew the rules. Yet we were transfixed. It was fast, immensely skilful, and the underwater action was occasionally brutal. The crowd were enthusiastic, non-partisan and clearly enjoying themselves as part of the Games. There were clutches of Italian water polo fans, and a louder Aussie contingent – many of them apparently the extended family, friends and team-mates of those competing in the pool. But in the main it was Brits, bemused yet amused by everything going on. This is surely part of the appeal of the Olympics – to be fascinated by sports that we know next to nothing about, and without the necessity for partisanship. Sport reduced to its essence – the joy to watch, and, for some of us, to participate in.

There was something else inside the Park that was quite different to the sports culture we've become too used to: inside the stadiums there were no adverts, no corporate branding at all, just the Olympian five rings and London 2012 logo. The commercialisation stopped once we entered the park. Not entirely of course – there were the merchandising

megastores and the giant McDonald's concessions. But there was no
trackside advertising, no sponsor's logo on the kit of every athlete, no
stadium naming rights sold off to the biggest bidder, no hoardings
filling every space of our vision. This was No Logo land, where the
Five Rings were preserved for what their role should be – a symbol of
a great sporting occasion.

But my best Olympic day out was the cycling time-trial – no
tickets, free, just grab a space on the kerbside and a front row seat is
guaranteed. Precious little commercialisation –and we could bring our
own barbecue too. Best of all, a Team GB Gold Medal performance
as Wiggo flashed by to fulfil his and our dreams. He did it, we were
watching, and it hadn't cost us a penny. How good is that?

Stretched around the single 27-mile circuit for men, 18 miles for
the women, huge crowds lined each side of the road. It was packed
at the hairpin bends, where the cyclists slow down, and for the final
few hundred yards before the finishing line, but just about anywhere
else it was easy enough to get a decent view, up and close to the fast-
moving action. Churches, community centres and more than a few
enterprising householders had set up sandwich and cake stalls in
their front gardens. This was an event that it was impossible for the
corporate sponsors to dominate; the only roadside branding permitted
was the Olympic Five Rings and 'London 2012'. Just like the Olympic
Park, here was a space where the visual backdrop belonged to sport
and not the advertisers. And the sometimes oppressive securitisation
of the main Olympic Park was also almost non-existent, with, in
the main, just volunteers and fluorescent-jacketed crowd marshals.
Cycling could have been one of the Olympic events most vulnerable
to disruption, and yet for long stretches not even a crowd barrier
separated us from the action. It was hard to see why the risk of a
protest, or something much worse, was considered so low here in view
of the levels of security elsewhere.

A decent number of those watching had arrived by bike, and I've
never seen so many bicycles padlocked to any available immovable
object. A daring few arrived there early enough to pedal their way
round the route. What other sport would allow such a thing? And
once Wiggo had passed our vantage point, we huddled around those
with smart phones or laptops with Wi-Fi connections to catch his
final sprint to the line, and glory. Best of all, when the racing was over
thousands rode off home, and for this day, with Wiggo ruling the

world, not a car-driver in sight would think to tell us to get out of their way. On the roads of Kingston and Richmond this showed the kind of 2012 Olympics we all deserved to have.

THE OLYMPICS THAT MIGHT HAVE BEEN

Like hundreds of thousands of others I had a great time at the Olympics. But does that mean the Olympics couldn't have been better? Of course they could. There are a three key areas where improvements could be made.

First, at the core of any improvement would be an increase in the relatively small numbers of those who are actually able to see a 'home games' in action. After all it was hardly a secret that interest amongst the British sporting public was sky-high, as Brits applied in advance for an astonishing 22 million tickets.[23]

Take the cycling time trial. Why on earth was it held during the working day, thereby excluding all who couldn't take the time off to watch? The crowds would have been multiplied many times over if this event had been held in the evening, as summertime would have enabled, or at the weekend. The same applied to the Triathlon, also staged on a working day rather than the weekend, the watching crowds therefore, though big, not as big as they might have been.

Year in year out, the London Marathon is run on an A to B course, 26.2 miles of pavement packed with supporters and onlookers, and much of this route passes through London's East End. So when the Olympic bid was won, many East Enders assumed that this would be the one event where they were guaranteed a front row seat, with no ticket required. And for the Olympic boroughs of Tower Hamlets, Newham and Hackney, here was a chance to show off their neighbourhoods to a global TV audience for the best part of two and a bit hours. No chance. As soon as they could, the London Organising Committee moved both the men's and women's Marathon routes to central London, and the potential 26.2 miles of free pavement space was cut by 75 per cent, since the race would now be run four times round the same six-mile lap.

Over and over again, decisions were made that seriously reduced the numbers who could watch the few free-to-see events that there are in the Olympic programme – road cycling, marathon, triathlon and race-walking.

My last day at the Olympics was spent watching the men's hockey Bronze Medal match, England vs Australia. The stadium in the Olympic Park was packed, but its capacity was only 15,000: the match clearly had a far greater potential audience than could be fitted in. For, although hockey doesn't have much of a spectator following in GB, as those 22 million ticket applications had definitively proved, the Olympics had changed the levels of interest for just about any sport in which a 2012 gold medal was at stake. And added to that was the fact that both women's and men's GB teams were genuine contenders. The hockey tournament was organised in the same kind of way as a mini football World Cup – with 12 teams taking part in each competition, divided into two pools to play group stage matches, with the pool winners and runners progressing to knock out stages to settle the medals. So far so familiar – yet any World Cup would share these games around venues to maximise attendance. Not London 2012. Every single game took place in the purpose-built and modest-capacity hockey stadium. Matches were scheduled to start from 8.30 in the morning to 9.15 in the evening. This was a programme guaranteed to limit the numbers who could attend. Yet across London there is Rugby's Twickenham stadium of 90,000-plus capacity, Arsenal's Emirates Stadium of 60,000, as well as Stamford Bridge, White Hart Lane, Craven Cottage and others – stadiums that could have hosted the tournament between them, with games being organised at the weekend and in the early evening, thereby vastly increasing the numbers who could watch – matched by a corresponding cut in the ticket prices. There would also have then been none of the expense of a custom-built hockey stadium – it is hard to imagine that laying hockey's artificial surface over the grass of rugby or hockey pitches would have cost anything like as much money.

Another example was the boxing finals. These were held at the Excel centre, with a capacity in the low thousands. Yet it is quite common for major world title boxing fights to be staged in football stadiums. Most recently Ricky Hatton defended his world belts at Manchester City's stadium, which has a capacity of over 40,000. Here again London's football and rugby stadiums could have been brought into use, thereby multiplying the number of tickets available.

Of course no stadium in the world could have fitted in all those who wanted to watch the London 2012 athletics, swimming and track cycling. But by imaginatively reconfiguring London's rich resources of stadiums, and creatively thinking about the routes of free-to-watch events, as well as about issues of timing, the numbers who could have been part of the Games might have been massively increased. One consequence would have been that the Olympic Park would have become less of a central venue for the Games, but even if it had consisted solely of the Olympic Stadium, Pool and Velodrome (incidentally the three permanent features of the Park post-2012), the concentration of these massive Olympic sports would still have accorded the Park the kind of event-status that organisers, broadcasters and spectators crave.

In my view this failure to conceive of a Games model whose core objective is being there reveals a fundamental lack of ambition on the part of the organisers. Provided the ticket sales targets met the income stream level required they seemed satisfied. Yes, plenty did get to see the only 'home' Olympics of most of our lifetimes, but plenty more didn't. They could, and should, have been able to do so.

A second problem is that, in terms of the global picture, in sport after sport the parade of medal winners remains drearily predictable. In rowing, of the fourteen gold medals available just one was won by an African nation – South Africa – and one by an Asian nation, China. Of the thirty yachting medals, China managed a silver and Brazil a bronze, but not one medal was won by an African nation. Of the eighteen Equestrian medals, none were won by African or South American nations, though there was a solitary bronze for an Asian nation – Saudi Arabia.[24]

And in numerous other sports entire continents lacked any medals. Canoeing, hockey and modern pentathlon – no medallists from Africa or Asia. Diving, fencing and gymnastics – no medallists from Africa. Compare this to athletics – where Jamaica came third in the medals table, Ethiopia fourth and Kenya fifth, and medals were won across a spread of countries, including the Dominican Republic, Turkey, Grenada, the Bahamas and Algeria; or boxing, where Cuba was third in the medals table, and medal winners included boxers from Kazakhstan, Mongolia, Thailand and India; while the men's and women's football medal-winning teams included Mexico, Brazil, Japan and South Korea.

Of course the Olympic Medal Table isn't intended to be a chart of equality. It lists the winners. Losers don't get a mention. Yet understanding what is common to middle and long-distance running, boxing and football matters in terms of our appreciation of what the Olympics represent. Each of these sports needs next to no kit, equipment or expensive facilities. The rules are simple. No particular physique is required to be successful (in boxing this is aided by the weight divisions). And each of these sports has a world-wide and well-established professional level that represents an aspirational route of poverty. None of these factors apply to a very large number of Olympic sports, and thus the countries that win the medals remain unchanged, Games after Games. This wasn't something that London 2012 could change – for example by adding more events for the most universal sports, and reducing the numbers of those which prove incapable of becoming more universal. But this is the kind of challenge that Olympism more widely should face, for the sake of a better Games.

A third area where there is considerable room for improvement is in protecting the symbolism of the Olympic Five Rings – one of the most recognisable symbols in the world. No other sporting event has a symbol that comes close to matching it for instant familiarity. Few of even the most committed football fans could sketch FIFA's badge, yet we all know what those Five Rings signify. History helps of course, given that the Games date back to 1896, but most crucial here are those gold-medal winning moments every four years via which we can measure out our progress through childhood, adolescence, adulthood and family life. That's why it matters when this symbol of sport becomes just a logo to flog fast food, fizzy drinks and the rest. The sport becomes not only commercialised but commodified too, the Five Rings just another corporate brand. Of course modern sport doesn't come cheap, but the major sponsor of London 2012 was you and me, the British taxpayer. The companies who bought up the right to have the Five Rings splashed over their products and adverts couldn't have funded the Games on their own, and didn't come anywhere close to doing so.

The Torch Relay represented all that is wrong with this selling off of the Five Rings. Everywhere it went the torch carriers were preceded by a parade of sponsors' open-top buses, branded from beginning to end in adverts for whatever they were trying to sell. Contrast this with the increasingly popular Park Runs.[25] Non-profit making, low resourced, run for fun by most, as a race by some, tens of thousands join one in a local park every Saturday morning. The kind of practical legacy the Relay could have represented would have been linking each leg of the torch's journey with just such a run, or walk or cycle ride, if preferred.

For the physically inactive that first step towards participation is so often the hardest. The number one legacy claim of the Olympics was to 'inspire a generation' into participation in sport. The relay instead became a self-congratulatory parade around Britain for the organisers and their media entourage, with the rest of us looking on, participation defined as spectating. We know the Olympic Five Rings have an incredible pulling power: these Games managed to get the British public watching Handball for goodness sake. Think what the relay might have been – the biggest single exercise of mass participation in sport, with the Olympic Torch out in front.

But the Olympics bidding process makes it almost impossible to mount a challenge of these kinds to the International Olympic Committee model. By 2012 so much was already in place for the 2016 Games that next to no lessons of how to change the model in any significant way could be learned from London – not that the IOC would permit this in any case. And before the end of 2013 the 2020 host city will be chosen, and by then the 2024 bidders will already have begun their jockeying for position. No deviation from the IOC diktats allowed.

The same vocabulary will be used in each and every bidding cycle. Regeneration, inspiration and participation. Yet there is next to no assessment by either the IOC or future bidders of whether these claims have been fulfilled. Instead the IOC demands that the Games be organised in a manner that serves their interests, prestige and profile – never mind how this might serve the interests of the host. None of this will change until bidders do what sports economists Robert Baade and Victor Matheson describe as 'the obvious': 'they must take steps to counteract the monopoly power of the IOC. It is in the collective interest of potential host cities to devise means to change the nature of the bidding process'.[26] Their advice for bidders is:

They must be realistic about what the Olympics offer. Thorough investigations of past experiences will not only provide a filter through which promises of booster can be run, but it might well indicate the most effective methods for integrating Olympic infra-structure needs with the present economy and a vision of its future. In the absence of careful and direct planning, cities that succeed in hosting the Olympics may well only find fool's gold for their efforts.[27]

Despite all the fun we had, when it comes to the mantra of Regeneration, Inspiration and Participation there is to date no evidence that London 2012 will deliver. What data already exists points in the opposite direction: there has been no sustainable jobs increase, a continuing decline in physical activity, and precious little inspiration beyond those already involved in sport. Yet Rio, and whoever comes next, will follow a model nearly identical to that of London – reproducing in large measure the ways previous Games have been organised and with the same result.

RUNNING FOR FREE

For Alan Tomlinson, the opening ceremonies matter 'because of how universalising rhetorics of world sport – usually stressing peace, harmony, past-present continuity, rebirth and hope for youth – are woven into the[ir] textures'.[28] I watched the opening ceremony with a group of fellow left Olympics malcontents on a big screen at Bethnal Green's Rich Mix arts centre, and we whooped and hollered when the Tolpuddle Martyrs and the Suffragettes made their appearance. Then Windrush, and then, best of all, the NHS. But Alan is right, whatever the universal ideals, theirs or ours, this was the theatricality of rhetoric. Trade union rights, ending sexism, cuts and privatisation imposed on the NHS – nothing much was likely to change as a result of the show. This isn't to decry how much we enjoyed it, our discontent slipping away as the feel-good factor so expertly conjured up by Danny Boyle took over. Yet only eight months later Boyle revealed exclusively to the *Sun*: 'I think it would be naive to say it could last'.[29] The front page splash featuring Danny's interview was treated to the sobering banner headline, 'OLYMPIC SPIRIT KILLED BY RECESSION'. What price the best firework display of our lives now?

The day after London 2012 was over, caller after caller on Nicky Campbell's BBC R5 morning breakfast show phoned in to say they couldn't care less about what the Games had cost each of us in terms of our taxes. £200 a head? £300 a head? Money well spent was the near universal response. This in an era of austerity and cutbacks. Something was shifting in the political mood. If the nanny-state could put on a good party then let nanny spend, spend, spend. There may have been little or no connection with the case for public expenditure on hospitals, schools, welfare and all manner of other vital services. But nevertheless the effect of the Games was welcomed and celebrated, and its funding out of our taxes enthusiastically endorsed. This was a truly collectivist Britain, dressed still in its Team GB colours. There seemed a sense of happy realism about what the callers were saying. Never mind those claims of regeneration, participation and inspiration: it was as if nobody had been fooled by them in the first place.

In his excellent book chronicling the sins of modern football, *Richer Than God*, journalist David Conn sums up neatly the way the game has been commodified:

> All around us is a celebration and injunction to watch other people playing sport, the hype that supporting a professional football 'club' is compulsory, Sky TV's relentless persuasion that paying £50 a month will provide endlessly exciting hours on the sofa, the newspapers, whose sections are wholly about following the skills of a very few, and almost never about helping people play sport themselves.[30]

As he also adds:

> ... it is seen as a great credit to England that we are exporting around the world our multimillion pound Premier League, for more people in other countries to watch on television.[31]

For the duration of the Olympics and a chunk of the Paralympics, football briefly lost its absolute dominance in the shaping of sports culture in this country. But within days of the closing ceremony that domination was re-established, and it's been the same ever since. Football has led the way in the transformation of modern sport into a business, and it has grabbed the biggest share of the spoils too. But the Olympics has never been very far behind, and sometimes it has even been ahead in this particular race. This is a process founded on the commercialisation of sport's traditions and the commodification of sport's practice. The result, in the words of that wonderful quote from Marx is: 'All that is solid melts into air, all that is holy is profaned'.[32]

Cycling perhaps offers a potential counter to the commercialised and commodified meltdown Marx was presaging. What other sport can you use as a way to get to work, to school or college, doubling up for a shopping trip with an added handlebar mounted basket or decent pair of panniers? We can do it as a family, use it as a basis for a day out, or, for the more adventurous, make it the basis of a holiday. We can cycle for a good cause, or challenge ourselves to beat clock and body by completing a hundred-mile century ride. It means we never have to stand in a queue for a bus or wait for an overcrowded train. We can sail past cars stuck in a traffic jam and keep our carbon footprint small into the bargain. With Wiggo, Cav and Froome's success in Le Tour, Lizzie Armistead and Emma Pooley on the roads, and Chris Hoy and Victoria Pendleton being overtaken by a new generation headed up by Laura Trott on the track, we have the poster boys and girls of aspiration as well. It's a potent mix. Yet the Olympics and elite success are only one part of cycling's potential to engage those not active, or to get those who are so already more active.

We may well be in the middle of a cycling boom. There are certainly reports that suggest this is so.[33] Jackie Ashley nominated 2012 as the 'The Year of Cycling', though at the same time pointing to some of the messy contradictions that remain:

> A quarter of us, roughly, are obese, children as well as adults. Our urban air is filthy. We are using too much carbon. But the great thing is millions of us are getting the message. Real revolutions come from below, and this one is too. That's perhaps the greatest message from 2012, the year of the bike.[34]

In the early 1980s it was the running boom that was making similar headlines. Accompanied by the success of Coe, Ovett, Cram and Elliott on the track, jogging became a social phenomenon, the first London marathon was run, and almost every city and town could boast a fun run of sorts, many raising funds for good causes. In the USA Jim Fixx's *Complete Book of Running* became a bestseller, and pretty soon reached a world-wide readership. In GB it was the late and anything but great Jimmy Savile who helped popularise the link between running and reducing the risk of heart disease. A radio one DJ, chomping on his trademark cigar, wrists and chest covered in what today we call bling, the message seemed to be that if Jimmy could do it then anybody could – and many did. By the 1990s commentators were dubbing the era 'the Age of Sport'.[35] Yet the twenty-first century has seen Britain report record levels of physical inactivity and obesity, with all the health problems associated with both. Some run, cycle or swim, most don't.

Mark Rowlands, a philosopher of running, in his book *Running With the Pack*, makes two key observations of the sport. Firstly, for runners, what we do has a variety of instrumental purposes.

> Different people run for different reasons: some because they enjoy it, some because it makes them feel good, look good, because it keeps them healthy, happy even alive. Some run for company, others to relieve the stress of everyday life. Some like to push themselves, test their limits; others to compare their limits with the limits of others.[36]

But Mark then adds a second observation. That the appeal of running lies not in any of these reasons at all. In fact the point of running is that it is pointless:

> It is true that running has multifarious forms of instrumental value. However at its purest and its best running has an entirely different sort of value. This is sometimes known as 'intrinsic' or 'inherent' value. To say that something has intrinsic value is to say that it is valuable for what it is in itself, and not because of anything else it might allow to get or possess. Running is intrinsically valuable, when one runs one is in contact with intrinsic value in life.[37]

As I total up another week's running mileage I've come to realise that the appeal of an early morning run lies precisely in the fact that it has no purpose other than this intrinsic appeal. Yes my legs are muscular and fat-free, I can run a distance and in a time plenty half my age couldn't even start. But the instrumentalism of running will always disappoint. I've scarcely ever won a race, and despite all those miles I've still got a bigger waistline than I'd like, while running has left me less resistant to colds, flu and sundry other viruses.

So why do I run? Because it's free and it is freedom. It is the most basic form of sporting activity. I run because I can. But the reason I can is in large measure socially constructed. I have a lifestyle which enables me to put ninety minutes or so aside most days for a run. I'm male, so the dark mornings from October through to March don't hold too much fear for me. Today I live on the edge of the South Downs – and my gravest worry nowadays is that a randy Bull might take an unnatural fancy to me. But for twenty odd years I ran along the towpath of the River Lea, circumnavigating what was to become the Olympic Park. In those two decades there were two shootings along my route, and on a couple of occasions I was chased by the deranged and the inebriated. Fortunately I have a decent finishing kick, which can come in useful when you least expect it. And when I started my running I went to a school with a playing field to run round, next to a heath: the basic facilities to nurture my childhood enthusiasm existed. I've never joined a running club – this is a sport you can do individually or collectively – but when I wanted to race there were events I could easily and cheaply enter, and family and friends to provide the transport and support I sometimes needed. I have come to value and protect the time I spend on my runs, but in order to do so I had to have had the time to start running in the first place.

All sports are socially constructed, some more than others, but their construction remains rooted in something more than is ever revealed by a scoreline or a race report. London 2012 failed to recognise this key idea, and that's why the case for legacy, inspiration and participation was so spurious and artificial, right from the outset. Sport for most of us is pointless. Most participants will never win a race, let alone a medal, and are unlikely to break a record. But that doesn't mean that as an activity sport has no social value. The playful, the recreational, should be a cornerstone of any vision for an equitable society. The best Olympic Games ever will be the one that has the practicalities of inclusion and participation as its central organising principle – this is what should be the measure of its ambition. But this requires a revolution in both sports culture and political culture – how we define sport, how we define politics. London 2012 scarcely impacted on either process.

London 2012 was one big party, and we can be thankful for that. For a precious few it will have changed their lives. For most it hasn't. You can't keep politics out of sport. And we shouldn't keep sport out of our politics either. Sport *is* politics.

NOTES

1. Paul Sinha, 'So Long, farewell, auf wiedersehen, goodbye', 12 August 2012: www.sinhaha.wordpress.com.
2 George Orwell, 'The Sporting Spirit', *Tribune*, 14 December 1945. Republished in Ian Hamilton (ed), *The Faber Book of Soccer*, Faber& Faber 1992.

3. SWP, 'Anger Hasn't Gone Away', Party Notes, 6 August 2012: www.swp. org.uk.
4. Marc Perelman, *Barbaric Sport: A Global Plague*, Verso 2012, p120.
5. Garry Whannel, *Blowing the Whistle: The Politics of Sport*, Pluto 1983, pp15-16.
6. Ibid, p14.
7. Stuart Hall, 'The First New Left: Life and Times', Oxford University Socialist Discussion Group (eds), *Out of Apathy: Voices of the New Left 30 Years On*, Verso 1989, p25.
8. Ibid, p26.
9. Alan Tomlinson and Garry Whannel (eds), *Five Ring Circus: Money, Power and Politics at the Olympic Games*, Pluto 1984.
10. Jonathan Freedland, 'Time To Find Out Who We Are', *Guardian*, 27 July 2012.
11. Jonathan Freedland, ' London 2012: We Glimpsed Another Britain, So Let's Fight For It', *Guardian*, 10 August 2012.
12. Stephen Duncombe, *Dream: Re-imagining Progressive Politics In An Age of Fantasy*, New Press 2007, p9.
13. Mark Perryman, *Why The Olympics Aren't Good For Us And How They Can Be*, OR Books 2012.
14. John Sugden, 'Watched by the Games: Surveillance and Security at the Olympics', in J. Suden and A. Tomlinson (eds), *Watching The Olympics: Politics, Power and Representation*, Routledge 2012, p239.
15. Ibid, p239.
16. Stephen Graham, 'Olympics 2012 Security: Welcome to Lockdown London', *Guardian*, 12 March 2012.
17. Richard Williams, 'Help for Heroes is a Worthy Cause But Spare Us the Moral Blackmail', *Guardian*, 22 November 2010.
18. David Cameron, Munich Security Conference speech, 5 February 2011.
19. Daniel Burdsey, 'They Think It's All Over … It Isn't Yet', in Daniel Burdsey (ed), *Race, Ethinicity and Football*, Routledge 2011, p5.
20. Rushanara Ali, 'The Olympic Legacy Has Failed To Bring Jobs to London's East End', *Guardian*, 27 January 2013.
21. Will Self, 'This Is England?', *Guardian*, 9 March 2013.
22. Mark Steel, 'Cyclists, Women, Refugees – Vindicated at Last', *Independent*, 9 August 2012.
23. James Pearce, 'London 2012: Many Tickets For Olympics Remain Unsold', 25 May 2012: www.bbc.co.uk/sport.
24. For the London 2012 medals table and for individual 2012 sports, see http://www.bbc.co.uk/sport/olympics/2012/medals/countries.
25. See James Brilliant, 'Parkrun, The Running Revolution Coming Soon To a Park Near You', *Guardian*, 11 March 2013.
26. Robert A. Baade and Victor Matheson, 'Bidding for the Olympics', *International Association of Sports Economists Paper 007*, 2000, p34.

27. Ibid, pp34-35.
28. Alan Tomlinson, 'Staging the Spectacle', *Soundings* 13, 1999, p170.
29. Grant Rollings, 'Olympic Spirit Killed By Recession', *Sun*, 22 March 2013.
30. David Conn, *Richer Than God*, Quercus 2012, p354.
31. Ibid, pp365-366.
32. Karl Marx and Frederick Engels, *The Communist Manifesto*, Verso 1998, p38.
33. See London School of Economics, *The British Cycling Economy*, LSE 2011.
34. Jackie Ashley, '2012 Was The Year of Cycling', *Guardian*, 30 December 2012.
35. See Martin Jacques, 'Worshipping the Body at the Altar of Sport', *Observer*, 13 July 1997.
36. Mark Rowlands, *Running With the Pack*, Granta Books 2013, pix.
37. Ibid, pxiii.

THE WONDER STUFF

Billy Bragg

Danny Boyle set the bar for London 2012 in the opening ceremony and he set it high. Instead of giving us the embarrassing spectacle of a Britain desperate to convince the world that it was still a force to be reckoned with, we were presented with the image of a self-effacing people who embrace change and diversity, and find success when they marry collective effort with individual genius. Could our athletes and Olympic volunteers follow the arc of Boyle's narrative and deliver an event to make us all proud?

In the following weeks, it was difficult not to be drawn in. After a few nervous days when it seemed that only our reputation as good losers was going to be enhanced, it all began to come together. There was edge-of-your-seat excitement, shout-out-loud triumphs, girlie screams and man-hugs. An unforgettable Saturday evening in the Olympic Stadium provided the nation with a communal experience rare in these days of modern multi-media. As a result, a feeling of national pride swept over the country, so warm that it pushed the rain clouds away.

Yet there were some who struggled with this new-found national pride. People who had never felt such emotions before looked at the massed Union Jacks being waved, heard the constant refrain of 'God Save the Queen' and felt decidedly queasy.

The long tradition of internationalism has resulted in the left having a blind spot when confronted with expressions of national identity. Many don't bother to differentiate between nationalism – wanting self-determination for your country – and patriotism – taking pride in your country. Some even go so far as to be positively patriotic about any country that is opposing Britain at sport or in politics.

This is ironic, given that patriotism, like socialism, comes in many varieties, with nuances that are deliberately ignored by detractors. Up close and personal, individual identity is a many-layered construct in which we choose to define ourselves by those things that make us proud to be part of an imagined community. In so doing we construct our own narrative of events, which helps to provide a sense of belonging to our family, locale or country.

Beyond our personal control there exists a grander narrative, which society seeks to enforce through education, tradition and the promotion of certain values. We in turn define ourselves in relation to this version of our national identity – some embrace it, finding comfort in being part of a greater construct, while others reject it completely.

The question we might ask ourselves, as the warm glow of the London Olympics fades in an era of harsh austerity, is whether the euphoria of those two weeks caused a shift in the grand narrative of Britishness.

In the summer of 2012, we witnessed two distinct forms of patriotism on display. The Queen's Diamond Jubilee required us, as subjects, to be interested in the spectacle of an old married couple standing on the deck of a barge while it slowly proceeded down the Thames in the pouring rain. Here was patriotism as duty – we were expected to be respectful for no other reason than Elizabeth Windsor is our monarch. The message being sent was that, while the Queen is on the throne and God is in His heaven, we can be proud to be British.

The patriotism displayed in the Olympic Stadium was much less dutiful. Here we were invited to engage not only with the members of Team GB, but also with the possibility of their defeat. Her Majesty could be on her throne and God in His heaven, but if Mo Farah got boxed in on the final bend of the race, then our sense of national pride could come crashing down. In that moment, between the all-to-familiar sense of disappointment and the unexpected elation of victory after victory, something shifted.

The shock waves were felt far and wide. Morrissey flew into a rage, denouncing the 'blustering jingoism' of the Olympics, his knee-jerk reaction blinding him to the fact that jingoism is defined by its bellicosity, and the crowds in the stadia were anything but hostile to foreigners. Peter Hitchens came closer to correctly judging the mood when he complained that the Olympics showed that Britain had forgotten that it was once a monarchist Christian country.

This scale of this change was reflected in Danny Boyle's opening ceremony, which took the date of the last London Olympics, 1948, as the beginning of modern Britain. It was the year that the NHS was founded – Boyle had his nurses dance in late 40s uniforms. It also saw the first wave of post-war immigration – and there was the Empire Windrush, sailing into the stadium. Harder to express in such a pageant was the fact that in 1948 the Royal Mint removed the title of Emperor of India from our coinage. From now on George VI would only be D:G:BR:OMN:REX – by Grace of God, King of Britain.

In the years since, although Britain has changed fundamentally, those who have taken it upon themselves to enforce the national grand narrative have clung ever tighter to a version of events that has come to be known as 'Our Island Story'. This portrays the British as a people who are white, homogeneous, monarchist and Christian, whose forefathers ruled the greatest empire the world has ever seen – a mind-set neatly symbolised by the Union Jack.

That's why some felt uneasy when they saw the massed flag-waving in the stadium. Yet here was also, before us on the running track, three good examples of how our society had benefited from multiculturalism, how the collective provision of free education and healthcare had helped these individuals to achieve their full potential. Jessica Ennis, Greg Rutherford and Mo Farah are the embodiment of the diverse Britain of the twenty-first century. But where was our symbol of who we think we are? That question was answered by the athletes themselves – as soon as they won their titles, they reached for the Union Jack.

When the BNP raise our flag, they are asking us to share their prejudices which seek to divide our communities. When it is held aloft by a mixed-raced woman, a ginger haired guy and an immigrant named Mohamed in the Olympic Stadium, they are asking us to share in the success of a state-funded, multicultural project that brings people together. And for the millions watching on TV around the world, they are challenging the traditional image of Britishness.

Those who cling to 'Our Island Story' have long relied on the fact that we on the left have been inept at constructing a counter-narrative capable of uniting the British people in a sense of national pride. Danny Boyle, with his 'Isles of Wonder', has provided us with our own founding story, and our athletes and Olympic volunteers have offered us a glimpse of who we really are. Can a new spirit of engaged and transformational patriotism emerge from this experience? One that seeks to build a fairer, more inclusive tomorrow, rather than constantly rehashing a narrow vision of the past?

Like a photo taken of a family holidaying together on a sunny beach, the London Olympics offered us a snapshot of who we can be. We remain a nation of quirky individuals, but we now know that when we rise together – like the flames of Thomas Heatherwick's Olympic cauldron – we are capable of creating something unique and impressive. Something that makes us all proud.

An earlier version of this chapter first appeared as a blog 'Did The Olympics Make You Proud To Be British' at www.billybragg.co.uk.

THE BEST OLYMPICS NEVER

Alan Tomlinson

In its last issue of 2012 the *Guardian* asked of 2013 'what can we do to match the Olympics?' – perhaps mainly as an excuse to show on the front page yet another photo of the firework display over the Thames for the Olympic celebration, itself resonant of that other national extravaganza of the year, the Queen's Jubilee. These would be the abiding images of 2012 for Britain – colourful celebrations of national pride and tradition. This was a year in which for once, back in August and September, the national press in the United Kingdom had been united on a dominant public issue of the day: the media had come together to massage the public ego in an orgy of self-congratulation about the unadulterated success of the Olympic and Paralympic Games. *The Sunday Times* set the tone in its editorial on the final day of the event, under the heading 'A nation united by our golden Games': the Olympics had 'engendered a sense of wellbeing and benevolent patriotism that has further united the nation'.

On the day after the closing ceremony, headline writers and lead editorial voices were as one, exuberant and triumphant, from the posh to the popular. According to the *Daily Telegraph*: 'We lit the flame; we lit up the world'; and the paper extolled the 'wonderful advertisement for the glories of this country and its capital city', while Mick Brown recalled the 'two weeks of unbelievable spectacle that surpassed our wildest dreams'. Other front-page headlines shared the same ecstatic moment of celebration. In the *Daily Mirror*: 'Goldbye! One billion watch star-studded finale to greatest Games'; in the *Sun*: 'We're world beaters ... Dream GB'. *Daily Star*: 'Best of British, Amazing farewell to Games'. More muted was the *Independent*'s 'That's all, folks' on its souvenir issue pullout, and 'What a swell party that was!' in the main paper. 'Goodbye to the glorious Games' declared the *Guardian* on its main page, setting in sepia, in its Olympics 2012 special supplement, the 29 gold-medal winning individuals and teams around the acclamation 'Golden Britain'.

And the hyperbole was not from just the specialist sports writers. Voices unfamiliar to sporting commentary and the sports pages were drawn into the excitement and debate. Writer, poet and literary critic Blake Morrison recalled being inspired as a ten-year-old by grainy images of the Rome 1960 Olympics on television, restaging events on his own in his backyard in rural Yorkshire. Initially sceptical about the winning bid, he had remained so up to the eve of the event, when stories of security mismanagement were to the fore. Now resident in South London, he had been particularly concerned about the ground-to-air missiles being installed in his backyard in metropolitan Blackheath. The costs were spiralling, corporate sponsors were gobbling up privileges, an Olympic bus driver couldn't operate his satnav, the weather was wet and grim. This was hardly the stuff of dream-inspiring spectacle:

> I was wrong. Most of us were wrong. The last two weeks have been amazing … I'm embarrassed to admit how many times my eyes have welled up. And even more embarrassed that the cause has usually been a British medal … pride of some sort seems to have affected most of the country … What's wonderful about the crowds waving their union flags inside Olympic venues or sitting in front of giant screens across the country is how diverse they are, yet how united … The Games have been the most inclusive event in Britain in my lifetime.[1]

Particularly once the gold medals started coming for the Great Britain squad on the fifth day, the Games offered 'an escape from reality' … 'for 17 days we could forget' the mess of the economy, the tensions of international conflicts, the shenanigans of national politics. Ticketless, but transformed into Olympic superfan by the wholesale coverage of the event on free-to-air television, Morrison exploited to the full the 'right to roam' that was offered by the 'unprecedented freedom' of the red button in what was the first-ever fully digitalised Olympics.

Everywhere I went in London and across England during the Olympics and Paralympics, I found people expressing similar sentiments to those of Morrison. London 2012 – and especially so once the sun came out and stayed out for close to the duration of the event – literally put a smile on people's faces; affluent families who could get tickets spent the cost of an annual holiday on an afternoon in the Olympic Stadium, whatever the competitive line-up; commuting fans took to the streets of London for free glimpses of cyclists or marathon runners; people clamoured to simply spend some time – any time – inside the Olympic Park; 'did-you-see' became the opening gambit of gossiping fans as livetime took precedence over the time-shifting mechanisms of our contemporary media. What were people chatting about at their kettles and worksinks, at the now proverbial water-cooler, if not the next rowing or cycling team's prospects, Bradley's sideburns, Jess's all-round talent, or the recovery time Mo needed for the merciless double of the 5000 and 10,000 metres? This was the WOW factor at work, as those sucked in to the spirit of the event talked it up to unanticipated levels of all-embracing import and significance.

Not everyone, of course, could get there, or get off work, or access the red button options and permutations. Not everyone – even as Team GB was pipping the Russian Federation to third place in the gold-medal table – thought that the £9 billion (minimum) cost of the Games was worth it. A Guardian/ICM poll reported on the final Saturday of the Olympic Games that 55 per cent of Britons saw the Games as 'well worth' the investment, and as having done a valuable job of cheering up the country during hard times; but 35 per cent, despite the smiles and the medals, still believed that they were 'a costly distraction from serious economic problems'. And in Scotland, opinion on the worthwhileness of the Games was evenly split, with 42 per cent agreeing, and 42 per cent not agreeing that the money, time and effort were worth it. Younger people were generally more in favour of the Games than older people, and professional (AB) social classes were 'keenest', with 63 per cent seeing the Games as a good thing.[2] Not everyone joined the party then. But more than enough did – particularly in the media spotlight of the venues and the Olympic Park itself – for talk of a consensus of support to be credible, a shared and extensive reading of the Olympics as a collective endeavour staged for the good of us all. London 2012 in this sense sustained the historical claims and values of Olympic enthusiasts and apologists through time. The city/country could combine a cultural-historical pedigree of commitment to sport (for both the articulation of national pride and the cultivation of individual character), with an all-embracing multicultural and projective vision of the contemporary relevance of the Games.

London 2012, just like other recent Games, was based upon an alliance-cum-contract between the city and the global brand of the IOC – with the national government signing up to cover contingencies in the eventuality of economic or security crises. To many people it is difficult to understand why informed and experienced politicians and professionals come to sign up for such a project – one that will always escalate out of control in costs, and can guarantee none of its projected benefits, whether these be home-nation medal tallies or tourist numbers. But my argument is that understanding the source of this willingness to take on the Games helps a wider understanding of the whole Olympic process. It is the special trick of the Olympics that there is always competition from hopeful host cities; and it is the magic that it continues to generate – for however transient a period of time – that provides an answer to the mystery of its attraction.

THE MYSTERY AND THE MAGIC

Team GB exceeded all expectations at the 2012 Games. Nervous Olympic planners, administrators and enthusiasts had aimed for fourth place, to equal the performance at Beijing, where China, the USA and Russia took the top three slots. But once the gold medals started to accumulate, it became clear that, counting just golds, in line with IOC protocol, the athletic might of the Russian Federation could be matched and bettered. The nineteen British golds of Beijing were eclipsed by the twenty-nine at London 2012 – five more golds than Russia's total (though Russia's overall medal total of 85 was well clear of Team GB's 65). Without these stirring results, the chemistry of the Olympian summer might have been hugely different; modest results would have led to serious questioning of costs. But as the medal count mounted, the seats filled up, and the carnivalesque crowds material-ised, an aura of sorts settled over the event. Women boxers? Taekwondo champions? It was not just the rowers, the cyclists and the equestrians who were doing it for Team GB – the old country was also competing with success in new spheres. Or in older spheres with revitalised competitiveness – Andy Murray taking tennis gold, and the virtually unknown Greg Rutherford taking long-jump gold with the shortest winning jump in the event since 1972. But who cared about records when yet another gold was won on that transformative Super Saturday? Tony Blair had promised a 'magic and memorable' Games, to 'do justice to the great Olympic ideals'.[3] And once the gold medals started coming for the host nation, the magic truly began.

Part of the mystery of the Olympics lies in its longevity, its survival and growth across what is now three different centuries. This partly stems from the rhetorical tone set for Olympic discourse by Baron Pierre de Coubertin, founder of the modern Games, right from the very beginning. At his 1894 congress to launch the modern Olympic Movement in Paris, he toasted his own vision: 'I raise my glass to the Olympic idea, which has crossed the mists of time like a ray from the all-powerful sun and is returning to shine on the gateway to the twentieth century with the gleam of joyful hope'.[4] But it is remarkable that such messianic sentimentality has been successfully reworked in an informed world of global media and digital communications that guarantee unprecedented levels of access to information and material. And what explains this longevity is the suspension of disbelief by a willing public, the readiness of people to not just watch, but to participate in the magic show. The turning point in recent Olympic history has been its adoption by an increasingly globalised media that is ready to embrace its rituals of idealism and rhetoric – particularly after satellite transmission made live coverage possible at the Tokyo 1964 Games. World media can now beam in and celebrate across the globe the skill and techniques that have made the opening and closing ceremonies such a quadrennial highlight for the national and global audience. These ceremonies have now become an essential part of the whole magical show. And the magician's key technique is sleight of hand – along with getting us to look one way rather than another, shifting our perceptions in a split second, and undermining our commonsense understandings. Designers and producers of Olympic ceremonies have become adept at such techniques, and London 2012 was no exception.

The London opening ceremony gave Oscar-winning movie director and northern Englishman Danny Boyle the opportunity to provide the nation and the world with a vision of British history and the making of an increasingly multi-cultural British nationalism. Its brilliant conceit was the green hillock up which the common people, the industrialists and the politicians could all climb, in times of turbulence and dramatic social and cultural change; the mound acted as a people's platform, accessible to all at the different points of British history. Boyle's people's history also downplayed the city of London, cleverly avoiding the danger of a self-congratulatory smugly self-satisfying and solipsistic promotion of the host city itself. And after all the hoo-hah about who might light the cauldron's flame – which Olympic veteran or contemporary superstar? We were given neither. Instead Boyle had stayed faithful to the 2005 winning bid's emphasis on youth, with a squad of six youthful athletes of the future taking the stage for this climactic moment. Nineteen-year-old athlete Adelle Tracey was one of these. A beneficiary of Dame Kelly Holmes's mentoring programme, she recalled how 'gobsmacked' she was when Danny Boyle told them what their secret task was actually going to be: 'The whole concept of 'inspiring a generation' really worked'.[5]

Danny Boyle's colleague, designer Thomas Heatherwick, had designed a cauldron that was integrated into the stadium – an echo of its placing at the 1948 Games, its gradual emergence serving to integrate it within the stadium, and helping to convey the feel of an intimate film set. The cauldron constructed itself on the spot, including 204 copper petals, symbolising each of the participating nations/teams, one to be taken home by each nation as a memento after the Games, a symbol of unity and the overcoming of difference. Sarah Crompton wrote of the 'originality and breathtaking beauty' of the cauldron:

> The technical execution was equally stunning: the creation of each shape by traditional British craftsmen; the delicacy of the long, stainless-steel tubes holding each petal; the way the flame passed from outer to inner rings; the rise of the pieces upwards to make a rose of fire. The blaze appeared magically suspended in mid-air.[6]

The tone was set. The opening ceremony became the perfect vehicle for a magical meaning-shifting excursion from the travails, tensions and demands of everyday life. Clive James wrote of Sydney 2000 that 'the opening ceremony ... had stunned the world and given Australia confidence in its new position as a mature nation'.[7] Such are the big – and barely testable – claims that are made for these spectacles. In fact they are nowhere near as different from each other as the publicists and enthusiasts claim. The opening ceremony at Sydney shared much with London 2012's opener: a people's history; in-house national jokes and humour (in Sydney this was dancing lawnmowers, a tongue-in-cheek take on the tidiness of suburban Australian lawns); and the depiction of ethnic and multicultural diversity in the remaking of the modern nation. Olympic spectacle of this sort must balance regional (city-based), national and global interests. It is projected to the world-wide audience, but it celebrates much that is local and even peculiar to the host culture and city. I spoke to numerous young people from South Korea, China and the USA about the London 2012 opening ceremony, and most were baffled by its innate Britishness – a baffle-ment which turned quickly into boredom. But the magic was beginning to work for the UK audience, bonding an often disunited Kingdom into a popular front that was soon to be cheering on its Stella McCartney-clad athletes and volunteers alike.

IDEALS AND IDEOLOGY

The messianic vision of Coubertin – Rénovateur of the modern Olympics – is rooted in a vocabulary of transcendence, and an aspira-tion to rebuild the youth of the world, both physically and morally: what he called the *rebronzage* (the burnishing) of his nation after the humiliation of defeat in the 1871 Franco-Prussian war:

> I shall enlarge its vision and its hearing by showing it with wide horizons; heavenly, planetary, historical, horizons of universal history which, in engendering mutual respect, will bring about a ferment of international peace.[8]

It is of course worth noting that such universalism is sometimes compromised by history, politics and human agency; and reactions to winning, hosting and staging the Olympics have altered over time. Expectation can turn to mistrust; agreement can escalate into euphoria; and forgetting can be superseded by nostalgia.[9] In the case of London 2012, we entered the euphoric phase from the second Saturday of the seventeen days, when three athletics Gold Medals were won in just one evening. (At the Atlanta Games in 1996 the British team collected just one gold medal in the whole Games, won by rowers Matthew Pinsent and Steve Redgrave. Euphoria? We never even got started.)

Even in London 2012 things started slowly. The publicity machine worked well in the build-up during the Olympic torch's journey across the country. But at first the competitors did not seem to be meeting national expectations. World champion cyclist Mark Cavendish disappointed fans and commentators on the first weekend, finishing only twenty-eighth in the men's road race. The gold medal went to Kazakhstan's 38-year-old Alexander Vinokourov, banned for two years after testing positive for blood doping during the 2007 Tour de France. A bemused British media cast him more as cheat than champion.

But Olympic silver medallist rower Cath Bishop assured me that the picture would change very soon as the rowers were coming, and indeed they did. On the fifth day of competition, in Bishop's old event, Helen Glover and Heather Stanning took Britain's first gold medal in the women's pair. Then Bradley Wiggins took gold in the cyclists' time trial, and a trickle became a flood of home-nation successes. The nation/country was more than ready to party by the final weekend of the event, as it approached its greatest medal total since the more parochial times of London's first hosting in 1908. And more events were to come – including the monumental triumph of Mo Farah in the men's 5000 metres. But at this point Coe gave his preliminary overview of the event:

> We have broken all records. We really have got the platform to inspire the next generation. It's what we said we'd do. They are Games for everyone by everyone. People have been involved in their millions. It has been a unique opportunity to showcase this country. Coming off the back of the Jubilee weekend, we will look back on this and think there's probably never been a time like this.[10]

Paul Hayward, in the *Daily Telegraph* the day after the closing ceremony, praised the energy of the crowds, a force that would become a dominant memory for millions, and called the Olympics 'an almighty advertisement for collective effort and shared experience', an expression of Britishness excluding no-one: 'If there is a single word to describe the quality at the heart of London 2012 it may be "soul". The Games had soul'.[11] Boris Johnson boasted after the opening ceremony, 'I reckon we have knocked Beijing – with all respect to our Chinese friends, and greatly though I admired those Games – into a cocked hat'; and, when the Olympics were over: 'London has put on a dazzling face to the global audience. For the first time since the end of empire, it truly feels like the capital of the world'.[12] But it wasn't just the home nation writers, journalists and politicians waxing lyrical and hurtling towards the extremities of hyperbole on London's achievements. The Mayor of Rio de Janeiro, Eduardo Paes, complimented his London equivalent Johnson: 'You just did the greatest Games ever. Everyone's looking at London. This was already a great city and it became even a greater city so Rio will try to follow you. You did so great that we're going to have lots of trouble, lots of work, but we're going to deliver great things in 2016 in Rio de Janeiro'.[13] (Mayor Paes was clearly prac-tising the word 'great' for his turn in 2016.)

It was the custom of previous IOC president Juan Antonio Samaranch to fuel the expectations of hosts through a model of continuous improvement in the profile – and finances – of the Games and the IOC. It became a Samaranch tradition to comment on the Games in the closing ceremony speech. He called the Summer Olympics in Los Angeles 1984 and then Seoul 1998 the 'best' Games; and he called the Barcelona 1992 Games (staged in his own home city) the best yet: 'Thanks Barcelona. Thanks Catalunya. Thanks Spain. You have achieved it. These have been, with no doubt, the best Games of the whole Olympic history'. There were exceptions to this tale of superlatives. In Atlanta 1996 Samaranch was more circumspect, telling the city 'Well done' for staging a 'most exceptional Games'. In this muted response he was probably responding as much to the bombing in the Centennial Olympic Park – and the woeful local transportation system – as to the athletic competition. But at his outgoing Olympics at Sydney in 2000, he was back on song, glorifying the event as 'the best Olympic Games ever. They could not have been better … a perfect organisation'. In this he was writing a testimonial to his own achievements in the Olympic story.

Samaranch's successor as IOC president, Jacques Rogge, changed the style, offering a more studied judgement than his predecessor; he avoided comparisons and superlatives, but he continued to frame the respective Games in an incremental developmental narrative. Athens 2004, his first Summer Olympics as President, received a carefully worded response: 'You have won! You have won by brilliantly meeting the tough challenge of holding the Games. These Games were unforgettable, dream Games'. Beijing 2008 was acknowledged as a 'truly exceptional Games' which gave birth to 'new stars' and 'true role models', whose achievements were marvelled at, and whose 'warm embrace' of each other showed the world the 'unifying power of sport'. At London 2012, Rogge's last Summer Olympics as president, he thanked the Organising Committee which, 'well supported by the public authorities, did a superb job'. The 'wonderful volunteers, the much-needed heroes' of the Games were praised for their smiles, kindness and support. Public and spectators were thanked for providing the soundtrack to a Games at which a festival spirit had characterised all venues. 'The best of British hospitality' had been shown to the world. Plucking words from the British national anthem, he dubbed London 2012 the 'happy and glorious Games'. But never did he say that they were the 'best'. They might have written 'a new chapter in Olympic history', but in IOC-speak that's what all Games do. Their biggest legacy has now become the next Olympiad cycle itself, the next Games, the succeeding version in this sustained narrative of idealism and universalism.

Writing soon after the Games, Rogge added a little history:

> The foundations for London's achievements were firmly built on the knowledge and expertise of previous Olympic organisers. Massive urban regeneration projects undertaken by Barcelona in 1992 and Sydney in 2000, environmental and sustainability standards set by Lillehammer in 1994 and Vancouver in 2010, and programmes to encourage volunteerism and youth participation by the Beijing 2008 organisers are just a few of the success stories that London used as a springboard.[14]

But while the IOC may have shifted away from baseless self-promotion, Mayor of London Boris Johnson let it be known that he 'wouldn't dissent' should it be put to him that the London Games were the best ever. In this he presaged a triumphalism that spread like an epidemic across the country, wholly inappropriate to the context of the Olympic spirit of mutual respect and inter-cultural understanding. In September, after the conclusion to the Paralympic Games, Johnson upstaged Prime Minister David Cameron at the Victoria Memorial in London, thanking the people whom he'd joined for 'one final tear-sodden juddering climax', to salute the victories of the previous fortnight: 'this was your achievement, you brought this country together in a way we never expected. You routed the doubters and you scattered the gloomsters, and, for the first time in living memory, you caused Tube train passengers to break into spontaneous conversation with their neighbours about subjects other than their trod-on toes'.[15] This was a host city party, with a lot to celebrate.

Meanwhile the sponsors were also counting their gains. To take just one example of the magic the Olympics bring for multinational companies, Proctor & Gamble, one of the eleven worldwide partners (elite sponsors), was proclaiming the success of its 'P&G Family Home'. They had converted a 68,000 square-foot brick warehouse in London's Borough Market to create their 'Home', which was host to thousands of visitors throughout the Games. It could hold 400 guests at a time, and staged 150 separate events, 100 of them specifically for National Olympic Committees. The idea had been launched in Vancouver during the 2010 Winter Olympics, when the company had offered luxury facilities to mothers and fathers of Olympians, and the repeat in London was judged a huge success: 'This is really beyond our wildest dreams', commented Marc Pritchard, P&G's Global Marketing and Brand-Building Officer.

P&G had refined its concept of boosting its various brands through offering them to athletes. It had its own beauty salon, with hair and nail care taken care of by Cover Girl, Pantene, and Max Factor products. Team GB members could pop in for a free nail job. And while the women were drawn to the salon, a 'man cave' – equipped with pool-tables, video games, table football, darts and big-screen TVs – offered barber services, 'haircuts and shaves using Gillette razors and Old Spice lotions'. For Pritchard, Gillette was 'one of our best brands to activate'. 'They even created a special gold razor for this. We gave Ryan Lochte and the swimmers gold-plated razors with encrusted crystals'. And if you needed a quick freshen-up orally, the Family Home had Oral B and Crest toothpaste on hand. Two news rooms were also based in the converted warehouse, 'pumping out press activities and huge social media and broadcast relations'. According to Pritchard: 'We have a great relationship with NBC, Tencent in China, with BBC. We've created probably close to 1 billion impressions a day around here. It was a really good opportunity for us.'[16]

RECURRING RENAISSANCE

There is now no shortage of candidates to pick up and run with the Olympic torch for the next round of Games, each blending their own

national character with what has become an almost spiritual cosmopolitanism. The concluding statement in Istanbul's bid-book for the
2020 Summer Games calls up historical, geographic, political, and
religious themes:

> Istanbul occupies a truly unique place in the world. Geographically,
> culturally and symbolically, it sits at the junction of East and West,
> representing the best of all worlds. In this secular Muslim society all
> people, regardless of race, culture, gender or religion, celebrate their
> nation's enlightened approach to inclusiveness and respect for
> humanity. The potential to create harmony by celebrating differ-
> ences through the lens of Olympic and Paralympic Games is
> profound, uniting all participants and guiding the way for the
> future.[17]

Madrid, defying the realities of economic crisis, has persisted in
staying in the race, and is bidding for a third successive time. Alejandro
Blanco's letter at the end of its bid book mobilised long-standing arguments to justify the candidature:

> We propose an organisational concept responsible towards all stake-
> holders, society itself and the management of resources: financially
> sustainable and environmentally friendly Games. Madrid 2020 will
> enthuse the generation of today, showing the way to the future for
> new generations.
>
> Madrid is a peaceful, open and vibrant city, which guarantees a
> safe environment for athletes and for the entire Olympic Family,
> receiving everyone with open arms. Our firm will to host the 2020
> Games is a proof of our commitment to the Olympic Movement, the
> interests of which we undertake to safeguard, as its development is
> also our development. We are ready to take on the honour and
> responsibility of delivering the Games. Games full of passion and
> enthusiasm, both inspiring and providing opportunities for a whole
> generation of young people and which will be the light of the future.[18]

Tokyo, bruised from its loss to Rio in the race to host 2016, and in the
wider context of the national tragedy of the March 2011 earthquake
and tsunami on its Pacific coast, stressed its progressive, global image
and status:

Tokyo is committed and fully prepared to deliver on its vision for 2020: to bring together innovation and inspiration in the heart of the world's most forward-thinking and safe city. We will unite the power of the Olympic and Paralympic Games with the unique values of the Japanese people and the excitement of a city that sets global trends. And deliver a dynamic celebration that will help reinforce and renew the Olympic Values for a new generation – and so contribute to more young people worldwide sharing the dreams and hope of sport.[19]

So there it is, again. The local, the national and the global, all woven together into the same formula. None of these cities will be able to keep to costs; all are professing the same principles, ideals and commitments. All of them have designers and showmen and spectacle entrepreneurs for 2020; all of them are capable of dazzling an entirely digitalised world for the required 17 or so days. We know that whoever wins this will happen, whatever the global or national crisis – it must happen, since to stage the Olympics is an imperative once the offer is accepted. It remains somewhat mysterious as to why such projects and promises continue to be made, and are given such degrees of credence. But that's where the magic comes in. And Rio knows that the magic can work again when it stages the Olympic show in another time, another place; it will still be peddling hope, still carrying on the same (though appropriately nuanced) rhetoric and ritual that has kept the modern show on the road for close to a century and a quarter.

THE MAGNIFICENT TRIVIA OF SPORT

Sport at its highest level embodies the principles of excellence, grace, beauty ... but it's still a form of magnificent trivia.[20] Olympic excellence conveys splendour, and unrivalled and always aspiring human accomplishment, in the context of the strong appeal of the sporting spectacle – but it is a spectacle which also assures a consensual infantilisation on the part of the onlooker, who is open-mouthed in wonder, temporarily oblivious to the wider context and meaning of the spectacle. It is top-level sport's abiding appeal that it can draw us into a Never-Never land, combining an escapist focus upon the action with a willed immersion in the magnificently trivial. Meanwhile the world changes little in substance: the armed conflicts continue, economic rivalries threaten global stability, Britain loses its triple A financial status/rating, and the multicultural conviviality of London 2012's party fades as the moment of inclusive ecstasy recedes. Never mind. The Olympic show, for the sake of all who have invested so much in it, must go on, and move on. Next stop Rio.

I am grateful to the British Academy for funding my research, conducted from 2007 to 2010, on ' The construction and mediation of the sporting spectacle in Europe, 1992-2004', Award Number SG:47220, which has informed historical and sociological dimensions of this chapter; and to Royal Holloway College, University of London, for inviting me to address the symposium on 'Olympics and the "'isms'" in London, 25 July 2012, when I rehearsed some of the arguments that frame this chapter.

NOTES

1. Blake Morrison, 'The Olympic triumph: astonishing, moving and magnificent', *Guardian*, 11 August 2012.
2. Tom Clark and Owen Gibson, 'Britons back the feelgood Games', *Guardian*, 11 August 2012.
3. Tony Blair, quoted in Mike Lee, *The Race for the 2012 Olympics*, Virgin Books 2006, pxiv.
4. Norbert Muller (ed), *Pierre de Coubertin, 1863-1937: Olympism; Selected writings*, International Olympic Committee 2000, p532.
5. Adelle Tracey, 'Eyewitness – The Opening Ceremony', *Observer*, 19 August 2012.
6. Sarah Crompton, 'Thomas Heatherwick: A burning desire to change the world', *Telegraph*, 31 July 2012.
7. Clive James, 'G'night Sydney', *Independent*, 3 October 2000.
8. Pierre de Coubertin, quoted in Marie-Thérèse Eyquem, 'The Founder of the Modern Games', in Lord Killanin and John Rodda (eds), *The Olympic Games: 80 Years of People, Events and Records*, Barrie & Jenkins 1976, p138.
9. These phases were identified by Chris Kennett and Miquel de Moragas, on the basis of their research on the Barcelona 1992 Summer Games: Chris Kennet and Miquel de Moragas, 'Barcelona 1992: Evaluating the Olympic legacy', in Alan Tomlinson and Christopher Young (eds), *National Identity and Global Sports Events*, State University of New York Press 1996.
10. Quoted in Gordon Rayner, 'The Finale: We can't slow down now, Coe tells Team GB: Games chairman urges athletes to keep on breaking records and finish on a high', *Daily Telegraph*, 11 August 2012.
11. Paul Hayward, 'London, you're beautiful: These Games will be remem-

bered as a triumph for warmth, civility, excellence and enthusiasm', *Daily Telegraph*, 13 August 2012.

12. Boris Johnson, 'London and Team GB – take a bow. You've dazzled the world', *Daily Telegraph*, 13 August 2012.
13. Eduardo Paes, quoted in Rayner, op cit.
14. Jacques Rogge, 'Was London 2012 the best Olympics ever?', *Guardian*, 23 November 2012.
15. Quoted in Michael Savage, 'One final tear-sodden climax', *The Times*, 11 September 2012.
16. All quotes from Ed Hula, 'P&G sets standard with London home for Olympic families', *www.aroundtherings.com*, 30 August 2012.
17. Istanbul 2020 Bid Book, Volume 3, p137.
18. Madrid 2020 Bid Book, Volume 3, p128.
19. Tokyo 2020 Bid Book, Volume 3, p124.
20. See Alan Tomlinson, *Sport and Leisure Cultures*, University of Minnesota Press 2005.

FRAUD OF THE RINGS

Eliane Glaser

'Olympics sparkle at height of magical British summer', reported Reuters. For the *Guardian* the Olympic fortnight was 'one of dreams and wonder'. Their 'real legacy', announced the *Mirror*, 'will be dreams and memories, inspiration and magic'. 'Look back in wonder' proclaimed an *Independent* photo spread. The euphoria of August 2012 was a willed rejection of British cynicism, naysaying and self-perceived incompetence. But now that this economic predicament is once again re-established as disastrous, that momentary summer madness can be revealed for what it was. That is, if we bother to analyse it.

It's become a self-evident cliché that we live in a 24-hour news culture: a neutral fact of fast-paced modernity. But that goldfish-memory culture has a political effect. It means that events are rarely properly mined for their underlying significance. The relentless onward march of the Twitterati renders London 2012 old news. And that's great for those who had an interest in making political hay out of the Olympics while the sun shined. But it's only now that the hysteria has subsided that it's possible not only to test those airy claims of 'legacy' and 'Olympic bounce', but also to see how the manic enthusiasm of that heady fortnight relates to the broader context of austerity.

In my book *Get Real* I describe how contemporary culture is full of airbrushed illusions, which not only distort reality but disguise things as their very opposite. Spending cuts that disproportionately target the poor are not announced as the product of Conservative ideology, but are dressed up in the rhetoric of 'people power'. 'We are the radicals now', explains right-wing Old Etonian David Cameron, 'breaking apart the old system with a massive transfer of power, from the state to citizens, politicians to people'. In a world increasingly determined by digital technology, we discover a retro fondness for quilting and embroidery. As food production becomes ever more industrialised, we are fed a diet of TV programmes about allotments and home baking. As the environment is ever more modified and destroyed, we worship David Attenborough as a national treasure.

When I look for examples of this insidious combination of deception and self-delusion, I am guided by the insights of cultural critics like Antonio Gramsci, Louis Althusser, Jean Baudrillard and Theodor Adorno. But that way of thinking has been on the wane since the 1990s. Ideology critique, as it was once called, is not really happening in the media and public conversation; not even – or rather especially – when it comes to an event as culturally freighted as the Olympics. It's as if in the twenty-first century we now consider ourselves to be savvy and sophisticated citizens, adept at interpreting adverts and media messages. But if we're all so firmly on the case, why did revelations that many reality TV programmes are in fact 'faked' create such a furore in 2007? And why did the discovery that many 'beef' products actually contain horsemeat come as such a surprise in early 2013? I don't think it's an accident that ideology critique has fallen out of fashion as covert forms of ideology are taking hold – in the era of Twitter, Facebook, and hyper-real computer games; and of ever more sophisticated spin, PR and viral advertising campaigns. Ideology critique has become passé at the precise time when we need it most.

THE USES OF ENTHUSIASM

While the Games seemed at the time to be an escapist holiday from austerity, a kind of temporary blissful blip, the crucial point for me was that this 'feel-good factor' actually lent austerity a cosy little alibi. Just as the 'bit of fun' defence of Page Three girls does a lot of anti-feminist spade-work, a huge amount of political capital was extracted from Olympic cheer. David Cameron's stated desire to 'bottle' the Olympic spirit was telling, because it distilled attempts by politicians and corporations to commodify the games; to turn what many valued as a kind of transcendent experience into something with a market price. The Olympics were justified from the start in financial terms, by the contribution they would make to economic growth.

What I'm really interested in, however, is how the Olympics were made to bolster Coalition austerity in a much less tangible way. They were portrayed as having nothing to do with politics, thus enabling the politics to operate at a much more covert level. If Olympic enthusiasm now looks embarrassingly overrated, it also seems to me to be deeply pernicious.

I know it's annoying to say I told you so. But right from the start I was a cynic, a curmudgeon, a party pooper. Way back in 2005, watching the demented reaction to Britain's winning bid on TV, my heart sank. I thought, here comes seven nightmarish years of feeling like I'm back in a school games lesson, geekily uncomprehending as to why my classmates should so relish running laps round a freezing, muddy field. And with my snarky attitude towards the assumption that everyone should be into sport came a creeping sense of stigma: to lambast what looked to me like groundless celebration felt like being the fat kid who gets picked last for the team.

PROPAGANDA, BOYLE STYLE

In the run-up to the Games, my irritation blossomed into a full-blown allergy: to the corporate carve-up of East London, to the looming transport disaster for ordinary working Londoners, to the blanket clockwork media coverage. And then on the night of the opening ceremony, things got even worse. Up till then I had felt part of a small but significant band of naysayers. But on that first night, almost all my fellow dissenters melted into the crowd. As the hegemony of the 'fun' school sports day became complete, dissent was now indistinguishable from not being a team player.

And that was down to Danny Boyle and his remarkable extravaganza. It wasn't just that it was a thrilling and moving show, as even I am compelled to admit. It was that it celebrated things that lefties like me hold dear, from trade unionists to NHS nurses. Fifty suffragettes marched through the stadium, Dizzee Rascal provided the banging backdrop for a multi-racial romance, and it all looked very convincingly like a two-fingered riposte to the Coalition's austerity agenda.

But look again at the imagery of that opening ceremony, and a rather different interpretation opens up. Let's consider for a moment the meaning of the word propaganda. It seems at first sight that propaganda means simply a crudely overt message: the Nazi games of 1936, the Soviet games of 1980 and the Chinese games of 2008. Some commentators described the 2012 opening ceremony – and indeed the games as a whole – as being redolent of propaganda. To the *Daily*

Mail's Stephen Glover, Danny Boyle's show was a piece of 'Marxist propaganda'; while the lanes reserved for IOC officials were branded Soviet 'Zil' lanes. To have an opening ceremony tell our Island Story in such a brazen and heavy-handed way seemed a bit, well, North Korean.

But there's another meaning of the word propaganda that we don't tend to register very much any more; at least not consciously. And that is a form of communication that's sneaky and subliminal. We associate Communists with propaganda not just because they were so overt about their political messages, but also because – as in *The Manchurian Candidate* – there was something rather sinister and mind-gamesy about those messages. They involved manipulation rather than straightforward hectoring. Brainwashing isn't about being shouted at; it's about being influenced in more subtle ways. So propaganda actually has one meaning that is directly opposed to the other; that radically undermines the other. If you want to find out the truth in the world of Orwell's *Nineteen Eighty-Four*, you look to the opposite of what the authorities are telling you: the Ministry of Peace promotes war, the Ministry of Plenty oversees famine. We may consider ourselves to be living in a more transparent society than that of Orwell's dystopia. We may regard ourselves as more sophisticated and savvy than the citizens of Soviet Russia. But in fact the brand of propaganda that characterises the modern West is in a way more insidious than that of either the USSR or Nineteen Eighty-Four, because it is disguised by a comforting illusion of liberal openness.

So when Danny Boyle's ceremony celebrated NHS nurses, it seemed like an unarguably good thing. But what if the ceremony had the very opposite effect? Of giving us a false sense of security that we were, as a culture, valuing the NHS; when at that very moment a government of neoliberal ideologues was allowing the free market to spread its corrosive logic through this institution that we hold so dear? Similarly, broadcasting to the watching world what appeared to be a national affection for Tolpuddle Martyrs and Jarrow Marchers created a somewhat misleading impression, at a time of wholesale erosion of trade union rights and the mainstream media's universal demonisation of those claiming unemployment benefit. We were offered an ostensibly subversive spectacle, with a clubby, house-party vibe, Mr Bean undercutting the pomp and ceremony, and even the Queen demonstrating that she was not above putting in a cameo appearance. But what if this inclusive, progressive performance was actually a remarkably effective mechanism for bringing dissenters into the comfy, corporate Olympic fold? A way of stifling those voices with a matey, sentimental hug?

It all reminded me of Boyle's *Slumdog Millionaire*, a feel-good film that celebrated unlikely rags-to-riches success, and which made Western viewers feel more comfortable about all the other children eking out a rubbish-heap existence in poverty-stricken Mumbai. The performers in Boyle's opening ceremony did reflect Britain's actual diversity, but there was something a bit public relations, a bit Benetton-ad, about the harmonious image that was being projected.

And if Boyle's pop-video liberalism wasn't subtly coercive enough, there was also the sporting response from Coalition politicians keen to get in on the act. Boris Johnson illustrated just how seamlessly the Right could assimilate Boyle's symbolism. 'The thing I loved was the heavy political stuff', he enthused. 'I loved the emergence of the urban proletariat'. Boris's embrace was designed to stifle any anti-establishment potential Boyle's ceremony hoped to convey.

EYE-CON

Similarly co-opted were the Olympic 'role models' – Mo Farah, Jessica Ennis and the other 'homegrown heroes'. It goes without saying that they were instantly commodified through commercial sponsorship and 'image rights' deals. And the celebration of these genuinely brilliant athletes was oddly double-edged: it promoted the idea not only that elite sports are accessible to all but also that racism, sexism and other forms of discrimination are a thing of the past. 'Mo makes racist slurs seem distant memory', announced *The Times*. 'Stop complaining' is the implied flip-side of these 'good news' stories.

'London 2012: The year of the Woman'; 'London 2012 Olympics: The Women's Games'; 'London 2012: Was this the Women's Olympics?' ran the headlines. So why was there more debate about American gymnast Gabby Douglas's hair than her gold medal-winning performance? Why did the Japanese and Australian women's basketball and football teams fly into London in economy class, while their male counterparts flew in business? And what is it with the gross discrepancy between male and female athletes when it comes to funding, media coverage and sponsorship deals? 'Ennis, Farah, Murray:

Here Ends the State School Myth', ran the headline to a *Guardian* article of 5 August; but in reality 37 per cent of medal-winners were privately educated, as compared with the 7 per cent nationally who attend private schools. Journalists covering the Paralympics received a special guide instructing them to avoid discussing disability, or the issues around it, where at all possible. 'We believe information on impairment is irrelevant to an athlete's achievements', the booklet declared. 'If you want to include it, try to make sure it is a reference rather than the focus of the article'. The success of minority athletes was recruited to serve the iconography of Thatcherite aspiration; a retort to those grumpy sceptics who claim that there are still barriers to achievement.

'THE PEOPLE'S GAMES'

Despite being sponsored by an elite roll-call of banks and multinational corporations, including Lloyds TSB, Dow, McDonalds, Procter & Gamble, Coca-Cola, and BP, the 2012 Olympics was referred to – by Danny Boyle and others – as 'The People's Games'. The Paralympics were very visibly sponsored by ATOS, the private firm notorious for assessing whether or not disabled people are entitled to their benefits. These 'People's Games' had dedicated limo-lanes for IOC officials, to whiz them from Hamleys to the Ritz. For all the talk of public access and 'transparency' around ticketing, a disproportionate number of VIPs attended the high-profile events.

The Olympic volunteers were held up as emblems of solidarity and egalitarianism, but they were also used as proof, by David Cameron, of Britain's Big Society 'can-do' attitude. At a time when benefits claimants and interns are being forced to work for nothing, the volunteers became an unwitting advertisement for unpaid labour. And for all the rhetoric about the volunteers 'making' the Games, the reality was top-down stage management by the organisers.

The Games were the epitome of manufactured spontaneity; products of a world in which corporations recruit the imagery and ethos of 'grassroots' 'alternative' counterculture. Tesco silently owns a 49 per cent stake in the 'family-run', 'artisan' coffee chain Harris & Hoole; T-Mobile's adverts feature a funky 'flashmob dance-athon'; and a Vodafone ad campaign, entitled 'our power', claims credit for the Arab Spring. So it was an easy step for the commercialised and elitist Olympics to conjure a hollow spectacle of 1960s liberation; a blissed-out Festival vibe that seemed to channel 'people-power' but with any actual substance drained out.

THE IDEOLOGY OF LONDON 2012

We live in a weirdly post-political era. Not only is there little difference between the main political parties, but even the word ideology has become a kind of insult. We are not motivated by ideology, our politicians claim; we are just doing what works. Right and left are supposedly outdated categories, and divisiveness and tribalism are frowned upon. Politicians are no longer motivated by competing ideals about how to run society; they are motivated by 'working together in the national interest'. But to maintain that our political culture is post-ideological is itself an ideological manoeuvre; one that conceals the rise of a particular ideology: neoliberalism.

It's often forgotten nowadays that the word ideology, just like the word propaganda, has an overt and a covert meaning. Ideology refers to an explicit set of political ideas, but it also refers to ideas that are transmitted under the radar. The Olympics did indeed convey a potent political message; it's just that it was a message framed as a break from the political 'real world'. Not only was the coalition imposing spending cuts that targeted the poor, but we were now supposed to stop worrying about that and go out and enjoy ourselves. 'I think it's given the country a tremendous lift', eulogised Cameron'. 'I think it's brought the country together'. He made criticising austerity seem unsporting. But if Cameron's vision of the Olympics bringing the country together was an underhand reinforcement of his 'we're all in it together' line, the 'togetherness' of the Games was also coded as socialist. And if there's one thing worse than bread and circuses, it's when the circuses are labelled Progressive.

The mythology of sport

Kate Hughes

When I was 12, I was marched into a large school hall with my class-mates. We sat in front of an ancient, black and white TV and watched grainy pictures from the Mexico Olympic Games. That day a window to a new world opened for me. By the time I was back in my classroom, I knew what I wanted to do and what I wanted to be. London's vision is to reach people all over the world to connect them with the inspirational power of the Games.

Seb Coe, 6 July 2005

When traced back, the storyline of sport's mythical status begins in the era of *Tom Brown's School Days* and an educational regime in which sport was used as a means of promoting discipline, to prepare young men to serve their country, and, if required, to go to war.[1] Sport (particularly 'games' as played in the English public school system) was considered to encourage the development of courage, endurance, self-discipline, determination and self-reliance.[2]

Fred Coalter describes ascriptions of such status to sport as mythopoeic: they 'contain elements of truth, but elements which become reified and distorted and "represent" rather than reflect reality, standing for supposed but largely unexamined, impacts and processes'.[3] Indeed Richard Giulianotti suggests that there is considerable historical evidence that sport can also be a dysfunctional force that intensifies sources of social conflict, including 'nationalism, sexism, racism and other strains of xenophobia'.[4] Furthermore, stories about the sporting elite often provide evidence that participation can produce less desirable outcomes, including corruption, cheating, the use of recreational drugs and eating disorders.[5]

Most people, however, are content to let sport retain its more romanticised and positive image. And the 'mythopoeic' nature of sport has been central to the development of sport policy in the UK, from it first iterations in the 1960 Wolfenden report to the present day, when leading global organisations continue to reiterate all that is 'good' about sport. The United Nations' special advisor Adolf Ogi informed a Sport and Development conference:

> Sport teaches life skills. Sport remains the best school in life. With sport young people learn: to manage victory; to overcome defeat; to become team players and to be reliable and gain the other team members' confidence; respect for opponents and the rules; that for good results regular training is needed; and, to know their limits and themselves better. The positive lessons and values of sport are essential for life.[6]

International Olympic Committee President Jacques Rogge has identified the part the IOC can play in delivering the Millennium goals, and argues that: 'sport can play an important role in shaping a safer, more prosperous and more peaceful society'.[7] And later in the same document, the IOC's Director of the Department of International Cooperation and Development, Ganda Sithole, went further:

> Sport is able to unite where differing national passions, politics, religion and culture often divide. It can foster social integration and identity-building of minorities and marginalized groups such as street children, child soldiers, ethnic groups or people suffering from HIV/AIDS. Sport can also support local economic development and create jobs though the numerous income-generating activities that are linked to its practice. Sport also conveys positive messages and influences behaviour, just as it can promote self-esteem and interpersonal skills among people, especially young people. It can fight discrimination and raise awareness about women's rights. It has the ability to enable communities at odds with each other to build bridges between themselves. It helps the healing process in populations overcoming trauma and brings joy and fun to brighten up their lives. It can alleviate the negative effects of poverty.[8]

THE GAMES AND MYTH-MAKING

The Games has been linked to claims about its values from the earliest musings of its founder, Pierre de Coubertin. For Coubertin the goal of

Olympism was to 'place sport at the service of the harmonious development of man, with a view to promoting a peaceful society concerned with the preservation of human dignity';[9] while the Olympic values as set out in the Fundamental Principles of the Olympic Movement are: the joy of effort; fair play; respect for others, pursuit of excellence; and a balance between body, will and mind.

In recent years the IOC has had to put in some hard work to promote the idea that the Games can act as a catalyst for social good: the organisation and the Olympic Movement over which it presides have been subject to considerable criticism, particularly towards the end of the presidency of Juan Antonio Samaranch. Some of this criticism is based on the elitist model of growth and expansion being followed by the IOC in the development of the Games.[10] It has been suggested that the Olympic spirit had become a 'marriage of the spirit of capitalism with the spirit of sport'.[11]

Writing at a time when the IOC was reeling from revelations of internal corruption in the build-up to the 2002 Salt Lake City Winter Olympics, John Milton-Smith described Samaranch as 'aloof, arrogant and imperious', and as operating 'not as an inspiring leader but as a banana-republic dictator, cultivating a shameless culture of extravagance and excess around him'.[12] Earlier criticism of the IOC had outlined the freedom from surveillance enjoyed by its officials: at times it had provided sanctuary for those who had compromised themselves within their national communities.[13] Authors such as Andrew Jennings and Helen Jefferson Lenskyj had also added to this negative commentary, describing the Olympic movement as elitist and as abusing its power to exploit young people and their aspirations.[14] Milton-Smith suggested that to transform this situation would require 'reinvention', and a leader 'motivated by a heightened sense of civic duty', who would be able to articulate the Olympic values equally as well as plans and profits'.[15]

The arrival of Jacques Rogge as President in 2001 did, however, mark a noticeable change in the discourse of the IOC. Under Rogge's leadership, the IOC has actively sought to renew its image and to regain a focus on the values portrayed by Olympism. For example, in his address at the opening ceremony of the 2006 Turin Winter Olympic Games, he stated: 'Our World today is in need of peace, tolerance and brotherhood. The values of the Olympic Games can deliver these to us'.[16] And the notion that hosting the Games should be a catalyst for increasing 'social good' was advanced by an amendment to the latest version of the IOC Charter, which now refers to the creation of positive legacies in the host country.[17] Rogge has been a keen supporter of this aim:

> Legacies are the lasting outcomes of our efforts. They bring to life the Olympic values of excellence, friendship and respect ... Creating sustainable legacies is a fundamental commitment of the Olympic Movement.[18]

The IOC Charter as amended in 2007 specifically refers to leaving a legacy of 'sport for all' in the host country, and Rogge has subsequently has spoken of the potential of sport to combat obesity and social isolation, and to encourage a healthy society.[19] But in the build-up to the London 2012 Games these claims were criticised in the light of Games' sponsors such as Coca-Cola, McDonald's and Cadbury.[20] In the *Obesity Games Report*, the Children's Food Campaign pointed out that although corporate sponsors accounted for less than 10 per cent of London 2012 funding, they had been given an 'unrivalled platform to promote their unhealthy brands and products'.[21] Claiming that London 2012 had squandered the opportunity to create a positive health legacy, the CFC called on the IOC to promote healthy eating in their sponsorship deals, and for junk food to be excluded.

The contrast between the IOC's claims about promoting a 'healthy society' and its acceptance of sponsorship from junk food manufacturers is just one instance of a conflict between the IOC's ideals and its actions. Kevin Wamsley suggests that the contemporary Olympic Games have become the 'antithesis of the very ideals they ostensibly cherish'.[22] He then poses a number of difficult questions for the relationship between Olympism and the Olympic Games. Who actually gets on to the field of play? Does competitive sport at its highest levels balance the body and the mind? How can sport be a human right when the bidding process on its own costs billions of dollars, and require the building of both infrastructure and sport facilities that are inaccessible to the average citizen? What is interesting here is the very fact that, despite a lack of persuasive answers to such questions, the Olympic movement still retains 'core groups of loyal adherents and benevolent self-images that in some cases have exercised a virtually global reach for most of a century'.[23]

John Hoberman suggests that the 'halo effect' that has allowed an idealised view of the Olympics stems from its 'myths of origin' that are 'rooted in reverential attitudes toward the personal qualities of their respective founding fathers and the salvational doctrines they created'.[24] Hoberman also draws attention to the nature of the period when the Olympic Movement was founded, alongside other movements such as Scouting: at the end of the nineteenth century the origins of such movements were often based on array of concerns about social instability and class conflict.

THE GAMES AS A 'GIFT'

Iain MacRury argues that the 'Olympic Good' that has been attached to the Olympics enables the value of hosting the Games to go beyond the basic commodity character; it exists outside cost-benefit analysis – in 'gift-mode'.[25] The Olympic Games are seen to have the status of a 'gift', and this induces a different set of human relations. Gift mode enables Games organisers to go beyond the basic commodity-based question of what will they will cost and what we will get. The 'gift' that is gained by hosting the Olympics is then reflected in rituals such as passing the Olympic flame between hosts and nations: it cannot be given a tangible value. In staging the Games, the host community is bestowed with a *priceless* gift through its association with Olympism and Olympic values,

The IOC and their supporters seek to blend the mythopoeic nature of sport with that of the Games; to demonstrate all that is 'good' about sport, and how this can be delivered through the medium of the Olympic movement; and particularly how all this will be to the benefit of the Olympic Games host community. A simple version of the story-line goes. Sport has the potential to combat a number of social ills. Thus hosting the Olympic Games (the world's largest sporting event and, through Olympism, one that is set on a loftier moral platform) will 'gift' the host community with all that is 'good' about sport; it will inspire people to change deep-seated behavioural patterns, and thus take part in sport and thereby gain those positive characteristics to the benefit of all concerned. It should therefore come as no surprise that Lord Coe, in outlining the benefits to the UK of hosting the Games, described sport as a 'hidden social worker'.[26]

Here Coe neatly encapsulates the contradictions for those of us who are advocates of the worth of sport, given the distortion of this case by the ever growing claims of what sport's mega-events can achieve – the mythopoeic. Such events are now thought capable of curing a depressed part of a capital city from its economic decline, tempting a nation to put down the TV remote and put on the running shoes, and instilling a set of values founded on the collective good of the team rather than the needs of the individual. Of course sport can do a bit of each of these, but it isn't immune from the pressure of economic, cultural and political factors. Just like Coe's social worker, it is doing some good in the community, but it is not able to transform society on its own. At its best, sport privileges the local and the communal, where small, practical claims of impact have a degree of validity. But modesty isn't what a mega-event like London 2012 is all about. Instead we're treated to an Olympic spectacle that promises the earth yet delivers not very much at all.

NOTES

1. See Fred Coalter, *A Wider Role For Sport*, Routledge 2007.
2. See, for example, *The Wolfenden Report*, CCPR 1960.
3. Fred Coalter, op cit, p9.
4. Richard Giulianotti, 'Human Rights, Globalization and Sentimental Education: The Case of Sport', in *Sport in Society* 7 (3), 2004, p356.
5. See, for example, Simon Heffer, 'Don't be complacent – English cricket is on a sticky wicket, too', *Daily Telegraph*, 1 September 2010; David James, 'Don't let's get complacent about drug testing in football', *Guardian*, 15 March 2009; Mark Hodgkinson, 'Beijing Olympics: women athletes are going hungry for success', *Daily Telegraph*, 1 August 2008.
6. Adolf Ogi, Conference Address, Sport and Development International Conference, Magglingen 2003. Quoted in Giulianotti, op cit.
7. Jacques Rogge, *The Contribution of the International Olympic Committee to the Millennium Development Goals*, IOC 2010. The Millennium Development Goals, officially established following the Millennium Summit of the UN in 2000, set targets for, among other things: eradicating extreme poverty and hunger, achieving universal primary education, promoting gender equality and empowering women, reducing child mortality rates, ensuring environmental sustainability, and developing a global partnership for development.
8. Ganda Sithole, *The Contribution of the International Olympic Committee to the Millennium Development Goals*, IOC 2010.
9. *IOC Charter*, IOC 2007.
10. V. Girginov, 'Governance of London 2012 Olympic Games legacy', in *International Review for the Sociology of Sport*, 2011.

11. D. Adair, 'Le Musee Olympique: Epicentre of Olympic evangelism', in M. Phillips (ed), *Historians in the Museum: Representations of the Sporting Past in Museums and Halls of Fame*, Routledge 2011.

12. J. Milton-Smith, 'Ethics, the Olympics and the Search for Global Values', *Journal of Business Ethics*, 35 (2), 1999, p140.

13. V. Simons and A. Jennings, *The Lords of the Rings, Power, Money & Drugs in the Modern Olympics*, Simon and Schuster 1992.

14. A. Jennings, *The New Lords of the Rings*, Pocket Books 1996; H. Lenskyj, *Inside the Olympic Industry: Power Politics and Activism*, SUNY 2000.

15. J. Milton-Smith, op cit, p141.

16. J. Rogge, Address at the Opening Ceremony of the 2006 Winter Olympics, Turin 2006, in D. Binder (ed), *Teaching Values. An Olympic Education Toolkit*, IOC 2006.

17. IOC charter 2007.

18. Jaques Rogge, Speech given to 2012 Legacies Now, Vancouver BC, 27 February 2008, in *Olympic Legacy Guide*, IOC 2009.

19. Jacques Rogge, *Advancing the Games: the IOC, London 2012 and the future of de Coubertin's Olympic Movement*, Lecture to The Royal Society of Arts, Manufacturers and Commerce, London 2008, p9.

20. Brian Moore, 'There's a million reasons why Deighton should explain where the tickets have gone', *Daily Telegraph*, 9 June 2011.

21. The Children's Food Campaign, *Obesity Games Report*, CFC 2012.

22. Kevin Wamsley, 'Laying Olympism to Rest', in J. Bale and M.K. Christensen (eds), *Post Olympism? Questioning Sport in the Twenty-First Century*, Berg 2004.

23. Ibid, p234.

24. John Hoberman, 'Toward a Theory of Olympic Internationalism', *Journal of Sport History* 22 (1), 1995, p3.

25. Iain MacRury, 'Re- thinking the Legacy 2012: the Olympics as commodity and gift', *Twenty-First Century Society* 3 (3) 2008.

26. Tim Adams, 'Ready, Steady, Coe', *Guardian*, 27 July 2008.

Wearing Team GB's colours

Yasmin Alibhai-Brown

Mo Farah did it! And he is still doing it, nipping in and out of schools and events, smiling that smile, inspiring and, with others, subliminally reshaping the British identity. Some patriots are infuriated by this alteration of the national image, to them as devious and suspect as photographic digital manipulation. They still believe GB to be a white country, under constant threat from dark forces and faces. These stalwarts defending the idea of mono-cultural/mono-racial Britain are a minority, but powerful. More on them anon.

Cheers reverberated to the heavens as Farah won the Olympic gold in both the 10,000 and 5000 metre races, one of only seven men ever to do so. David Cameron tweeted '@Mo_Farah is an Olympic legend and a true British hero. We can all be proud of his extraordinary achievement'. But not even the PM quite gets the significance of his victory. The runner was born in Somalia in 1983 and came to London when eight years old. His eldest brother Faisal stayed behind and is a farmer on a smallholding without electricity. They are close. Two brothers, two lives, and a journey that changed everything for one of them. Today Farah, whilst remaining a devout Muslim, claims and extols his adopted country. His joyful embrace of Britishness, replicated by other Olympians of immigrant stock, has aroused the same rapturous national feelings in people who, until now, were wary of nationalistic celebrations and expressions. Not any more. For black and Asian Britons, seeing the mixed race and black competitors fiercely fighting for their own personal bests and for their country was the moment when history seemed to have turned a page. Was that real or an illusion or both?

In those heady days, while travelling on the tube I met a Somali family festooned in Union Jack kit. The mum had a red, blue and white band across her forehead under a tight, black head scarf; her sons had on t-shirts and caps, and held flags, and on her daughter's leggings were crowns, Big Bens, St Pauls and the colours of this nation. They were coming back from a halal restaurant after breaking their eighteen-hour fast during Ramadhan. They told me they were so happy because of Farah. They wanted their children to be like him, make this country proud of them. Near us a white family was just as joyous and for the same reasons. And I thought, this is brilliant, we are in it together. One stuck up passenger muttered disapprovingly that the happy Somalis were not British and had no right to the flag. Such grumblers couldn't spoil the biggest and best party our nation has ever thrown. When part-Jamaican Jess Ennis, black British boxer Nicola Adams and others of similar heritage got their medals, and wept with joy as the anthem played, along with millions of other migrants and their children I too threw myself into the warm pool of belonging.

We have had such winners before, like the super-driven medal holders Daley Thompson and Dame Kelly Holmes. But this time, because the Olympics was in London, the whole country got engaged and showed its most integrated, optimistic self. Since the 2005 July bombings the land has felt fragmented, mutually suspicious, with too many of its citizens falling in with white bigots and Muslim extremists. For a few weeks those malevolent forces had to retreat. And those grousing, neoliberal intellectuals and pundits who warned the centre would not hold because there was 'too much diversity' in Britain, went silent.

This moment is especially significant for me personally, and for my people the Ugandan Asians. It was forty years before London 2012, in August 1972, when Idi Amin announced he was expelling us from our beautiful homeland. Those who had British passports arrived in the UK, many with less than £100 in their pockets. At the time, Britain was in economic turmoil and the incomers faced overt racism, but there were also countless kind Britons, who gave the exiles clothes, homes, jobs and loans. This group has now achieved more and faster success than any other group of migrants since the Second World War. Many of them are millionaires and professional highfliers, and they are among the top in educational tables. What's more, like my mum, they are true patriots. My mum said England made her feel safe, independent and truly happy. Such loyalists have never approved of my carps against the country which gave them a second chance and refuge.

Whatever my criticisms, I too know that I would never have become the person I am, or developed so many skills, got so many rights, got into a profession I love, or found my voice, in Uganda. Asian women there lived like middle-class Victorian ladies here, as keepers of the home, with all other ambitions stifled. There was no democracy back there, not under the British nor under subsequent Ugandan leaders, no freedom of speech either, absolutely no dissent within communities or nationally. It hurts when indigenous Britons attack me for my skin colour or faith or for being an 'fucking Paki immigrant', but that is offset by the love I get from my English husband and white friends, some of whom have kept me going and fighting on, through some terrible personal times – times when I wanted to give up and die.

I am writing a book on England, and have found that even those immigrants who have suffered hardship and faced dreadful prejudice would not live anywhere else. As Ahmed, whose family moved from Afghanistan, and who is unemployed and depressed, told me in a small cafe in Kilburn: 'I don't want to go anywhere. This is my place. My daughter here will get the best education, they will not imprison her future. I can say what I want, pray if I want, am free like a human being should be.' What about anti-Muslim antipathy? 'Yes, it is there. I feel it on my skin. But still, for us this is the best place. Difficulties are everywhere my dear. Have you ever been to Pakistan or Afghanistan?'

In 2011, two French footballers of African descent spoke candidly about the difference between their country France and England, the nation they play for. Benoit Assou-Ekotto explained why England felt to him more open than France, where:

> even if you had only one drop of Moroccan blood, for example, you would represent it to the death. You would be fiercely proud of being African. But here it is different. People might say that their parents are from the Ivory Coast or Nigeria or whatever, but they are fiercely proud of being here and the society accepts that ... France has been unwilling or unable to accommodate the sons and daughters from its former colonies.

Fellow African footballer Sebastien Bassong agreed, and passionately:

> It's just a fact. In England it is more open and that's why people come here. They know they will get a chance no matter how they dress or where they're from. In England minds are more open and that's why

French players who play in England don't want to go back to France
... the way that English people think, they don't judge you.

There has been much talk about the post-Olympic legacy, about getting the young into sports and the health benefits of that. Just as important is the legacy of Britain's winning inclusivity. The games showed its diverse identity, made and remade by natives and strangers, through tough encounters and sheer determination, where pride beats prejudice. However, it is important not to be swept away by post-Olympic optimism. This extraordinary festival of good will does not mean racism and anti-immigrant hostility have vanished. and that all playing fields are now level. Or that ghettoised communities are letting the walls fall. For every grateful, relatively happy settler in Britain, there is another who never got near the good life, whose talents and hopes and self-esteem were crushed.

A year on from the Olympics the euphoria has subsided, replaced in part by more sober contemplation of what happened then and where we are now. Since those uplifting games there have been some nasty examples of racism re-emerging in British football. We thought we had kicked that out of the beautiful game. Things get better, but the bad old ways reappear with alarming frequency. As the French novelist Alphonse Karr wrote in the early 1900s: 'The more things change, the more they stay the same'.

The multiracial team of athletes did represent the nation at its most diverse, confident and interconnected. But it diverted attention away from the internal conflicts, the lack of ease, the terrifying ethnic and religious antipathies, and the continuing, possibly worsening, racial discrimination faced by immigrants and their families. There is no anti-racism movement any more; equality as an ideal has been abandoned by the government and by black and Asian Britons too, exhausted, perhaps after so many decades of struggle. Doreen Lawrence, mother of Stephen, is one of the few public figures speaking out against racism and discrimination, which, she rightly says, has not been driven out of our institutions, the police included. Reports by the Runnymede Trust and academic departments attest to this fact, but few in power listen or care. In the last five years, of the main party leaders only Nick Clegg has made a major speech on racial disadvantage and discrimination. Diversity policies in the public and private sectors focus almost wholly on gender and gay rights- both of which I wholly support – and are unconcerned about race, religious and ethnic equality.

Though immigrants have been scapegoated in Britain since the sixteenth century, never before have they been so defenceless, naked and without allies in high places. When Enoch Powell incited his fellow countrymen to resist non-white immigration in his Rivers of Blood speech in 1968, he was sacked from the Shadow Cabinet by his Conservative Party Leader Edward Heath, and condemned by MPs and prominent names in the media. Today immigrants are repeatedly blamed and derided on the BBC4's *Today* programme, phone-in programmes and the right-wing press. Rarely are immigrants themselves or their dwindling number of supporters called upon to contradict what their detractors allege. The usual trick is to go into poor neighbourhoods, question disgruntled and frustrated white Britons about immigration (no prize for guessing what they say) and then get committed, effective anti-immigration lobbyists such as Frank Field or representatives of Migration Watch to add gravitas to the anti-immigration 'debate' – which is no debate at all. Incrementally, hostility against incomers has spread and now seems irreversible and, unlike before, no politician now dares to confront these attitudes. In their rhetoric immigration is decoupled from race by those who oppose it and also from long settled immigrants. Who are they kidding? Eastern Europeans, like Jews, black people and Asians, are depicted as the Other, who cannot be British, who steal jobs and women and is treacherous. As one Polish worker said to me: 'We are the new blacks, the ones it is OK to be racist about'. Refugees and asylum seekers are seen as even more dangerous than economic migrants. A large number are destitute, and most experience hatred.

Successful, long-settled migrants are praised by politicians and the media, but we are not fooled by that posturing and duplicity. That white woman who spat at me on the bus, and screamed I was a scrounger who should go back where I belonged, saw a 'coloured' interloper. How was she to know I have been here for forty years and never asked for benefits? Or that my taxes have contributed to state welfare payments to the poor and needy of all backgrounds?

Four decades after the US civil rights struggles and similar battles fought here in the UK by our own brave and resolute campaigners, racism is acceptable and normalised, but complaining about racism is thought outrageous. And the Olympics have, sadly, made disbelief even more likely. Just as Obama's presidency is used as proof that racism is no longer a problem in the USA, so it is with Mo Farah, Jessica Ennis and other medallists of colour on the British isles. These winners need to speak out about racial injustice. Like popular music, sport is one of society's greatest equalisers. As an activity it is a rare signifier of real and natural integration, cross-racial ease and meritocratic progress with talent breaking through barriers. But without mainstream political concern, effective legislative remedies and most importantly, powerful people imagining and articulating anti-racist ideals (not platitudes), all that optimism and promise of the Olympics will be squandered or turn to dust. We, who care deeply about our multifarious and vigorous nation, must not let that happen.

An earlier version of this chapter first appeared as 'Mo's joyful embrace of Britishness and Why These Games Mark a Truly Historic Watershed', Daily Mail, *12 August 2012.*

TURNING SUPER SATURDAYS INTO HAPPY MONDAYS

Andrew Simms

It was a weekend in February 2012. The part of the week still most associated with doing, or watching, sport. I love sport. There was a time in my mid teens when doing it became slightly out of hand: training three times a week at the local athletics club, judo once a week, hockey twice a week. Then there was an assortment of table tennis, tennis and badminton to fill in any time left over. Life was like a mini-Olympics, but better. It avoided the jingoism, commercialism and excessive pressure to perform that are tangled around the five Olympic rings. I *played* sport in exactly that sense, it was *play*, not a means to an end. It had its own purpose. It was an end it itself. Sport as play was an intrinsically satisfying way of being, not motivated by some deferred, hoped-for outcome, like weight loss, a medal or fame and corporate sponsorship. It was fun. The point at which I lost interest in running, towards the end of my teens, was when the purpose of my athletics became geared to only one end, individual success and personal glorification.

I have a photograph of my daughter, Scarlett, aged five, running across the long, dreary raised pedestrian walkway over the platforms of Clapham Junction railway station in London. A late winter sun casts dramatic, elongated shadows on the ground. Scarlett is running fast towards me, so fast that in the picture she almost bursts out of the frame. Exploding with joy, she leaves behind a shrinking perspective of shadows that stretch into the distance. I look at this picture and think two things, first that we are born to run, and second that this is what sport should aspire to.

In this way, argues the philosopher Mark Rowlands, even if they are unaware that they are doing so, children grasp innately what is important and valuable in life – which is, as he puts it, just another way of understanding the meaning of life.[1] 'We think of childhood as a time of preparation for the important part of life that comes later', writes Rowlands. 'I suspect this gets things the wrong way around ... Children know that what's worth doing in life is worth doing for its own sake. And everything else is merely unfortunate. This is something we forget when we begin the great game of growing up.' Rowlands describes his adult life, like that of many others, as resembling a complex journey to relearn this simple yet elusive understanding.

Back on that Saturday in February 2012, once more confronted with the great game of growing up, I couldn't let it lie. It was Olympic year in the city where I lived, and I was losing count of the layers of wrong that were obscuring the sporting event itself.

The Olympics were sold to the International Olympic Committee and to the British people as delivering the rebirth of part of London. This promise of creating lasting value for communities was key to winning the good will and assent of the IOC and general public. Yet, the emphasis on the occasion's *legacy* sounded like an increasingly desperate defence of something that, rather than resurrecting poor neighbourhoods in East London, might instead be the death of sport. All our memories are now coloured by Danny Boyle's glorious, zeitgeist shifting opening ceremony and the medals carried home by Team GB. These make it hard to conjure and understand the issues which caused concern in the months before – few, if any, of which were ever addressed.

Back then, braced for the imminent Olympic deluge, in one irritated, slightly splenetic burst of tweeting, I began, 'Apologies, I'll pluck these 15 thorns now, then say no more.' And, as I sent them, my layers of concern about the event were:

#tweet 1/15 Suspension of free speech: under special powers it is illegal for local people visibly to criticise the Olympics. Incredible but true.

#tweet 2/15 They were imposed on local communities and businesses who had no ultimate choice over the 'regeneration' of their neighbourhoods.

#tweet 3/15 They went massively over their initial budget.

#tweet 4/15 The polluting, climate-wrecking, renewable-energy-dropping, oil giant BP, is their 'sustainability sponsor'.

#tweet 5/15 Having fast food giant McDonalds as a sponsor makes a mockery of the healthy sporting example the event is meant to set (oh, and Coke).

#tweet 6/15 Dow Chemicals is a sponsor although still embroiled in dispute over the lethal Bhopal disaster.

#tweet 7/15 Vast numbers of tickets went to corporations & dignitaries rather than ordinary punters, the people who are paying for it.

#tweet 8/15 Special traffic lanes will put the interests of VIP traffic flow ahead of the needs of some emergency services.

#tweet 9/15 The broken promises about mass sporting activity for young people.

#tweet 10/15 The broken environmental promises.

#tweet 11/15 The broken promise about the outside race routes that should have gone more around the host boroughs.

#tweet 12/15 They mask a global trade in muscle biased toward rich countries. Results flatter national resources. Why not redistribute Olympic cash?

#tweet 13/15 Other parts of the country needed the new infrastructure much more than the South East.

#tweet 14/15 The fact that to enter the Olympic area you're channelled through a shrine to crass consumerism – the appalling symbolism of Westfield.

#tweet 15/15 It is a monument to hypocritical, pompously self-justifying, elite vain glory. Shame when sport is such a good thing.

For a time, these kinds of issues seemed set to define the London Olympics. It appeared a disaster waiting to happen. But then came Danny Boyle's opening ceremony and a big haul of medals for Britain. Together they swept public dissatisfaction beneath the freshly laid turf of the Olympic Park. Something shifted in the general consciousness. A collective hysteria sounded by the starting gun chose no longer to dwell on inconvenient truths. The mantra of the 'Summer of Sport' allowed no place for songs sung in a minor key.

Yet neither the opening ceremony nor the home team successes materially changed the underlying problems. Few people asked how, if better designed, an Olympics could be a far greater force for good. Or – given that we felt good about the Olympics in spite of all the flaws – how much better such events could be if they were improved. But the downsides are real, and they matter if you care about the individual and communal benefits and transformative potential of sport.

THE FEELBAD

There's a tendency for the perception of success surrounding an event to cast an invisibility cloak over its bad points, however serious. The greatest danger is that any feelgood spun from the event then becomes like an ephemeral spell of good weather, while beneath the surface of public awareness deeper machinations go unaddressed that will change the climate for the worse in the long run. Time after time, the ends of staging the event were used to justify means that undermined the possibility in the long term of celebrating and spreading general well-being, and the intrinsic value and enjoyment of sport.

Under extreme duress and very specific conditions, such as war or the complete breakdown of civil order, most Western democracies restrict the freedoms of which they are proud, such as the right of assembly and free speech. In the UK, they did it for the London Olympics.[2] In the name of the 'war on terror' over the last decade and more, all sorts of extra powers have accumulated to the police and security services. Enough, surely, to allow the safe policing of even a very large sports event. But The London Olympic Games and Paralympic Games Act (2006) went further. In order to protect the Olympic brand it allowed for the banning of advertisements which might compromise either the event itself or its official sponsors. But it also permitted the banning of advertising of a 'non-commercial nature, and … announcements of notices of any kind'. This could include any material deemed critical, or even just casting the event in a negative light. The Act gave a 'constable or enforcement officer' the power to enter land or premises 'if they believed any sign or advert that fell foul of the law was being displayed or produced, and to take possession of and destroy the materials'.

This is what you might call 'extreme brand policing', and even Mayor of London Boris Johnson warned of the 'insanity' of it being overzealous.[3] The police also had powers within the so-called Olympic Dispersal Zone to effect the removal of children or adults in groups of two or more if a constable decided that their presence would cause a bad atmosphere or 'intimidation, harassment, alarm or distress', as the human rights watchdog Liberty put it. Another group championing freedom of expression, Index on Censorship, drew attention to the suspension of a spoof Twitter account set up by the self-styled Official Protestors of the London 2012 Olympic Games, *Space Hijackers*.[4]

Autonomy and a sense of creative control of your environment are important aspects of our well-being. When they are hemmed in, we feel worse. These restrictions, long before the opening ceremony, were likely to produce a 'feel bad' rather than a 'feel good' factor. Yet another was the wittily dubbed 'East End Missile Crisis'. This came about when the Ministry of Defence planned to deploy surface to air missiles at several sites across London on the roofs of residential blocks of flats, including Fred Wigg Tower in Waltham Forest, not far from the Olympic site. After this story emerged, rather than feeling secure, residents felt threatened – and protested, marched and petitioned against the proposals.[5]

The Olympic movement's mantra of inspiration for youth, international togetherness and legacy (now 'sustainable legacy' even) attempts the triumph of assertion over truth. And the enormous scale of the Olympic promotional machine and its attendant benign media coverage means that it might easily succeed in this, were it not for the unforgettable, even darkly poetic, nature of some of the contradictions that emerge.

Some were obvious and the subject of critical analysis. Accident-prone giant oil company BP, having shed most of its interests in renewable energy, became the sustainability partner for the Games, and subsequently proclaimed a new golden age for oil, in spite of worsening climate change. A wave of Western obesity sits on the doorstep of junk food companies Coke and McDonald's, both sponsors and suppliers to a Games that was meant to inspire a generation to healthier living

In July 2012 it was reported that a long running legal case against the huge multinational pharmaceutical firm GlaxoSmithKlein had come to a conclusion. In a settlement described by the Deputy US Attorney General James Cole as 'unprecedented in both size and scope', the company admitted, amongst other things, bribing doctors and promoting antidepressants for use on children and adolescents that had not been approved for such use. This mattered, because drugs affect people at different stages of physical development in very different ways. Indeed, the scale and seriousness of the wrongdoing was such that a fine of $3 billion was levied for what the BBC described as the 'largest healthcare fraud settlement in US history.[6] GSK were guilty of the doping of children and teenagers with unapproved antidepressants. Less than two weeks later GSK announced a multi-million advertising campaign to highlight its role as provider of anti-doping testing equipment for the London 2012 Games. Employing several well-known athletes, adverts carrying the slogan 'The crowd is my only drug' ran throughout the Olympic and Paralympic Games.[7]

Equally brazen, and unforgivable to many athletes and volunteers at the Paralympics, was the choice of dedicated sponsor for their event, Atos. This company has been centrally involved in the controversial 'work capability assessments' that have been commissioned by government in order to pressurise people in receipt of social security benefits to return to employment. Work capability assessments target, and many believe intimidate and victimise, people with disabilities. The assessments are outsourced to Atos, who are paid a reported £110 million a year to carry them out. And, as so many of their assessments are contested, a further £60 million is spent on administering appeals. Many people who have been told they are fit to work have died before being able to do so, and many more have died during the process of assessment. To the large number of people in Britain with disabilities Atos has become a public enemy, and yet it was imposed as a sponsor of the Games.

Seeing the winds of commercialism and a brutal, global economic ideology blow around the Olympics would have been an irony not lost on Pierre de Coubertin, the founder of the modern Olympic Games. Coubertin tried to instil an educational doctrine into the Olympics, as a counter to the growing international culture of materialism, but he was to be disappointed. Already, by 1911, the high cost of staging the Olympics was restricting the hosting of the event to an elite few countries. Far from encouraging global togetherness, some sports historians argue that the growth of the Olympics is based on a logic of exclusion, because it 'undermines the two main tenets of sustainability – sharing and dispersing Olympic development benefits across communities and sports'.[8]

At the national level, regardless of political promises of a legacy for all, actual funding follows a narrower logic of success in individual sports. Thus, for example, swimming is widely regarded as one of the best forms of exercise; it is low impact and good for people of all ages. But that counts for little when British swimmers fail in the pool. After what was considered a poor result in London 2012, British swimming lost £4 million in funds.[9]

To allocate a sport's national funding on the basis of a winner-take-all approach premised on the success of elite athletes is to directly contradict the generalisation of sporting participation. This is for the simple reason that, by definition, you can only have one winner at a time. Every other, non-gold winning sport, is condemned to the 'feel bad' of reduced or no funding and is unlikely to develop.[10] Athletics saw its money increase post-2012 by £1.7 million. Good news for elite athletes, certainly, but what about the sporting grass-roots that has to deliver the public legacy, and provide the means through which an inspired nation can turn inspiration into reality? Such policies serve to promote the myth – effectively debunked in Malcolm Gladwell's book *Outliers* – that success comes largely from exceptional, isolated individual endeavour, rather than being the product of an intricately linked web of opportunities that allows advantages to accrue, such as easy access to community sports facilities and coaching.[11]

Toni Minichiello, UK athletics coach of the year in 2012, warned that, in spite of renewed interest among young people, a failure to prepare since London was awarded the games in 2005, has left athletics clubs under-resourced, and forced to put children on waiting lists. According to Minichiello:

> Having enough capacity and enough coaches is a desperate struggle … You've got to have enough qualified coaches at an appropriate level to take them on. The coaches need to be of a level to deliver the quality those kids need to keep them invigorated and keep them coming back.[12]

At the very least, after 2012 it seemed that even for successful sports like athletics, delivering the legacy and capitalising on new enthusiasm would rely heavily upon a massive increase in volunteering at sports clubs.[13] Any lasting health and well-being benefits from London 2012 would represent a triumph over both historical precedent and a weak-to-negative evidence base that such events can deliver.

Thirty-one sports were funded as part of the UK's push toward London 2012, but on its eve only six had experienced a 'statistically significant increase in participation' over the previous four-year funding period. Fifteen saw reduced involvement and ten saw no change.[14] This should, of course, have been no surprise to government. Back in 2002, the Department of Culture, Media and Sport stated clearly that 'hosting events is not an effective, value for money, method of achieving a sustained increase in mass participation'.[15] In 2007 the House of Commons Select Committee on Culture Media and Sport went further, suggesting that there was reason to believe that the Olympics would have a negative effect on the take-up of sport outside London, because of the preferential focus on the capital.

Targets for increased participation were missed and abandoned in the run up to 2012, but an assessment by Sport England at the end of 2012 did show that the number of people taking part weekly in sport had gone up. Crucially, however, the key objective of inspiring younger people into sport was missed: there was no increase in taking part by people aged 16 to 24. That is an extraordinary fact. Hundreds of millions spent, a cultural triumph at the opening ceremony and an unprecedented medal haul from elite athletes, yet somehow a generation were left stoically uninspired. This failure to deliver an uptake of sport among young people suggests that Olympic planners got their design values, priorities and practical implementation wrong.

The economic wheels that drove London 2012's downside turn relentlessly, but they are largely obscured by the folk memory of what went right with the Olympics. Because, notwithstanding this critique, *some things* did go right. Is it possible that we can take lessons from the successes that might allow us to redesign the more destructive economic drivers?

FEELGOOD

In a society like Great Britain, where most people have most of their basic material needs already met, factors other than merely increased consumption determine whether our life satisfaction is high or low, rises or falls. Extensive research from a range of disciplines, and surveys across age, gender, demographic and geographical boundaries, identify five types of behaviour that are strongly associated with greater life satisfaction.

These include: *connecting* with people around you, family, friends, colleagues and neighbours, at home, work, school and in our local communities; *being active*, day-to-day, by going for a walk or run or just stepping outside; *taking notice* of the world, like the concept of mindfulness, it involves being open, attentive and curious; *carrying on learning* is another, trying something new without worrying whether or not you'll become a world champion; and, lastly, *giving* enhances personal well-being, and encourages the reciprocity that helps make communities more convivial, resilient and adaptive.

From the content of the opening ceremony to the shared spectacle of the games themselves, from the brief explosion of popular sporting activity to the thousands of Olympic volunteers who made it run smoothly – it is not difficult to see that, over the course of the Games, several of the behaviours linked to well-being were triggered and celebrated. It surely would have been strange if most of us didn't feel better while the Games were happening. We were hanging out with friends, had an easy topic of conversation to share with strangers. We took acute notice of something out-of-the-ordinary that was happening, and learned about sometimes exotic sports and unfamiliar sportswomen and men. And those much praised volunteers set a tone of unusual and extraordinary helpfulness in public spaces.

Amid the disorientation and dislocation of the digitised and globalised modern world, truly grounded, unifying moments of collective joy, grief or purpose are harder to create and experience. And, given that the structure of how we communicate militates against a sense of common purpose, the moments when, culturally, we do come together become all the more powerful. At these moments, instead of creating fragmentation, modern communication channels can amplify quite spectacularly the sense of being part of something bigger.

The Olympics is irresistible to all forms of media. It is one of the very few truly global events, in which even the world's poorer countries have some stake. High Olympic ideals coexist cynically with compromised sponsors who burnish their reputations on the Olympic rings, but when the London 2012 opening ceremony began in the largely brand-free interior of the London 2012 Olympic Stadium, a global audience of billions found themselves watching something unexpected and extraordinary.

Instead of praising individual athletes, or the more usual national bombast of official histories paraded around an arena, the ceremony was a witty song of praise to the triumph of bold, creative and collective endeavour. The person in charge, film director Danny Boyle asked himself a simple question – what is good about this nation, Great Britain?

In a culture dominated by passive consumerism and reality television, his answers caused many to pause and think twice about themselves and the world around them. But where did the 'feel-good' factor come from? Jody Aked, a researcher on human well-being connected to the New Economics Foundation (where I am a Fellow) suggested to me that one element could be the very way that the Olympics, and especially the opening ceremony, disrupted normal routines.

> There is some value in an event which is a positive catalyst for changing norms and attitudes. Other cultures have festivals and fiestas as regular fixtures in the annual calendar. They give up work all the time to spend hours hanging out, celebrating. We in the UK do this very rarely.

Certain patterns of behaviour that are typical in the Anglo-Saxon economic model – such as long hours at the desk in an unfulfilling job, with little or no time for friends or even family – are not supportive of well-being. Thus, as Jody pointed out, 'The potential of something like the Olympics to open up space for things and activities in our lives that are more well-being enhancing is probably a good thing.'

BE JUST AND FEAR NOT

The opening ceremony performance celebrated the establishment of universal primary health care, the creation of the open, public domain of the World Wide Web, children's literature, music and comedy; it lauded industrial development (while noting its costs) and raised the struggle for justice and universal suffrage. A single Suffragette banner held aloft in the show seemed to capture the tone of the whole celebration, 'Be Just, And Fear Not'.

Beyond the point where basic material needs are met, other factors have a more profound effect on our well-being than simply getting richer. Taking part in communal activities and meaningful work makes us feel better about ourselves. Knowing that we, as part of a society as well as individuals, can accomplish things such as the creation of the National Health Service, increases our sense of agency, and this in turn feeds into well-being. Appreciation of music, literature and other forms of culture allows us to develop more fully, further adding to how good we feel about ourselves. Comedy works through its powerful neuro-physiological effects, and Danny Boyle's ceremony had a lot of that. And positive feedback from identifying and associating with a higher purpose further contributes to well-being– and the explicit references to causes of social justice will have pressed that button.

The opening ceremony, by accident or intuition, was a giant happy pill. What's more, there was something that was even more shocking for a country enduring the prospect of long-term austerity and cuts to valued services – the reminder that something other than markets and commercialism was axiomatic in our lives, and of how society gets the best from itself. This was a disruption to the threadbare but still powerful and negative norm. Here, proudly paraded before a global audience of billions, was a very different way to appraise the true wealth and success of a people – that had nothing to do with the size of bonus pay, model of car, or the trajectory of national income.

The celebration showed that it is possible for a people to be enterprising without the enterprise needing to be in the shape of the selfish, market individualism beloved of conventional economic theory. It said there is something prior, deeper and better that motivates us. Whisper it in the context of a giant sports event, but anthropologists, biologists and behavioural economists have converged in recent years on the notion that human co-operation and empathy has a lot more to say about our success and resilience as a species than does competition.

In *Supercooperators: the Mathematics of Evolution, Altruism and Human Behaviour*, Martin Nowak, a professor of biology and mathematics at Harvard University, writes that he is 'struck – perhaps awestruck – by the extent to which humans cooperate ... no animal species can draw on the mechanisms [of co-operation] to the same extent as seen in human society'.[16] A more optimistic and hopeful view of human nature than that generally assumed by mainstream economists.

COULD DO BETTER?

Toward the end of the Games, there were huge billboard adverts displayed on the London Underground thanking commercial Olympic sponsors. Without them, the adverts said, not a single one of the pulsating moments of the games would have been possible. But how much did these companies actually contribute to the costs of the event? A third, a half, more?

In fact, when the layers of secrecy and commercial confidentiality were peeled away, it turned out to be about just 6 per cent. It was a bit more if you included the IOC's global partners, but a bit less if you priced in the value of volunteers' freely donated time, and items like the late delegation of armed forces personnel to stand in for the failed private security provider, G4S. The overwhelming bulk of the estimated £11.3 billion cost of the games was met by the public.

Yet in return for the proportionally small contribution of sponsors, the public had to give up seats, pull over in traffic, bow to the brand police, and generally be deferential. It was our Games, that we paid for, but we had to struggle to remember that. This is all part of the extraordinary triumph of 'perception management' over reality, with all the enormous implications that has for politics, reaching far beyond sport to the nature of the social contract in 'austerity Britain'.

Towards the end of 2012 an interview with Sebastian Coe was published in the *Guardian*.[17] Interviewer Decca Aitkenhead extracted an extraordinary admission from Coe, and one which showed how the most powerful politics succeeds by creating the impression that it is not deliberately political at all, that it is more a state of nature.

Coe: I don't wake up each morning trying to figure out what kind of Conservative I am; for me it's quite instinctive. I actually don't believe in big government and half the time I'm never quite sure I believe in government, generally.

Aitkenhead: But without government we wouldn't have had the Olympics.

Coe: No, that is true. That is true.

In the spell of a politics with such a pathological lack of self-awareness, private interests are able to purchase the reflected glory of a society's achievement, and pass it off disproportionately as their own. Why does it matter? Because it creates a distorted view of what the public sphere, as opposed to the market, can do. It reinforces the view that only markets are dynamic, that only they should be relied on to make things happen, whereas planning and public purpose and resources should not – which is the opposite of the reality. This issue could not be more important. It is at the very heart of public policy and political debate.

In 2010 David Cameron spelt out his priorities for government, which were to use 'all available policy levers' to make it easier for the private sector to 'create a new economic dynamism'. The following year Cameron announced that he was 'taking on the enemies of enterprise', which included the 'bureaucrats in government departments' and town hall officials. Chancellor George Osborne argued that the public sector was 'crowding out' the private sector and needed cutting back. Behind this logic is an economic model that believes the path to happiness and fulfilment is paved with individuals consuming more stuff. Yet the Olympics revealed the opposite, that feeling good came from communal experience and the celebration of collective endeavour.

The economy is littered with evidence that Cameron and Osborne's premise is flawed even on its own terms. We can see it in the way rail privatisation led to a dramatic rise, not fall, in public subsidy to Britain's railways, and in the fact that healthcare is typically much more expensive and less comprehensive in countries with heavily privatised systems such as the United States, as compared to the NHS. Some of the our largest private care-home providers had to be saved by public intervention, and the private banking system that underpinned the whole economy is only standing today due to massive public bail-outs. The astonishing confidence trick of neo-liberal economics has been to distract everyone, including the left, from the logical conclusion to draw from its demonstrably failed markets: that there are other and better ways to get things done

The great and, for some, shocking reminder that came from London 2012 is that it is us, and the governments that we elect, who can make really big things happen. In spite of the unaddressed flaws that undermined its potential, we saw that once a decision has been taken forces align: the money gets found, rules are set to ensure success, people mobilise, deadlines are met and we accomplish.

No insight could be more important now, at a time when the

political mainstream tells us we have no choice but to tear up the social contract of a caring and cooperative society, and burn the climate in the name of an economy designed around the conspicuous consumption of a wealthy one per cent.

To rebuild an economy ruined by the excesses of financialised global markets, hold together societies scarred by inequality, and turn around the prospects of global warming, it will take the equivalent collective effort – and rewarding togetherness – of an Olympics every year. Our challenge is that we cannot rely on a Danny Boyle performance every time to bring us together as a nation. But if we make the principles, values and experiences celebrated in his opening ceremony central to our politics, we may create and maintain a warmth within and between us that lays the foundations of a better future.

Fortunately, not only do we now know that we can do it, we know we can feel better for trying. We have nothing to lose, and a world to win. As the poet Carol Ann Duffy put it in her appreciation of the collective experience of the London 2012 Olympics, 'We sense new weather. We are on our marks. We are all in this together'.[18]

NOTES

1. See Mark Rowlands, *Running With the Pack*, Granta Books 2013.
2. See the 'Freedom Games' campaign at www.liberty-human-rights.org. uk.
3. Roger Blitz, 'Warning on Olympic Brand Insanity', *Financial Times*, 20 July 2012.
4. Padraig Reidy, 'Olympic Organisers Shut Down Space Hijackers Protest Twitter Account', 23 May 2012: www.indexoncensorship.org.
5. David Baker, 'Don't Play Games With Our Lives', *Daily Mail*, 30 June 2012.
6. See 'GlaxoSmithKline to pay $3bn in US Drug Fraud Scandal', 2 July 2012: www.bbc.co.uk/news.
7. Mark Sweney, 'GlaxoSmithKline Launches Anti-Doping Ads', *Guardian*, 16 July 2012.
8. Vassil Girginov & Laura Hills, 'A Sustainable Sports Legacy: Creating a Link between the London Olympics and Sports Participation', *The International Journal of the History of Sport*, 25, 2008.
9. Aidan McCartney, 'Swimming Funding Suffers Dip', *Daily Mail*, 18 December 2012.
10. See 'Mixed Fortunes as UK Funding For Rio Olympics Revealed, 18 December 2012: www.itv.com/news.
11. Malcolm Gladwell (2009), *Outliers*, Penguin, London

12. Owen Gibson and Anna Kessell, 'Toni Minichello Says Athletics Cannot Cope With Post-Olympics Surge', *Guardian*, 22 November 2012.

13. James Hall, 'Parents Need To Get Involved To Ensure Olympic Legacy', *Daily Telegraph*, 19 August 2012.

14. Paul Kelso, 'London 2012 Olympics: Sport England Claim Participation Surge', *Daily Telegraph*, 22 June 2012.

15. DCMS, *Game Plan*, DCMS 2002.

16. See Martin Nowak and Roger Highfield, *SuperCooperators: Beyond The Survival Of The Fittest*, Canongate 2012.

17. Decca Aitkenhead, Interview with Sebastian Coe, *Guardian*, 11 November 2012.

18. Carol Ann Duffy, 'Translating the British, 2012', *Guardian*, 10 August 2012.

STREETS OF FLAMES AND
SUMMER GAMES

Ben Carrington

For a brief period in early August 2011 cities and towns across England were ablaze, sparked initially by the fatal police shooting in north London of a black man named Mark Duggan. Shortly after, *Private Eye* sought to capture the public discontent following the violent disturbances that had shaken the country. Its front-cover headline read 'Olympic Rehearsal', next to the widely criticised 2012 Olympic logo. Underneath the headline, a photo taken from a scene in East London shows officers from London's Metropolitan Police in full riot gear facing a large group of hooded youths, whilst, in between, flames leap from the shell of a burning car. We see a multi-racial and predominately male crowd engaged in violent civil disorder as a seemingly passive police force look on, all framed by the anticipated grandeur of the forthcoming London Olympics. Above one of the youths a speech bubble can be seen with the following words: 'This is the worst opening ceremony ever'.

Whilst the magazine's cover was of course meant as a satirical commentary, it nonetheless brought to the fore a number of important issues: the nature of urban policing and the security state; the ways in which young people were regulated and disciplined, and their reaction and resistance to these processes; and the role of sport, leisure and recreation in maintaining social order, as well as the potential of using sport to address wider social justice issues.

CONSUMPTION, CONTROL AND SPORT

With the advent of commercialised forms of popular leisure and entertainment in the nineteenth century, a perceived breakdown of the moral order became an increasing concern for Europe's middle and upper classes – as well as the related challenge to the authority of ruling elites (including the church). What become known in Britain as the 'rational recreation' movement was an attempt by Victorian moralists to instil better (meaning bourgeois) values and mores amongst the working classes, through the provision of morally improving leisure activities that eschewed the often violent behaviour of the sports crowd, the lewdness of the music hall, and the associated 'sins' of gambling and drinking. The concern for Victorian reformers, notes the sports historian Richard Holt in his book *Sport and the British*, was how to separate the 'potentially respectable and stable work-force from the "dangerous" classes of unskilled, casual labour'.[1] This was a twin process that involved providing 'acceptable' leisure activities for some, whilst prohibiting others; thus animal sports such as dog fighting were outlawed, but not comparable middle-and upper-class blood sports such as fox hunting. Any leisure activity associated with working-class crowds became suspect and subject to state surveillance. In contrast, sports such as cricket were deemed capable not only of advancing the project of Empire abroad by bringing English civility to the colonial natives, but also of civilising the domestic working-class masses.[2]

Football, with its populist appeal, was always more problematic. Self-organised forms of street football between towns and villages – which were raucous affairs that often resulted in serious injury and sometimes death – were outlawed, as were even casual games played in the streets. At the same time middle-class reformers sought to codify the game, issuing official rules and regulations that governed how football should be played, leading to the establishment of the Football Association in 1863; the aim was to ensure that newly professionalised working-class footballers, as well as those playing at amateur levels, would do so under middle-class control and tutelage. Of course, the working classes resisted these processes and continued to engage in disreputable leisure activities beyond the permissible boundaries established by the rational recreationalists. Richard Holt, for example, quotes one young man who had the temerity to engage in casual street football:

> I remember one Bank Holiday Monday I was kicking a ball about in the street when a little later a copper came up to me and said 'What's your name? … You've been round here footballing'. Anyway some-

thing was said and he hit me over the head with the bloody truncheon
… I was done for breach of the peace, footballing in the street.[3]

By the mid-twentieth century, the 'new' forms of commercialised
leisure had created a 'mass culture' that bore little organic relationship
to traditional forms of folkloric culture. In the years following World
War Two, European cultural elites began to fear this emerging
consumer revolution, and what they saw as the Americanisation of
European culture, as American films, music and celebrities saturated
Europe, young people in particular were quick to embrace thee products and styles of the US that threatened to displace Europe's deeply
embedded class-based cultural distinctions and social hierarchies.
Nothing better illustrated Europe's decreasing authority than the
emergence of an increasingly global consumer culture that was dominated by American (and not European) corporations and commodities.
And embedded within these products came the related ideals of individualism and 'consumer choice', driven by both elaborate marketing
strategies and the entrepreneurial spirit of American companies,
backed by the strength of finance capital from Wall Street. This new
mass culture was viewed by many intellectuals across the political
spectrum and on both sides of the Atlantic as amoral and vulgar,
appealing to people's base instincts, and lacking artistic merit, intellectual depth or true aesthetic quality; its very popularity was a marker
of its lowly status and questionable social relevance.[4]

NOT JUST CRICKET

In the same week that several English cities and a number of small
towns were in flames, and as political leaders and commentators struggled and failed to make sense of the disturbances that had caused an
estimated £300 million in damage, the England men's cricket team
defeated India to become the world's leading cricket nation. It was
hard during the latter days of August 2011 not to be struck by the
visual contrast between the urban looters that were paraded across the
broadcast and print news media as a sign of multiracial English criminality, and the all-white England Test team. The visual narrative
seemed to imaginatively restore, if only for a short while, a sense of
English confidence, framed in the national psyche as cricket still is,
along with village greens, old maids cycling to Holy Communion,

warm beer and the vistas of Empire. This was now updated for the post-colonial moment, and embodied in the masterful brilliance of Matt Prior, Andrew Strauss and Jimmy Anderson.

In an article for the *Daily Telegraph* entitled 'The resurrection of English cricket can inspire us all', London Mayor Boris Johnson argued that the discipline shown by England's cricket team, and their success, should serve as a model for England's inner-city youth. According to Boris, the primary lessons to be learnt were that concentration, patience and hard graft were the keys to turning around your life. The problem, he suggested, was that the young men (for him this was a largely male issue) who rioted were probably oblivious to England's recent sporting triumph. 'That is sad in itself', Boris lamented. 'But it is also part of a wider problem. It is not just cricket they lack, but any set of rules about how to behave'.[5] Echoing Education Secretary Michael Gove's endorsement of the use of corporal punishment, Johnson argued for the return of a 'culture of discipline, of standing up when any adult walks into the room; of taking your hands out of your pockets when you are talking to an adult; of addressing your teachers with respect'.[6] If discipline was what was needed to address the cultural and moral malaise underlying the disturbances, then sport was what these young men most required if they were to reacquaint themselves with the protestant ethic. Boris declared, 'There are all sorts of ways of teaching young people self-discipline and respect for rules, not least competitive sport – and especially cricket, where one wild swipe is usually punished with ignominy'.[7]

He concluded his article thus:

> Of course kids mainly want to play football. But doesn't it make sense to induct them into a game at which England has shown it can triumph, as well as one where we are a chronic disappointment? Cricket may be a small part of the answer. But it is not to be despised: you are more likely to give young people boundaries if you teach them to score them. And unless we expand inner-city cricket, the gulf will widen between two nations – the one that has the chance to play cricket, and one that doesn't even know England is winning.[8]

The kids may want to play football, but what they really need, according to Johnson, is cricket, a sport with proper middle-class boundaries and social mores. Having beaten the Indians and shown the former colonial subjects who really was master, cricket had finally returned home as a twenty-first century mode of rational recreation for the uncivilised inner-city youth; it could therefore now help prevent the country breaking into a proxy civil war and further separating the 'two nations' – the civilised, law abiding, cricket-loving subjects on one side and the feral, law-breaking, sports shoe-stealing masses on the other. A few days later as if on cue, on Test Match Special, David Cameron would repeat Johnson's call for the England team to serve as a model for the nation's wayward youth.

POLICING THE OLYMPIC CRISIS

The disturbances of August 2011 created anxiety amongst the political class not just about the state's ability to maintain law and order at home, but also about Britain's image overseas, a situation that was heightened by the fact that preparations were already well advanced for the 2012 London summer Olympic and Paralympic games. The newspaper headlines told their own story: on 9 August the *Guardian*'s headline read 'Mayhem Engulfs London', next to a dramatic photo of a woman leaping from a burning building in Croydon as police officers below attempted to catch her; *The Sun* used the same photo with the headline 'DESCENT INTO HELL'; whilst the *Daily Mirror* pictured hooded youths attacking police cars under the title 'YOB RULE'. As the violence spread from London to other towns and cities the following day's *Guardian* led with 'London in Lockdown but Violence Flares Across the UK', above a photo of riot police running down Market Street in central Manchester, whilst *The Times* proclaimed 'London Simmers as Flames Spread', with a photo of a Birmingham police officer in full riot gear holding back a police dog as a car burns. The *Daily Telegraph*'s 10 August headline stated simply 'Anarchy Spreads'.

England's international friendly game against Holland, due to take place on 10 August, was cancelled, whilst a number of other professional sports events assessed whether they had adequate security measures in place if the violence were to continue. The English Football Association issued a statement on behalf of the team: 'The squad would like to appeal for calm and an end to the disorder that has been going on'. Richard Williams, in the *Guardian*, noted that the disturbances occurred just as London was showcasing a number of Olympic sports:

So there has been one unexpected addition to the programme of test events for the 2012 Olympics now taking place across London. Last weekend, by the Serpentine, it was the triathlon. This week, in Wembley Arena, the badminton. On Tuesday it was beach volleyball at Horse Guards Parade. Next weekend, from historic Westminster to the leafy Surrey Hills and back, it will be the road cycling. And, right now, perhaps in a high street near you, the riots.

He pointed out that London had won the 2012 Games 'on the back of its young people'; the significance of Britain's urban culture had been symbolised by London 2012's official 'street art' logo, and there had been promises that a vote for London was a vote for youth develop-ment and opportunity. Yet, as Williams pointed out, in the six years since the bid there had been little in the way of tangible dividends for the younger generation in the London boroughs of Newham, Tower Hamlets, Waltham Forest and Haringey:

> Meanwhile, youth centres are closing. Eight of 13 have gone in Haringey alone. And school sports programmes in the UK are severely curtailed. Some of the young footballers who would have been playing at Wembley on Wednesday are on salaries of more than £200,000 a week. The nearest most of this week's rioters will get to that is a pair of looted trainers.[9]

Paul Hayward in *The Observer* made a similar point, adding:

> If Blairite Britain conceived the Olympic bid as a billboard for British modernity then the former prime minister's heir, David Cameron, is left to reassure Japanese or Californian visitors they will not have to brave a war zone next summer. By then, draconian prison sentences will have been imposed on many youngsters who made stupid first-time errors of judgment (and many who deserve a long spell inside) while unemployment and inequality continue their upward trajectories. A paramilitary police force will have it all cleaned up by then, and the so-called underclass who the Games were meant to inspire will be demonised or incarcerated.[10]

In another article in the *Observer* – and no doubt in part as a response to such criticisms – Tony Blair argued that the disturbances were not symptomatic of any broader societal problem or moral malaise but rather lay with a small number of dysfunctional families. Keen to reassure the wider international public, if not specifically the IOC, Blair added that 'The spirit that won the Olympic bid in 2005 – open, tolerant and optimistic – is far more representative of modern London than the criminality displayed by the people smashing shop windows'.[11] Blair was, of course, seeking to defend his and new Labour's legacy. If the generation that were born in the 1970s, grew up in the 1980s and came of age in the 1990s could rightly be called Thatcher's children, then Blair's children were those who were born in the 1990s, grew up in the first decade of the twentieth century and came of age in the summer of 2011. These were Blair's kids, coming home to loot.

Given their timing, the disturbances produced what could be described as an 'Olympic crisis' – one that necessitated an authoritarian response in order to restore not just civil order but the very legitimacy of the police, and by extension the power of the state. During the height of the August troubles, 16,000 police officers were deployed, the biggest ever in UK policing history, with a further 450 detectives specifically dedicated to finding those involved after the event, resulting in around 4000 arrests.[12] A *Guardian* newspaper analysis of the first 1000 cases to appear before the courts revealed a hyper-punitive reaction by the state. Figures showed that 70 per cent of those who came before a magistrate were remanded in custody awaiting a Crown Court trial. Of those sentenced, a staggering 70 per cent were given immediate prison terms (against a norm of 2 per cent). Those who had committed public order offences received sentences 33 per cent longer than normal, whilst those convicted of assaulting police officers were being given jail time that was 40 per cent longer than usual.[13]

Many commentators argued that the disturbances could not be understood as political, at least not in the traditional sense, because, beyond the initial protest at Mark Duggan's death, after which the first disorder began, the rioting seemed to lack a clear and recognisable motive. Unlike the riots of the 1980s – which even Conservative pundits miraculously tried to reclaim as somehow having been an understandable response (if still wrong) to high unemployment and overt police racism towards black youth of the time – these riots were quickly framed as consumption riots. According to sociologists Richard Sennett and Saskia Sassen, 'the rioters seem motivated by a more diffuse anger, behaving like crazed shoppers on a spree', whilst Zgymunt Bauman similarly suggested that the events were not so much driven by hunger or destitution but were, rather, 'riots of defective and disqualified consumers'.[14] Jon Cruddas and Jonathan Rutherford would later suggest that:

> The riots were a carnival of nihilism and hedonism, but targeting the shops had its own political logic. For every opportunist looter grabbing something free because they could, there were ten who knew the humiliation of being second-class in a culture of conspicuous consumption. Foot Locker isn't just a shop that sells trainers, it's a source of positional goods. Our consumer culture teaches the young that you must own in order to achieve status, and in order to own, you need money.[15]

On BBC's *Newsnight*, historian David Starkey suggested that although those involved in the disturbances from towns like Reading, Gloucester and Gillingham were clearly white, black culture (and by extension black people) was still to blame. Starkey suggested that the 2011 riots had finally fulfilled Enoch Powell's 'Rivers of Blood' prophecy, namely that violent conflict would be the inevitable result of immigration from the Commonwealth:

> His [Powell's] prophecy was absolutely right in one sense. The Tiber didn't foam with blood, but flames lambent wrapped round Tottenham and wrapped round Clapham, but it wasn't inter-communal violence, this is where he was completely wrong. What's happened is that a substantial section of the chavs ... have become black. The whites have become black. A particular sort of violent, destructive, nihilistic gangster culture has become 'the fashion' and black and white, boy and girl operate in this language together. This language, which is wholly false, which is this Jamaican patois that's been intruded in England. This is why so many of us have this sense of literally a foreign country.[16]

For Starkey, as for many others on the right (and some on the liberal left), 'black culture' had infected and undermined white working-class culture to such an extent that this foreign influence had now altered forever nativist language, mores and behaviour. Starkey implied that rioting itself was somehow 'new' to (white) British political culture, an external malevolent intrusion into the indigenous society, or at least its youth. He dismissed the underlying pattern of police harassment of young people and the continuing high levels of unemployment and that further exacerbated wealth inequalities, and the general sense of youth disenfranchisement. Instead, he concluded that the explanation lay simply and squarely with black culture.

Melanie Phillips continued this line of argument, suggesting that the 'violent anarchy' was a direct result of the left's culture wars: 'The married two-parent family, educational meritocracy, punishment of criminals, national identity, enforcement of the drugs laws and many more fundamental conventions were all smashed by a liberal intelligentsia hell-bent on a revolutionary transformation of society'.[17] In this vacuum of moral relativism, feral youth lacked appropriate moral boundaries, and thus the ability to even recognise that looting was wrong, and had next to no respect for the law. If this moral collapse was not bad enough, these issues had been 'compounded still further by the disaster of multiculturalism', which, according to Phillips meant that children were no longer being taught about their national culture:

> So not only were they left in ignorance of their own society, but any attachment to a shared and over-arching culture was deliberately shattered. Instead of forging social bonds, multiculturalism dissolved them – and introduced instead a primitive war of all against all, in which the strongest groups would destroy the weak.[18]

But as later analyses would show, those involved had not suddenly been engulfed by mindless criminality; these were not simply BlackBerry Messenger-orchestrated gang rampages, and the rioters certainly were not being driven to loot because they had downloaded too many Vybz Kartel songs from iTunes.[19] Contrary to much of the on-the-hoof media reportage, researchers found that few of those who participated in the disturbances were involved with 'gangs', and they were more politically conscious than initially assumed. And as Gary Younge commented, many of the young people interviewed were 'considerably more likely than the public at large to say poverty, inequality, government policy and policing were behind the riots'.[20] Indeed, awareness from personal experience of police malpractice, and a general hostility towards the police, were overwhelmingly identified as a key reason for the events of August 2011. 'The 2011 riots', concluded Gary, 'would probably win gold as the year's most destructive, least coherent protest of disaffected youth against indifferent elites, economic hardship and police brutality'.[21]

In their landmark book *Policing the Crisis: Mugging, the State, and Law and Order*, Stuart Hall and his colleagues argued that the 1970s moral panic that was produced around the crime of mugging needed to be understood as a political response to the wider crisis of hegemony affecting the British state. They suggest that the specific term 'mugging', or stealing from the person, was invented and amplified by the media, triggering a panic that required a strong law and order response by the state. They show how the supposed mugging epidemic became associated specifically with black British communities, so that by the mid-1970s mugging had become defined as an essentially black crime, produced in black ghettos against innocent white victims. With growing levels of unemployment, media stories about immigrants living off the shrinking welfare state, attacks on 'welfare scroungers' by politicians, and the related growth of new far right organisations like the National Front, there was a perceived need for the police to oversee potential so-called 'trouble spots'. As Stuart and his co-authors put it, 'Policing *the blacks* threatened to mesh with the problem of policing *the poor* and policing *the unemployed*: all three were concentrated in precisely the same urban areas ... The on-going problem of policing the blacks had become, for all practical purposes, synonymous with the wider problem of *policing the crisis*'.[22]

The neoliberal reordering of the social contract that had sustained the welfare state throughout the post-war period has developed extensively since the period when *Policing the Crisis* was published in 1978. Today, as Les Back and his colleagues note, it is the presence of 'the immigrant', fears of terrorist acts and the threat of multiculturalism that is seen to necessitate the policing of diversity and those communities deemed to be 'out of control'.[23] The Olympics served to accelerate the draconian forms of policing and scrutiny already in play, producing a state of emergency that normalised the mobilisation and surveillance practices not just of extraordinary numbers of police and private security personnel, but, critically, of the military too – even if that required the stationing of surface-to-air missiles on the roofs of tower blocks in East London against the wishes of the actual residents.

A POST-EMPIRE GAMES

The Olympics came to London in the context of a national debate over race and multiculturalism, which both questioned what it means to be British and identified sport as a way to shore up and provide substance to Britishness. At the same time the British state was facing ongoing economic and geo-political challenges, including the after effects of the invasion of Iraq, the occupation of Afghanistan and the general-ised war on terror.

These issues were brought to the fore the day after IOC President Jacques Rogge's announcement that London would host the thirtieth Olympiad – when the 7/7 terrorist attacks took place in central London. Much of the initial commentary as to why London had been awarded the Games had suggested that the decision to include thirty inner city children from the East End of London amongst the 100 representatives each city was allowed in the voting hall had helped sway the IOC voting members. London's pitch had been that the games would produce a legacy that would benefit the youth of London directly, and inspire the nation more generally. The news coverage thus praised London's (and Britain's) successful multiculturalism, and the role that sport in particular had played in producing both 'social cohesion' and 'community integration'. However, once it emerged that the four bombers were 'home grown' terrorists, the debate quickly shifted towards examining the role of multiculturalism in 'fanning the flames' of terrorism. Many commentators suggested that state multiculturalism had fragmented British society. Rather than assimilating into British values, minority ethnic communities had allegedly been allowed, if not actively encouraged, to celebrate their difference from the rest of mainstream society. Thus, within twenty four hours 'multiculturalism' had shifted from a signifier that embodied all that was great and strong about Britain, to one that embodied all that was wrong and weak with contemporary British society.[24]

In the years after 7/7 the backlash against multiculturalism gathered pace. For example, in February 2011, speaking at the annual Munich Security Conference, David Cameron warned of a persistent threat to the British way of life: radical Islamism had been allowed to take root due to the 'passive tolerance' of divided communities that had been accentuated by the ideology of multiculturalism. Speaking specifically about young British Muslim men who had been drawn to violence, and invoking a clash of values between western modernity on the one hand and traditional Islam on the other, Cameron suggested that such men 'also find it hard to identify with Britain too, because we have allowed the weakening of our collective identity. Under the doctrine of state multiculturalism, we have encouraged different cultures to live separate lives, apart from each other and apart from the mainstream'.[25] As a way to confront this situation Cameron proposed that Britain reassert a more robust national identity. By educating 'immigrants' about Britain's 'common culture', such groups would be able to more easily assimilate into Britishness. Cameron concluded by echoing similar arguments made by western European leaders such as the German Chancellor Angela Merkel and then French President Nicolas Sarkozy, 'Frankly, we need a lot less of the passive tolerance of recent years and a much more active, muscular liberalism'.[26]

Yet despite the assault on the values of multiculturalism from both the right and sections of the liberal left, the 2012 Games did in the end serve to reinvigorate a sense of the lived realities of contemporary multiracial Britain. In this regard the 2012 Olympic opening ceremony proved to be a particular success. Choreographed and designed by film-maker Danny Boyle, the general reaction was that opening spectacle of the Games had successfully portrayed the complexities, nuances and self-deprecating humour of British culture and identity.[27] Danny Boyle's historical narrative was rooted in the idea that modern Britain had been forged from the green and pleasant lands of the 'Isles of Wonder', driven forward by the foundries of industrialism, by the manual labour of the working classes and the entrepreneurial spirit of industrialists and inventors. Yet despite its aesthetic and emotional appeal, this was a story that failed to provide any account of Empire. References were made to the last time Britain had hosted the games in 1948, but just as Wembley has magically disassociated itself from its previous name, the Empire Stadium, so too did Boyle's national story disavow the existence of British colonialism. The painful legacy of Britain's involvement in the trans-Atlantic slave trade, which provided the basis for the nation's industrial strength, prosperity and wealth, as well as the colonial regimes that emerged soon after, was simply ignored.[28]

The centrepiece of the opening ceremony was Boyle's powerful homage to the founding of the National Health Service in 1948 as the institutional embodiment of British modernity. But 1948 also marks another symbolic moment of Britain's racial modernity, namely the post-war migration of Britain's black Commonwealth subjects to the homeland with the arrival of the Empire Windrush at Tilbury docks. And if Boyle was unable to account for the British imperial past (or even its existence), he was clearly aware of the need to acknowledge Windrush's legacy. In the opening ceremony the shift from the industrial revolution of the nineteenth century to the social revolutions of the twentieth was in part marked by a group of young West Indian women and men arriving onto the stage dressed smartly in suits and long dresses, carrying their luggage under their arms. This moment prompted Barry Davies, the commentator on the London 2012 official live feed, to announce to the viewers that 'others would come from other lands, in particular from the West Indies'.[29] How black Africans had ended up in 'the West Indies' before unexpectedly arriving in London from these 'other lands' in the middle of the twentieth century was left unsaid. This is imperial British history without Empire, blacks arriving from the colonies in a story without colonisation.[30]

And yet, when the opening ceremony depicted the contemporary period, the quintessentially twenty-first century British family portrayed featured a white mother and a black father, with 'mixed race' children. This is the mundane reality of a post-Empire London (and indeed much of Britain) in which a convivial multiculture is not so much celebrated or denigrated, reviled or respected, but simply lived as an unexceptional and uncontestable component of British life.[31]

UNION JACK BRITISHNESS

If the 1996 European football championships helped to generate a certain revival of overt expressions of Englishness and the re-emergence of the St George's Cross, then the 2012 London Olympics can perhaps be read as signalling the return of the Union Jack, embodied in the purposeful branding of 'Team GB'.[32] And the Olympians that came to be 'the face' of the Games, at least as far as British audiences were concerned, reflected precisely the multi-racial cosmopolitanism that Conservative populists, Ukip and the far right BNP had all in their different been railing against ever since the successful bid coincided with 7/7. Later, reflecting on the 2012 sporting year, Richard Williams would note:

> The summer told us a great deal about who we are and what, as a society, we have become, although there are no guarantees that the new understanding will be taken to heart. But surely the sight of Farah, who came to England as a refugee from Somalia, achieving his 5,000m and 10,000m double must have given pause for thought to critics of Britain's relatively open policy on immigration. Ennis, the daughter of a black father and a white mother, was another adding a new layer of meaning to the combination of flags making up the union flag draped around her shoulders.[33]

At the opening ceremony Sebastian Coe announced that he had 'never been so proud to be British', whilst Jacques Rogge, acknowledging this was the third time that Britain had hosted the games, thanked London 'for welcoming the world to this diverse, vibrant, cosmopolitan city yet again'. In the immediate aftermath of the 7/7 London bombings Trevor Phillips, then Chair of the Commission for Racial Equality, wrote that:

> the unity in diversity that won us the Games and that saw us through last week's dreadful carnage will be at the heart of the 2012 Games. By the time London is finished, everyone on Earth should want to know how we created the diverse, integrated society we have. The 2012 Olympic flame will illuminate some wonderful sport. But it should also light the path ahead for the future of our common humanity.[34]

Whilst Britain continues to wrestle with the legacy of its colonial past in shaping the present, and in the context of Conservative Party mobilisation of nationalist politics in its attempt to dismantle the welfare state and undermine a multicultural conception of British identity, it would be disastrous to ignore the importance of sport, and the 2012 games in particular, for producing a popular anti-racist retort to such ideologies. In this context and at this historical conjuncture, sport is arguably the most effective way to give meaning to a more expansive sense of Britishness, and as such it is necessary that we pay close attention to the political effects and possibilities of sporting practices and the powerful emotional attachments and discourses (however temporary) they generate.

THE OLYMPICS AS SPECTACLE

Alan Tomlinson notes that Olympic ceremonies are both 'magnificent trivia' and at the same time 'seriously revealing of the dynamics of globalisation and national identity as encapsulated in the mediated sports mega-event'.[35] Alan reminds us that such spectacles are all the more important to analyse precisely because the ideologies they contain can mask as much as they reveal about a society. In some cases, he suggests, 'these rhetorics are little more than fronts for ruthless and ambitious companies, or operate as apologetic justifications for dubious political regimes, or veil the real motives of corrupt land dealers and asset strippers complicit with or close to those running the events'.[36]

Exactly a year after Britain had seen the worst civil disturbances in generations, and an unprecedented punitive response by the state the nation celebrated the end of the Olympic Games as a crowning glory of British achievement and of a society at ease with itself. *The Sun* proudly proclaimed 'DREAM GB' underneath the words 'WE'RE WORLD BEATERS', whilst the *Daily Telegraph* more modestly, and echoing the closing words of Sebastian Coe, announced 'BRITAIN, WE DID IT RIGHT'. The front page colour photos of August 2011 showing parts of East London ablaze against the night sky were replaced in August 2012 with an explosion of fireworks lighting up the Olympic Stadium and surrounding areas. Boris Johnson noted in a *Daily Telegraph* article of London that 'for the first time since the end of empire, it truly feels like the capital of the world'.[37] The Olympics managed to unite Conservative anti-multiculturalists longing for the long lost days of Empire with a liberal left who saw in the Games and the opening ceremony in particular a celebration of the ideals of working-class solidarity and a successful multiculturalism. And yet, as the sports journalist Dave Zirin astutely observed, the progressive potential of the games had in fact failed: 'because all of this celebration of working-class sacrifice, multiculturalism and the glories of national healthcare was done at the service of an Olympics that deliver the harassment of black and brown Londoners, ballooning deficits, austerity and cuts to the very programmes like the NHS that Boyle was choosing to celebrate'.[38]

This is the great paradox of the London 2012 Olympic and Paralympic Games, and sport as a whole. As these Games showed, sport emphatically embraces moments of beauty and grace, moments that often cause us to laugh and cry, or sometimes to be shocked into devastating silence. Sport engages the ludic, the play element within, in order to show us what it means to be free – a freedom that exists, however temporarily, beyond the instrumental rationality of capitalism. Sport can and should be defended precisely on the grounds that it is no more or less than the structured pursuit of useless play. Not because it reduces crime or can prevent riots, or that it has health benefits, or that through education programmes it can reduce transmission rates of HIV/AIDS in various parts of the world, but rather because it holds on to, embraces and expands what it means to be alive, to be human, at this particular moment of neoliberal hegemony, where even to speak in such terms of play, joy and love makes some uncomfortable and others cringe.

And yet sport also enables deeply reactionary forces to claim these very same properties as somehow unique and particular to nationalist causes. The powerful spectacle of sports mega-events can be used by states to shift attention away from underlying crises, and as a way to reclaim legitimacy for its various disciplinary projects. The universalism of 'youth' can be invoked as the defining cause of sporting meritocracy by multinational corporations and political elites, whilst young people are left to struggle to maintain their human dignity at the margins of wealth-laden societies, and as the opportunities for social mobility decline year on year. In this regard, sport offers no guarantees as to the political outcomes it produces, and for that very reason it remains a contested, open terrain of social meanings and political affects.

WHOSE TEAM GB?

Les Back and his co-writers have suggested that, whilst there is 'no going back to monocultural Britain', there remains a 'reordering of the terms of inclusion' regarding who is given temporary admission to the imaginative boundaries of Britishness.[39] They argue that because of the alleged threat to the British way of life posed variously by 'terrorism', 'immigration' and 'multiculturalism', the state is able to justify intrusive modes of control ranging from the detention and deportation of 'aliens' to the internal surveillance and harassment of black and brown bodies. They describe 'neoliberal hierarchies of belonging (that) corrode the quality of our social interactions and the possibility of humanity'.[40] But we should also remember that moments of crisis also produce opportunities and counter-narratives. As problematic as it remains, it is through sport that we can find glimpses of what a post/colonial, confident and multicultural Britishness might look like, as it jettisons a conservative nostalgia for a class-ridden imperial white past. Sport has the capacity to create social bonds and identifications that cut across seemingly insurmountable racial, ethnic and religious divides. The sporting achievements of a Nicola Adams, or a Mo Farah, or a Jessica Ennis, enable us to reimagine the return of the Union Flag as something new, something different, something more inclusive. The waving of the Union Jack during the opening and closing ceremonies, and the heroic feats of humanity performed in between, produced moments when it was hard to imagine there being a scenario when there is not some black in the Union Jack. Whether or not sport provides the beginnings for a wider transformative politics will be determined in large part by the extent to which we can prevent the summer feats of 2012 from eclipsing the summer flames of 2011, so as to better understand the socio-political connections between the two.

Parts of this chapter draw upon and develop ideas first published in my book Race, Sport and Politics *(2010, Sage) and also from the introduction to* The Blackwell Companion to Sport *(edited by David Andrews and Ben Carrington, 2013). I would like to thank the participants at the 'Sport Mega-events and the Crisis of Youth Exclusion' symposium held at Goldsmiths College, London on April 20-21 2012, organised by the Open Society Foundation and the British Council where I presented an early version of this chapter. Finally Max Farrar, Michelle Moore, Simone Browne and Mark Perryman provided insightful feedback on an early draft, thanks to you all.*

NOTES

1. Richard Holt, *Sport and the British: A modern history*, Clarendon Press 1989, p137.

2. For histories of working-class leisure and resistance to bourgeois control, and the rational recreation movement, see Peter Bailey, *Leisure and Class in Victorian England: Rational recreation and the contest for control, 1830-1885*, Routledge 1978; John Clarke and Chas Critcher, *The Devil Makes Work: Leisure in capitalist Britain*, Macmillan 1985; James Walvin, *Leisure and Society 1830-1950*, Longman 1978; Chris Waters, *British Socialists and the Politics of Popular Culture 1884-1914*, Stanford 1990.

- 3. Holt, op cit, p140.

4. On the impact of the new American 'Market Empire' and consumer culture in challenging and ultimately displacing European cultural norms and taste cultures, see the historical accounts of Tony Judt, *Postwar: A History of Europe since 1945*, Penguin Books 2005; and Victoria de Grazia, *Irresistible Empire: America's Advance through Twentieth-Century Europe*, Harvard University Press 2006.

5. Boris Johnson, 'The resurrection of English cricket can inspire us all', *Daily Telegraph*, 22 August 2011.

6. Ibid.

7. Ibid.

8. Ibid.

9. Richard Williams, 'Could Disorder Erupt Again and Threaten the Olympics?', *Guardian*, 10 August 2011.

10. Paul Hayward, 'Riots force London to get real over 2012 Olympics', *Observer*, 13 August 2011.

11. Tony Blair, 'Blaming a moral decline for the riots makes good headlines but bad policy', *Observer*, 20 August 2011.

12. The scale of the disturbances was significant. In London alone, there were reports of looting, fires and confrontations with police in Tottenham (where the initial protest of the shooting of Mark Duggan had occurred), but also Wood Green, Enfield, Dalston, Waltham Forest, Brixton, Hackney, Lewisham, Peckham, Croydon, Notting Hill, Ealing, East Ham, Clapham Junction and Bromley.

13. Alan Travis and Simon Rogers, 'Revealed: the full picture of sentences handed down to rioters', *Guardian*, 18 August 2011.

14. Richard Sennett and Saskia Sassen, 'Cameron's Broken Windows', *New York Times*, 10 August 2011; Zygmunt Bauman, 'The London Riots – On Consumerism coming Home to Roost', *Social Europe Journal*, 9 August 2011. On the issue of consumer capitalism and commodity desire as a primary motivator of the disturbances, see also Neal Lawson, 'Violent Shopping', 30 March 2012: www.compasonline.org.uk

15. Jon Cruddas and Jonathan Rutherford, 'Out of the Ashes: Britain After the Riots', *New Statesman*, 2 January 2012.

16. See Ben Quinn, 'David Starkey claims "the whites have become black"',*Guardian*, 12 August 2011.

17. Melanie Phillips, 'Britain's Liberal Intelligentsia has Smashed Virtually Every Social Value', *Daily Mail*, 11 August 2011.

18. Ibid.

19. See for example the joint research project between the *Guardian* and the London School of Economics, 'Reading the Riots': http://www.guardian.co.uk/uk/series/reading-the-riots.

20. Gary Younge, 'Indifferent Elites, Poverty and Police Brutality – All Reasons to Riot in the UK', *Guardian*, 4 December 2011.

21. Ibid.

22. Stuart Hall, Chas Critcher, Tony Jefferson, John Clarke and Brian Roberts, *Policing the Crisis: Mugging, the State and Law and Order*, Palgrave 1978, p332.

23. Les Back, Shamser Sinha and Charlynne Bryan, 'New Hierarchies of Belonging', *European Journal of Cultural Studies*, 15 (2), 2012.

24. For a further analysis of this point, see chapter four in Ben Carrington, *Race, Sport and Politics: The Sporting Black Diaspora*, Sage 2010.

25. David Cameron, Speech at Munich Security Conference, 5 February 2011.

26. Ibid.

27. Writing in the *New York Times*, Sarah Lyall noted, 'With its hilariously quirky Olympic opening ceremony, a wild jumble of the celebratory and the fanciful; the conventional and the eccentric; and the frankly off-the-wall, Britain presented itself to the world Friday night as something it has often struggled to express even to itself: a nation secure in its own post-empire identity, whatever that actually is': Sarah Lyall, 'A Five-Ring Opening Circus, Weirdly and Unabashedly British', *New York Times*, 27 July 2012.

28. Boris Johnson too noted 'the lack of Empire', though his complaint seemed to suggest that this omission was problematic because Britain's colonial project should have been *celebrated*. He was quoted as saying 'I couldn't follow all of it but it was beautiful. We knocked the spots off Beijing. There wasn't much Empire in it but maybe that wouldn't have been the best thing to show in there'. See Patrick Sawer, 'London 2012: Opening Ceremony Wows the Queen and the World with Wit and Drama', *Daily Telegraph*, 28 July 2012.

29. This form of historical amnesia produces black and other similarly racialised groups as somehow exterior to Britain's history until 'they' suddenly arrive on 'our' shores, forgetting of course that such peoples were already and always British. As Back et al note, the 'colonial citizen-migrants who came to Britain after the Second World War were transformed from "citizens" into "immigrants" on their arrival', Back et al, op cit, p141.

30. For an excellent account critiquing the uncritical celebration of the 'originary moment' of *Windrush* and the pre-1948 histories of black settlement in Britain, see Barnor Hesse, 'Diasporicity: Black Britain's post-colonial

formations', in Barnor Hesse (ed), *Un/Settled Multiculturalisms: Diasporas, Entanglements, Transruptions*, Zed Press 2000.

31. See Paul Gilroy, *After Empire: Melancholia or Convivial Culture?*, Routledge 2004.
32. For a discussion of how 'Team GB' highlights the continuing contradictions of British identity see Gerry Hassan, 'Olympics to kick off with national confusion', *The Scotsman*, 21 April 2012.
33. Richard Williams, '2012: A Truly Remarkable Sporting Year to be Relished Over and Over', *Guardian*, 28 December 2012.
34. Trevor Phillips, 'Let's Show the World its Future', *Observer*, 9 July 2005.
35. Alan Tomlinson, *Sport and Leisure Cultures*, University of Minnesota Press 2005, p27.
36. Ibid.
37. Boris Johnson, 'London and Team GB – Take a bow. You've dazzled the world', *Daily Telegraph*, 13 August 2012.
38. Dave Zirin, 'Danny Boyle's Olympic Minstrel Show', *The Nation*, 30 July 2012.
39. Les Back et al, op cit, p150.
40. Ibid, p151.

A POSTCARD FROM RIO

Gavin Poynter

RIO, SUMMER 2016

It calls itself the 'Marvellous City'. It is. Breakfast at Favela Point is a particular pleasure.[1] Opened by seven local women in 2012, with help from the Elas Social Foundation, the café serves fresh bread in the mornings and homemade dishes like barbecued meat with rice, beans and salad throughout the day. Located at the last stop of the gondola development, part of the Porto Maravilha Public-Private-Partnership project that was built to revitalise Rio's Port Region, the café's location offers extensive views over the city that stretches below. It is situated in Providencia, one of the oldest favelas in Brazil.

Favelas were originally established as illegal settlements by rural migrants seeking work in Brazil's cities. By 2012, about 20 per cent of Rio's population (1.3 million people) were living in over 750 communities, many perched precariously on the mountain sides overlooking the city. Living conditions in the favelas are typically very basic, with inadequate sanitary conditions, makeshift and sporadic electricity supplies, high levels of unemployment and large areas dominated by drug cartels. For decades Brazil's middle classes have turned a blind eye to these communities. They were content to draw upon the cheap and readily available labour of those living in the favelas – until Brazil won the right to host the 2014 FIFA World Cup and Rio won its bid for the 2016 Olympic and Paralympic Games.

Preparations for hosting these events initiated an extensive and rapid redevelopment of four zones of the city, as well as its transport infrastructure and the favelas. When redevelopment of the favelas commenced in 2008, elite, specially trained, police teams, often supported by the military, moved in to remove the armed gangs and drug dealers that, since the 1990s, had dominated their street life. Once cleared, the police established a permanent presence in the districts, deploying teams of officers known as Pacifying Police Units (UPPs). When the UPPs were established, government aid sought to improve the education system and social infrastructure and, eventually, enterprise capital began to find its way into areas such as Providencia. Several favelas gradually re-joined the city. Pacification, shorthand for describing the end of the dominance of the criminal gangs and the introduction of social programmes designed to revive civil society, generated economic opportunities. Favela tourism took off; land values in several areas rose, and communities that had previously paid little in property value tax began to pay. Within some communities, activists came together to resist eviction or relocation that had been forced upon them by rising rent and land values.[2] Some, such as the women who opened the social enterprise at Favela Point, deployed their talents to secure a foothold in the new economy of their area. Many others were forced to move.

Where guns and violence had failed, rising property prices and commercial development succeeded. The favelas were pacified and several gentrified. Rio de Janeiro, despite concerns about its capacity to complete the extensive renewal of its urban and social infrastructure, delivered to the world the two biggest sporting shows on the planet. Budgets were set and exceeded. The Games organisers and city and federal government met the considerable challenges that arose, not least from the weakening of the nation's rate of economic growth. Now, in 2016, the city has turned its attention to fulfilling the sporting and social legacies that formed the narrative that legitimised and authenticated its hosting of these two global events. Rio's Olympic plans drew upon the experience of two previous hosts cities in particular –Barcelona and London. The former provided insights into the zonal re-development of the city, whilst the latter offered the framework of justification via the longer term legacy of urban renewal that the mega-event accelerates and, in many ways, compels. As Rio turns its attention to the long term, it is perhaps a useful moment to draw some lessons from London's legacy achievements, four years after it hosted the 2012 Olympic and Paralympic Games.

LONDON AFTER 2012

By its nature, the summer Olympic and Paralympic Games are a one-off spectacular, a stage on which the world's elite sportspeople come together for a few weeks, once every four years. Cities compete for the right to hold the Games, and the International Olympic Committee places significant contractual, including financial, requirements on the host nation and all preparations for the event have to be completed within seven years – the timescale between the awarding of the Games to the successful bidder and the opening ceremony. Putting on the Games is a costly affair; and harnessing the mega-event to the social process of city building serves to justify the vast expenditure that the sporting spectacle requires. According to the official discourse, the 'one-off' event catalyses its temporal opposite, a long term process of urban development and renewal – that is, in the wake of London 2012, now widely referred to as its legacy. In everyday usage the term suggests a gift, a bequest or inheritance, often passed within a family from one generation to another. But unlike the typical familial gift, the one bequeathed by the Games has to be paid for. In short, as London 2012 has revealed, harnessing the Games to the discourse of legacy provides the political and sporting elites that organises it a legitimising framework but also generates tensions, especially when it comes to delivering on the promised 'gifts' to those local communities whose daily lives have been most affected by their living within Olympic zones.

Like Rio de Janeiro, London's legacy plans required public and private investment to transform the Olympic development areas – in this case the Olympic Park and its borders – into an integral part of the city. The Park's location, East London, was an area long designated as one of the most socially deprived localities in England, and, post-2012, the main responsibility for achieving its conversion to legacy uses and contribute to the area's social transformation was given to the London Legacy Development Corporation. The LLDC, a not-for-profit company established in 2009 by central government, was re-established as a development corporation, and responsibility for it was transferred to the city-wide Mayoral Greater London Authority in the weeks leading up to the 2012 Games. The transfer of ownership of assets within the Olympic Park, and a wider area incorporating land on its borders, enabled the LLDC, along with local councils Newham, Hackney, Tower Hamlets and Waltham Forest (Greenwich, Barking and Dagenham were also designated as host boroughs but are geographically located outside the Park and its borders) to create a master plan for the conversion of the Park into a new zone of London with the postmark E20.[3] The four years that have passed since the Games have revealed the tensions between the social and commercial aspirations contained in the plans and the capacity of the partnership between public and private sectors to implement them; tensions that were intensified by the persistent weakness of the UK economy and, arguably, the flaws inherent in linking the mega-event to the complex process of urban regeneration.

The concentration of several sporting events and the Athletes Village into one location has considerable attractions for the IOC and event organisers. An Olympic Park provides the focus for the sporting festival, ensures that the majority of athletes share the daily experience of the Games and, consistent with the philosophy of Olympism, nations compete in a peaceful atmosphere of festival and celebration. But the festival setting lasts only as long as the Games; the task of converting the Olympic Park into an integral part of the host city presents considerable challenges – white elephants must be avoided, temporary structures must be removed, and the Park must be redeveloped as an urban space that effectively connects with its surroundings. The projected costs of conversion according to the LLDC Business Plan, was about £500 million in capital expenditure, £300 million of which was designated for infrastructure projects. Conversion was to take place over three phases, with the main public expenditure and key works undertaken over a period of three years.[4]

From the outset it was recognised that the ambitious plans for the legacy development of the Park required upfront public expenditure and effective collaboration between public and private sector partners (the LLDC directly owned less than forty per cent of the total area within the Park, the rest being owned by local authorities, the Lea Valley Regional Park Authority and private sector landowners, including Westfield and Thames Water). There was also a need for income from events and other activities as parts of the Park re-opened, and, most importantly, for the leveraging of additional private sector resources through the sale of the Park's publicly owned assets, or the contracting out of their management. The LLDC's task, therefore, was to manage potentially conflicting roles – fulfilling its commitment to social goals (providing affordable housing, employment opportunities for local people and developing a community infrastructure) whilst also maximising returns to the tax-payer and meeting the demands of investors and developers for whom the bottom line was scheme 'viability'. Over the critical three-year phase of the Park's conversion, in the absence of significantly higher levels of public funding, the balance between social and commercial goals tilted in favour of the latter. Scheme viability – the prospect of private capital achieving a profitable return on investment – established a pattern of development that privileged, for example, the housing needs and capacity to purchase or rent of inward migrating professionals and significantly limited the potential for public agencies to secure contributions from the private sector that could be used for public gain. The legacy development of the Olympic Village illustrates this fundamental weakness in the 'leverage' model, and captures the LLDC's dilemma.

Pre-games the Village was sold by the Olympic Delivery Authority to Triathlon Homes and a commercial partnership formed by Qatari Holdings (a subsidiary of the Qatar Investment Authority), and Delancey, an international investment company. Triathlon took responsibility for around 1400 homes and these were designated as affordable housing, with around half for social rent and the other half for sale through a range of 'affordable' options. As part of the Mayor of London's First Steps programme, for example, tenants in social housing in London boroughs could apply to move into the Olympic Village. Those seeking to rent could secure a discount of up to 30 per cent on the market rent for their property, though they had to be in employment and meet other criteria. And a similar, parallel scheme was operated by Newham local authority. In short, despite the limitations largely imposed by central government welfare policies, Triathlon's slice of the Olympic Village sought to address the demand for social housing and the aspiration to achieve the creation of mixed communities within the Park. But, as the Park's conversion gathered pace, such aspirations were much diluted. The first major mixed community development, Chobham Manor, provided about 25 per cent affordable housing – 10 per cent below the widely published target – and subsequent developments, to be completed by the early 2020s, are unlikely to achieve even this level. As the social or public gain dimension of the Games' urban legacy has waned, so the commercial has flourished, in pockets or 'hotspots', in the language of the estate agent.

Qatari Holdings owned 1439 housing units and developed these properties for rent. In 2012 such schemes were unusual, even in London. Institutional investors (for example pension funds and

Sovereign Wealth Funds – the huge funds built up by emerging economies such as China and Qatar) had a long history of investing in commercial rather than residential property markets; so the move into the latter reflected the growth of the sector that has arisen from the decline in home ownership in the UK, especially areas such as London, and the opportunities presented by the scale of development that took place with the construction of the Olympic Village.

The concentration of large numbers of housing units in one location facilitates sufficient scale to secure solid returns for the institutional investor on residential property. The property's scale enables the creation of a hotel-style development, incorporating concierge and retail facilities as components of the private rental living experience. The provision of such services pushes up rental values and is directly aimed at providing high standard accommodation for the mobile professional classes living in the global city. The Olympic Village conversion undertaken by the Qatari/Delancey consortium was an early example of this type of development in London. Others have rapidly followed. The consortium also purchased six adjacent development plots with the capacity to provide a further 2000 homes, and has recently completed the construction of a 50-storey residential tower (another hotel-style property designed for the high end private rental market) opposite a luxury hotel and flat development constructed by a consortium led by the Manhattan Loft Corporation. The MLC development contains three sky gardens, a pool, spa, rooftop restaurant and over two hundred apartments/lofts, the entry to which is shared with the hotel. Whilst undoubtedly improving upon the quality and management standards traditionally found in the UK private rented sector, this is not a model designed to meet the housing needs of lower income families. Its viability rests upon the implementation of a vision of housing provision that privileges exclusivity and affirms the higher social status of its residents.[5]

The Olympic – now East – Village has become part of a high-rise, high-density and high-price area of development around the transport hub that is Stratford. The vision for the creation of affordable housing has receded. As developers have privileged scheme viability, the proportion of the value captured for investment in social housing and public spaces has diminished, particularly on the south side of the former Olympic Park and within the developments on its borders. In the absence of significant levels of public investment post-2012 (far more than were earmarked in the LDDC's Business Plan), the social transformation focused on the needs of the local community has amounted to little more than a wish list. Its achievement was undermined by a combination of insufficient public resources to deliver an ambitious city building programme, the impact of government social policies that capped housing benefit support for the lower waged and unemployed (which put the purchase or rent of new housing units out of the reach of many local people), and the operations of a London property market in which the activities of international investors pushed up rent and property prices in iconic locations such as the Olympic Park and its borders.

As the excitement and public enthusiasm for the 2012 Games has become a distant memory, the spirit of the spectacle has been captured and commercialised in pockets of economic development in East London. The Park, now Queen Elizabeth Park, has become a 'destination' for popular cultural and sporting events, and a location for the consumption of leisure, symbolised by the Westfield Shopping Mall and the vast London ExCel exhibition centre nearby. The Olympic Press and Media Centre has become iCity, the site of an Infinity data store and the home of BT Sport, the telecom company's sports channel that began to transmit football's Premier League Games in 2013 from three studios on the site and for whom the Olympic Park provides an iconic sporting backdrop in what is an expensive and risky sporting enterprise. Such new sports media platforms enter a crowded and highly competitive market, as the failure of the Irish pay TV company Setanta demonstrated in 2009. Employment patterns in the local economies of what are now called East London's 'growth boroughs' (once the host Olympic boroughs) has slowly changed; there are more private sector jobs and fewer in the public sector but, with the best jobs going to mobile professionals, local residents have continued to work in the less skilled and lower paid service occupations.

Four years on from the 2012 Games, East London's regeneration has largely focused upon new developments located along the Lower Lea Valley, creating a corridor that connects Stratford with Canary Wharf. As Canary Wharf is now also expanding to include the recently commenced construction of Wood Wharf, a new location designed to attract high technology business services, the corridor has become a focus for international investors whose residential properties are designed for the high end of the housing market. Despite the commitments of successive governments since the successful bid to host the Games in 2005 to improve the lives and expectations of local residents, the process of creative destruction catalysed by the Games has tended to achieve the opposite – the replication of many features of London's pre-credit crunch economy, with its reliance on rising property and land values, its privileging of finance and business services and its creation of pockets of high price and high value housing.

OLYMPISM AND DISCOURSES OF LEGACY

London was the first host city to set out detailed legacy plans before the Games took place. A central component of its bid document was the harnessing of the public investment directly and indirectly associated with hosting the Games to the achieving of progressive social change in East London. Public investment in infrastructure did undoubtedly enhance the connectedness of East London to the rest of the city, and made specific areas, such as the Lower Lea Valley, attractive to private investors. But, as the role of private capital has moved centre stage, the ambitious programme of social renewal has shifted to the margins, with community gain increasingly reliant upon residual deals with developers. Dependence upon private capital to deliver public gain has produced socially regressive rather than progressive outcomes for local communities. Public investment has generated value creation that is concentrated in pockets of gentrification: public agencies engaged to deliver legacy have been unable to secure its socially equitable distribution.

The mega-event accelerates the process of urban change, reducing or removing planning barriers, whilst introducing a framework of contractual relations between the IOC and host city that places significant demands upon the latter to reconcile the creation of event-related structures to the longer term needs of the city. On the downside, London gained a new 60,000 capacity stadium but really doesn't need one; East London acquired more Four and Five Star hotels and a sprinkling of high-rise, high-value and high-price developments, but really does not need them; and many poorer families, caught in the twin traps of rising rent and land values and welfare benefit reform, had to move out of the East End. On the upside, the area's transport infrastructure has improved, the Olympic Park has re-opened in phases, and on time, and a new urban area continues to be created in the east. But it is an area whose future rests upon an economic model with shaky foundations – sporting events and shopping, industries that tend to bubble and burst, and a new mix of residential and commercial developments led by international investors in search of iconic locations.

The contradictions inherent in an Olympic movement whose philosophy rests upon the universal values of Olympism-human progress, cultural enlightenment and peaceful competition – but whose existence relies upon the commercial exploitation of its brand – have been reproduced in the narrative of the urban legacies achieved by London. Incorporating urban renewal and regeneration into the contractual framework of the Games's delivery may reflect the uncanny capacity of the IOC to re-invent itself as a force for 'good' in the wake of the negative impacts of bribery and corruption scandals surrounding the Games at the end of the last century; but it also creates tensions for the host city. The gift has to be paid for. The sporting festival serves to legitimise public investment that engineers social change, but in directions that support private capital's quest for new rounds of accumulation to be drawn from the city's economy. In the contemporary world, harnessing major sporting events to the process of city-building is a hazardous affair; the highly commodified character of each may diminish the social value of the other.

The potential provided by the legacy of London 2012 was, perhaps, only a fraction of that offered to private capital by the long-term economic prospects of Rio de Janeiro. Brazil's hosting of the 2016 Olympic and Paralympic Games affirms its arrival as South America's leading nation, and of Rio's status as a global city. Perhaps one tiny measure of the city's ability to achieve some kind of reconciliation between the competing social and commercial interests inherent in mega-event led regeneration will be its capacity to ensure that social enterprises like Favela Point, and the communities it serves, are, at the least, among the real beneficiaries of Rio 2016.

NOTES

1. Felicity Clarke, 'Favela Point Launches; Strength in a moment of uncertainty for Providencia', 29 March 2012: www.rioonwatch.org.
2. Katarine Flor e Glaucia Marinho, 'A favela agora virou a alma do negócio', 8 January 2013: www.brasildefato.com.br.

3. London Legacy Development Corporation, *London Legacy Communities Scheme*, September 2011.
4. London Legacy Development Corporation, *Business Plan 2012-13, 2013-4,* LLDC 2012.
5. Gavin Lucas, 'Hingston and Keep's Manhattan Loft Gardens Identity', *Creative Review*, 12 June 2012.

DRESSAGE FOR THE MASSES

Mark Steel

It may not admit it, but Conservative Britain took a pasting at the Olympics. To start with, some of the country's most revered heroes are now cyclists. This is marvellous, as there must be millions of *Top Gear* fans who see Chris Hoy whizzing round the track and think:

> Look at him blocking up that bloody velodrome, what if I wanted to drive across there? And the council have put all these cycle lanes round it, but if I smashed into one of those sprint heats with my 2.5 litre V6 Audi A4 and broke all their pelvises I'd be the one to get prosecuted, it's political correctness gone MENTAL.

There could have been a special London set of rules for the cycling races, with trucks cutting across the riders while a bloke with a red face yelled 'Pay your road tax you sideburned arsehole', and the commentator said 'Now they're coming to the tricky bend where sales reps zig-zag through the peloton while talking on their mobiles and Jeremy Clarkson reverses into them all while shouting "Oi Cavendish, you'd better not touch my wing mirror"'.

And one of the greatest British victories was the astonishing run by a man who came here from Somalia. So presumably the newspapers who, up until now, have campaigned daily against asylum seekers with headlines like 'They're Literally Pouring Into Britain Like Asylum Seeker Orange Squash', and 'Now They're Planning to Eat the Queen', will now say: 'When we insisted they should be sent back immediately, we meant sent back to the start of the track and encouraged to do one more lap so they're fit enough to win us a gold medal.'

Politicians will make statements such as, 'When we said we will be more vigorously menacingly ruthless than ever with any asylum seekers coming across the channel, we meant we won't allow any lorry in unless it's bringing at least six. "Go and grab a random bunch from

Sangatte" we'll tell the drivers. "You never know, one of them might end up getting silver in the archery".'

And Migration Watch will produce figures that prove that if the rate of immigration continues at current levels, by the next Olympics we'll win every single medal in everything, including sports that haven't been invented yet, like dressage on a forklift truck.

Another success of the Games was the growing enthusiasm for women's football. I went to the semi-final between France and Japan, where the fans were so gleeful they'd be evicted from the ground at an England men's match for being too amicable.

But there was something unsettlingly unfamiliar about the game. Because the women appear to have different rules from the men, in that as a free kick is awarded they don't all surround the referee and pull that 'Oh my God I can't believe it how can that be a foul I wasn't even in the country at the time' expression, and no one dives on the floor clutching their head claiming the defender has just given them brain surgery without an anaesthetic and therefore must be sent off and executed.

You could no more complain about the lack of skill than moan it's not worth watching women's athletics or tennis. There were 61,000 at this game, yet it's only a while ago that two of the most prominent football presenters in the country believed women had no place in the sport whatsoever.

Even more surprising was the sudden overdue affection for Andy Murray. Up until his gold medal, traditional tennis fans had seen him as not tennisy enough, and non-tennis fans had seen him as 'Not enough of a laugh', as if their coaching advice would be 'Stop worrying about winning so many points, and instead run round the court wearing plastic tits now and again'.

But in this Olympics his gold medal, and the raucous non Centre Court atmosphere in which he won it, went some way to burying this cynicism. He even finished third in the 2012 BBC Sports Personality of the Year awards for goodness sake!

During the Games much of the cynical attitude many people had towards sport in general evaporated, and people who've never shown an interest before were desperately applying for last minute tickets for events such as upside-down canoeing through a swarm of bees or vaulting over an ostrich.

The *Daily Mail* and Boris Johnson claimed Team GB's success was due to 'Conservative values' such as competition. But if medals were awarded on the competitive rules through which Boris and the Conservative leader attained their privileges, they wouldn't bother with the racing, since competitors would just inherit the medals, and then give an interview saying the trouble with the other runners was they expected something for nothing.

So a more reasonable suggestion would be for two medal tables to be shown each day. One showing the number that Britain has won, and one showing the number Conservative Britain has won – omitting the cyclists, the people they'd have prevented from coming here in the first place, the people who had to move abroad to train as facilities here were cut ... leaving them with the one for the Dressage. They can have that if they want.

An earlier version of this chapter first appeared as 'Cyclists, Women, Refugees – Vindicated at Last' in the Independent, *9 August 2012.*

SUPERCRIPS, CYBORGS AND THE UNREAL PARALYMPIAN

P. David Howe

A lifetime ago I was a Paralympian and participated in successive summer games between 1988 and 2000, representing Canada. At times I was successful in my chosen sport of middle distance running, and I also became personally involved in the politics of Paralympic sport when I was elected athletes' representative to the International Paralympic Committee Athletics Committee, from 1996 to 2000. The impairment that facilitated my participation in the Paralympics, and my interest in the cultural world surrounding this sport mega event, is mild right-sided hemiplegia. As an anthropologist with a certain level of participation in elite sport I began to explore the Paralympics as a research project as far back as 1986, when I was asked by a university lecturer to record 'field notes' during the summer following my first year at university. Since that time I have been mining this ethnographic material, and have continued gathering more – to give myself and others an understanding of the Paralympic world as I see it. During the 2012 Games I worked as a freelance journalist, using this as an access point to uncover with greater detail and clarity how the cultural politics of the Paralympic Games were changing.

There was a noticeable feel-good factor in and around Britain during the London 2012 Paralympic Games. And one of the things that amazed me is how the British media has now embraced Paralympic sport. Just over twenty years ago, at the 1992 Barcelona Paralympic Games, the BBC televised only a few live events, on *Grandstand*, its Saturday sports programme. At London 2012 I expected the spotlight to be much more intense, since with every passing Paralympiad there has been an increased media presence – and I was not disappointed.

Recent coverage from host nations – notably Australia during the

Sydney 2000 Games and Greece during Athens 2004 – had been good, but not as comprehensive as the coverage provided by the British media of the 2012 Paralympics. The 2012 organisers had some previous British experience to build on: since 2005 Britain has hosted the Paralympic World Cup in Manchester, and this has attracted a reasonable amount of media coverage, while offering athletes a chance to shine in at least three of the flagship sports (athletics, swimming and wheelchair basketball). And events such as the World Cup, and coverage of the London Marathon wheelchair race (which in 2013 hosted the International Paralympic Committee Marathon World Cup) have also kept the British public mindful of Paralympic sport between Paralympiads.

Nevertheless, the media frenzy surrounding London 2012 was even greater than I expected. There appeared to have been very little let-down in the carnival atmosphere at the Paralympic Games as compared to the Olympics. The host broadcaster, Channel Four, was different (the BBC had been the broadcaster during the Olympics), but it had sped on to do a similar good job for the Paralympics. The volume of coverage in both broadcast and print media in Britain surpassed any previous reporting at Paralympic level. Stories that attracted the greatest media attention, however, still had the tone of 'inspiration' about them. For, in the eyes of the International Paralympic Committee, the Paralympics are designed to empower people with disabilities; and this inspirational tone of reportage is a clear indication that media outlets are buying into the IPC's rhetoric. Any further details about Paralympic culture are often sketchy.

One element of the culture of Paralympic sport that was mentioned in the press but often poorly explained is the classification system. This is a structure – biomedical in nature – for competition that is similar to the systems used in the sport of judo and boxing, where competitors perform in distinctive weight categories. Within disability sport, competitors are classified by their body's degree of function, and it is important therefore that the classification process is robust, and that it achieves equity across Paralympic sporting practice, thereby enabling athletes to compete on a level playing field. However, establishing this level playing field through classifications is highly political, as there is never complete agreement among and within the International Organisations of Sport for the Disabled.

The IOSD is a management group of different disability specific federations, namely the Cerebral Palsy International Sport and Recreation Association, International Blind Sport Association, International Sports Federation for Persons with Intellectual Disability and the International Wheelchair and Amputee Sport Association, all of which were established with the explicit intention of creating opportunities for people with disabilities within their fields, and using sport as a vehicle for their empowerment. It was the International Organisations for Sport for the Disabled and their predecessors that helped to organise the Paralympic Games from 1960 through to 1988. These early Games were organised and run on a much smaller scale than they have been more recently under the influence of the International Paralympic Committee – whose rapid growth in the last few years has enabled it to establish an extensive network of 170 national affiliates.

The process of classification within sport for the disabled makes distinctions between the physical or mental potential of athletes, and attempts to achieve an equitable environment, whereby the successful athletes in each class will have an equal chance of accumulating physical capital. In reality, however, there are a number of factors that impact upon the accumulation of capital (both physical and cultural) in various classifications. The first factor is the number of athletes within a particular event. If there are only a handful of athletes, then the amount of capital that can be accumulated in most cases is limited. To the outside world the achievements of athletes in a highly contested event are generally seen as superior to the events with a small number of competitors. In the case of the Paralympic Games, it is the events for the severely disabled that are undersubscribed, and as such it is these athletes that are seen to lack capital; and it is these severely disabled athletes whose events in recent years have been removed from the Paralympic programme. Yet if Paralympism is to have a lasting virtue, it needs to consider the rights of participation in international competition of the most disabled populations.

In some classes there may only be six athletes from four countries (the IPC minimum for eligible events), suggesting that winners are less likely to receive the same kudos as an athlete who defeats twenty athletes. Another important factor in terms of whether winners ultimately gain capital from their involvement in sport is the nature and degree of their disability. Some disabilities are more acceptable than others, in part because they adhere more closely to the aesthetic cultural norms associated with the able bodied. An athlete's relative proximity to the mainstream norm can also be linked to how their disabilities occurred. For example, there seems to be a greater acceptance of acquired disabilities as compared with those that are a result of congenital deformity.

That being said, British Paralympic heroine Tanni Grey-Thompson is the exception to both these generalisations. Firstly, she has spina bifida, which is a congenital issue related to the spine (although she is a wheelchair user, and the wheelchair is in many ways the ubiquitous symbol of disability). Secondly, she has achieved celebrity status in a disability class that has not been very competitive: her class at the Paralympics (T53) was very small. Nevertheless she embodied the acceptable face of disability at the time she was competing – partly because the general public were not made aware of the small number of competitors in her races. That few are aware of this kind of detail is mainly because media reportage does not go into such details, or bother to examine the intricacies of her class. Tanni's status within the UK political realm remains currently unrivalled by any other Paralympian, and she currently sits in the House of Lords. She is more publicly involved with disability issues now than she ever was when she was an athlete; my belief is that, as a member of a marginalised community who had been 'accepted' into the mainstream, she was happy to take the applause as a competitor, while perhaps being rather uncomfortable about rocking the boat. One hopes that the ableist assumptions that gave her a voice might be better exposed now that she has a position of influence.

In some sports, like swimming, the classification system enables people from a variety of impairment groups to compete against one another. For example, one of the darlings of the Paralympics Team GB, Ellie Simmonds, whose disability is classified as Achondroplasia dwarfism, competes against individuals who are missing the use of several limbs. Ellie is in part a media darling because she has won races, but also because she is aesthetically pleasing. She was highly successful in London 2012, as she had been four years earlier in Beijing, but there was no mention in the media of the fact that she was competing against athletes with numerous limbs that were either uncoordinated or unusable because of a spinal cord injury – while she had no such impairment. We need to ask ourselves whether being of short stature is actually impairing in the context of sport, and whether there should be a Paralympic category for individuals who are of short stature? Such controversies surrounding classification are continually rumbling along in the Paralympic movement, but have yet to capture the imagination of the media.

As long ago as Sydney 2000 Australian journalist Richard Hind, writing for the *Sydney Morning Herald* on the eve of the Games, exposed the conundrum of reporting on the Paralympics that is still valid today. On the one hand, journalists will be dealing with athletes craving respect for their achievements, not merely acknowledgement of their courage and commitment. But on the other hand, the reporter who strays beyond the well-established territory of feel-good stories and heart-breaking profiles, and dares to make a critical assessment, risks automatic censure.

Stars like Grey-Thompson and Simmonds are spared the critical eye of the media because of their impairments – and this means that the public are not exposed to Paralympic sport in its true entirety.

There are certain types of minimally impaired bodies that are celebrated more than others.

SHOULD OSCAR BE A PARALYMPIAN?

South African amputee sprinter Oscar Pistorius is another example of an athlete who over the last five years has become synonymous with disability and sport. (Of course now he is now even more famous for the alleged murder of his girlfriend, but that will not be discussed here.) Until this tragic incident Pistorius was a global sports celebrity as the quintessential supercrip – a cyborg, part-man-part-machine, the embodiment of the empowered athlete. The controversy that surrounded him as an athlete centred on whether he should be permitted to compete in the Olympics. Pistorius has in the past successfully battled the International Association of Athletics Federations to have his prosthetic limbs considered legal for mainstream athletic competition, and thus was able to run in London 2012 Games. But the question that really should have been asked was whether or not Oscar should be permitted to compete as a Paralympian.[1]

Not surprisingly, Pistorius is a very successful Paralympian. On 2 September 2012, however, he was beaten in the T44 class for the 200 metres by Alan Oliveira of Brazil. There was a stunned and unsporting reaction from Pistorius, who suggested that his fellow competitor had broken the rules by wearing legs that were too long, thereby having an unfair advantage. Response to this outburst generally divided into two camps: those who saw it as unsporting, and those who sided with Oscar and questioned the International Paralympic Committee's rules and regulations on the use of prosthetic limbs – or 'blades'.

Pistorius apologised for the timing of his outburst, but he did not retract his concerns, which he had raised with the IPC before the Games. I am certain the IPC would have looked into this issue, but it is not within their mandate to report directly to individual athletes; but, because he had not got the response he wanted, Pistorius took his complaints directly to the media who had helped him develop the Oscar Brand so successfully over the last five years. I want to take a step back here to explore the history of the rise of the Oscar phenomenon, and to suggest that Pistorius himself has been taking advantage of the classification system that is central to the ethos of Paralympic sport.

In 2007, when the IAAF attempted to ban the use of the prosthetics limbs that Pistorius uses to run, it was seen by many as an infringement on the rights of the disabled. Pistorius himself was vitriolic when the IAAF banned him, arguing that such a stance would be counterproductive to the advancement of Paralympic sport. It certainly could have negatively impacted upon the Oscar Brand – but would it have been really bad for the Paralympic movement? I am all for Pistorius being eligible for the Olympic Games: my issue is the eligibility of his type of cyborg body to compete in the Paralympic Games. It could be argued that Pistorius and those impaired in a similar manner, such as Oliveira, should not be competing in the Paralympics at all, because it is unfair to the majority of athletes in their events.

The simple fact is that double below the knee amputees like Pistorius and his nemesis Oliveira have an unfair advantage over the single below the knee amputees who make up the majority of the competitors they race against. The dispute with Oliveira was about the length of Oliveria's blades, which the IPC says are legal. But to my mind the issue is all about balance. According to the IPC, Pistoriụs is a class T43 athlete (T stands for Track; the 4 represents the athlete's impairment category – amputee; and the 3 is the athlete's specific class – double below the knee). But many of the athletes that Oscar competes against in Paralympic competitions are single below the knee amputees (T44), and people in this category have difficulty in balancing the uneven ground forces between their human leg and the lower leg prosthesis during running. On the other hand T44 athletes generally have better starts than T43. Thus, over 100 metres in the men's T44/43 category, a British hero was born at the London 2012 Games – Jonnie Peacock, a single leg below the knee sprinter. Peacock beat Pistorius because of his bullet like start, becoming the fastest amputee in the world. The 100 metres is just a little too short for the bi-lateral below the knee athletes. However, once underway, the inertia of the balanced blades gives double below the knee amputees a huge advantage over 200 metres and 400 metres, as the uneven physical forces of T44 athletes makes them more impaired.

IPC rules state that a less impaired athlete cannot compete in a class with more impaired athletes because this makes the context inequitable. But modern technology makes having no lower legs an advantage over having one. And since there are not enough class T43 athletes running at an elite level for there to be a separate competition, I would argue that Pistorius should not be eligible to compete in the Paralympics. Many will think this is harsh, but there are countless other elite athletes with impairments who are not eligible to compete in the Paralympic Games for the very same reason – a lack of numbers to produce exciting yet equitable competition.

Since the formation of the Paralympic Games in 1948, athletes with Pistorius's impairment have usually competed using wheelchairs, in part because the technology available for walking and running was very uncomfortable during training and competition. There will come a time when there are enough athletes for Pistorius to compete with on a level playing field, but it is not now. And nor was it Athens eight years ago, when Oscar's achievement first came to the attention of the wider sporting world when he won so handily over 200 metres. Pistorius's unsporting comments may well have now drawn the IPC's attention to this discrepancy in classification.

CYCLONIC WHITEHEAD

Unlike Pistorius, Briton Richard Whitehead did not behave like a poor sport, and his gold medal winning performance in athletics in the 200 metres T42 category was celebrated as the man with no legs beating men with one. But my contention is that the technology used by Whitehead should also be considered as contradicting the rules of athletics, as well as being dangerous for his fellow competitors. For there is another potential problem of classification for the IPC here. Whitehead is a class T41 athlete, which means that he is a double amputee above the knees, but he ran in an event where the other competitors were T42 – single above the knee amputees. The T42 runners have a mechanical knee on their prosthesis leg, whereas Whitehead's prostheses are more like stilts without knees. As a result he runs in a cyclonic manner, which invades territory on the track reserved for other competitors.

After the event the *Guardian* wrote that Whitehead 'powered to victory with a stunning second half of the race as he stormed through the field with his prosthetic legs swinging from one side to the other'. Close examination of the race video shows how, particularly early in the race, Whitehead is breaking the plane of the lane line with every stride. The International Association of Athletics Federations (whose rules, with minor amendments, govern Paralympic Athletics) state in rule 163.3a relating to lane infringement: 'In all races run in lanes, each athlete shall keep within his allocated lane from start to finish. This shall also apply to any portion of a race run in lanes.' But in the race video you can clearly see that Whitehead's right prosthesis is close to the inside lane line, while his left is swinging over about 30 per cent outside the lane marking. As Whitehead builds up momentum on his running prosthesis, there will always be a danger that he will collide with another competitor – which is against the rules.

The issue of fairness needs to be addressed in this case in much the same way as in the debates surrounding Pistorius. Whitehead stands very tall, and while his fellow competitors have not publicly complained, the IPC should revisit the issue of combining T41 and T42, just as they should the T43/44 combination in the 'Oscar case'. Whether the degree to which Whitehead breaks the lines on the track gives him an advantage needs to be debated, and perhaps there needs to be an amendment to IAAF rule that is explicit regarding breaking the plane of the line. For athletes with two human legs it is clear that they cannot go out of their lanes, but to date we have seen very few athletes on the track who swing their legs in the cyclonic fashion of Richard Whitehead. What is certain is that a slow starter lining up beside Whitehead in the 100 metres T42 heats stands the very real risk of being tripped up by his running action.

And there are other anomalies in judging performance. In 2012, for the first time there was more than one Paralympian nominated for the BBC 'Sports Personality of the Year' awards show: Ellie Simmonds, cyclist Sarah Storey and wheelchair track racer David Weir all made the final shortlist of twelve. But by and large it is acknowledged by Paralympians that to represent their country is easier for them than for Olympians. To put it quite simply, mainstream sport development is like a pyramid with a wide base of club-level participants at the grassroots that provide a solid foundation for the elite sportspeople at the top. In the context of disability sport the shape is more like an obelisk, with a very narrow base. This is evident in the case of Sarah Storey, who was able to win two gold medals in the velodrome and another two on the road. This is partly due to her talent, but the lack of depth in Paralympic cycling also has to be a contributing factor. The same reservation could perhaps be made of David Weir, who won four gold medals, in distances from 800 metres to the Marathon. Nevertheless, the research I have conducted over the years suggests that his class – T54 wheelchair – is consistently the most competitive, both in the number of athletes involved and times on year-end IPC ranking lists. However, in David Weir's case it is the technology of the racing wheelchair that allows him and other athletes to perform over a wider range of distances than their ambulant cousins in the Paralympic and Olympic programmes.

VILLAINOUS SCROUNGERS OR HEROIC INSPIRATIONS?

Early in the London 2012 Paralympic Games, one of the sponsors, Atos, was targeted by members of the disability community and anti-cuts demonstrators; there were strong protests about the role that the company was playing in the evaluation of disabled people's rights to receive benefit payments. People were angry that the firm was carrying out 'fitness to work' tests for the Department for Work and Pensions at the same time as sponsoring the ultimate disability sporting event. Hundreds of people, some of whom were impaired, demonstrated outside the company's central London headquarters, before moving on to the DWP. There were a few scuffles with police after a small number of protesters occupied the lobby and attempted to blockade the front entrance of the department.[2]

The anger of the disability community arises from the widespread assumption that people on benefits are villainous scroungers – a view that the fitness to work tests has helped to promote. This representation of disability has been an almost constant since biblical times. And the contrast between images of disability benefit fraud and those of the heroic supercrip athletes was simply too much for segments of the disability community during London 2012.

Stereotypes of disability are sometimes reinforced by Paralympians: the inspirational tales told by the large number of current and former Paralympians who list as one of their occupations that of motivational speaker all too often reinforce stereotypes of disability. For me as a former Paralympian this is hugely problematic, and also, in so many of these cases (and I have 'listened' to hundreds of impaired motivational speakers as part of my research) ironic, given that most high performance athletes, regardless of whether they are impaired or not, lack the charisma to engage the public, simply because they are focused so much on their own training and event. But the effect of these motivational speakers and other contemporary Paralympians in the media is to place an extra burden upon the 'normal everyday' impaired population, urging them that they too should somehow live extraordinary lives. Those who are unable to work are then further marginalised.

A further problem is the way attention is sometimes focused on odds overcome rather than on sporting achievement itself. Thus the Helen Rollason Award at the BBC's Sports Personality of the Year is given 'for outstanding achievement in the face of adversity'; and Martine Wright, a player on the women's sitting volleyball squad, was presented with the award in 2012. Martine Wright lost both her legs in the 7/7 bombings of 2005, but had 'fought back' to compete in the 2012 Paralympics. (Sitting Volleyball is a sport that had both men's and women's teams representing Team GB in London, but both teams in fact performed poorly and have subsequently had their government funding cut.) While this is a genuinely heart-warming story, I believe that giving Martine the award was bad for the British Paralympic movement. Though Martine participated in sitting volleyball, she does not by any stretch of the imagination embody the ethos of a high performance athlete. Awarding her this accolade is thus a frank reminder that the Paralympics remains for some much as it used to be – it is simply about the ability to take part. And it also tells us something about how the BBC feels about the Paralympic movement. There is no doubt that Martine has overcome a great deal in putting her life back together following such a massive trauma, but her award also sent a negative message as to what Paralympic sport is about: that the sporting achievement of winning a Paralympic gold medal – competing at this elite level of international sport – is simply not recognised in the same way as Olympic competition; that after 2012 much remains virtually unchanged.

THE PARALYMPIC FABLE

The balancing of the 'imperfect' sporting body with a strong will is a story that is frequently played out in the supercrip fables that are the celebrated inspiration tales of Paralympians. These stories celebrate the will of athletes that allows them to live as normal a life as possible. It is even becoming commonplace to see the classification of bodies into equitable categories as a normative activity. Such a process is of political importance, since the IPC, though distancing itself from the explicit discussion of the politics of Paralympism, has tried to make the process of classification appear as scientific and therefore as neutral as possible.

But it is the bodies that most resemble a normal sporting body (Storey); are cute (Simmonds); or which have been through the process of cyborgification (Grey-Thompson, Pistorius and Weir) that remain at the centre of the media gaze. Paralympic journalists appear to be a shy lot, afraid to rock the ableist boat. And that means that reportage at IPC events leans towards the positive, not the critical. They appear to all buy into the IPC dictum 'Empower, Inspire, Achieve', and the vision 'To Enable Paralympic Athletes to Achieve Sporting Excellence and Inspire and Excite the World' – which clearly are important in establishing an ideology of the Paralympic movement. Journalists are ready and willing to highlight the hypocrisy surrounding the Olympic movement, but there is still strong resistance to do the same regarding the Paralympic Games. But until the press feel at liberty to expose the Paralympic movement warts and all, the Paralympics will continue to be simply a sideshow – a freak show. Until they do, the Paralympics will always play second fiddle to the Olympic Games, because they will have done little to really change the public's perception of disability.

NOTES

1. See P. David Howe, 'Cyborg and Supercrip: The Paralympics technology and the (dis) empowerment of disabled athletes', *Sociology*, vol 45 (5) 2011.

2. See Esther Adley, 'Paralympic sponsor Atos hit by protests', *Guardian*, 31 August 2012.

THE WIGGO EFFECT

Zoe Williams

Wednesday 1 August 2012 was an incredibly English, unEnglish day, that marked the start of a surge of national pride as unfamiliar to me as it was unarguable in its popular magnitude. The sides of the road, at the entrance to Hampton Court Palace, were six or seven deep with an excited but reserved crowd. Some Dutch people had painted themselves entirely orange, like Goldfinger retold as comedy, and that was noticeable because it was so unlike the rest of the spectator cohort, who seemed almost too polite to state their allegiance. Even in an English summer, the sun seems like a special guest; imagine our surprise when it hung around for the whole day. If cycling is the most democratic of sports – and we'll establish that beyond any reasonable doubt, shortly – then the time trial is its most democratic incarnation.

I have a few quibbles with the way time trials are run. When they all start separately, there's no sense of scale. It's like taking a picture of a baby bat without a pound coin next to it. You can't tell how small it is (the bat), and you can't tell how fast they're going (the cyclists). The only comparative judgment you can make is that none of their thighs are as big as Chris Hoy's (they don't need the big thighs. You only need them if you're planning to cycle sideways up a vertical slope).

But two things act as metaphor for the character of both the sport and its riders: not only is it free to watch, but there is no vantage point that is better than any other. All anybody is going to see is a whizz of lycra. All anyone can infer is that their guy is still in the race. Princess Anne stood in a VIP area as Bradley Wiggins took his heroic seventh Olympic medal, and I don't think she would have seen any more than the people standing on Weston Green roundabout.

Wiggins himself always stresses this as one of his sport's most admirable aspects – the fact that anybody can watch it. For as long as it is performed on roads, cycling will never be a rich man's sport, and its stars will never take on that precarious, nervy aspect of the formula one racer or football star, whose wealth seems to hold them in thrall to money, turn them into rich men's playthings. Cycling sponsorship, even at its most febrile – the Tour de France caravan – never manages to pervert the purity of this sport.

In JM Coetzee's book, *The Childhood of Jesus*, he creates an allegorical version of heaven, where a character tries to buy a ticket for the footie, and a friend says, 'It's a game. You don't need to pay to watch a game'. Sometimes I find socialist utopias a little bit annoying. Professional football wouldn't exist without people who'd pay to watch it. But then you look at cycling and realise that excellence doesn't have to look like the Premier League.

Bradley Wiggins has been skint for long stretches of his career. When he signed to the French team *Francaise des Jeux* in 2002, he described settling into his tiny bedsit with the cold, dread sorrow of a kid arriving at borstal. Even after the Athens Olympics in 2004 – the year he was awarded an OBE, the year he became the first Briton in forty years to win three medals at one games – he was, famously, still sometimes hunting for quids down the side of his sofa, to buy a pint of milk. It is not easy, being at the top, never mind the middle, of a non-glitzy sport, a non-neoliberal, non-market-dominated sport, a sport where money doesn't talk – or rather, it does talk, but there's a lot less of it. If it were up to me, I'd want Bradley Wiggins to have as much money as Wayne Rooney. But there is something intoxicating about the sight of human endeavour that is operating on a plane separate from money; someone whose wagon has come unhitched from the engine of commerce. If you're not riding for money, what are you doing it for? You're doing it for love. So we stood at Hampton Court and watched love affair after love affair, flashing past. It is difficult to stay aloof from that, even while it may not be necessary to paint yourself orange.

GOLD MEDALS AND THE COLLECTIVE GOOD

Overall, the Olympics did something really important for the left, and cycling was at the apex of that. Moving away from the romance that spurs the riders, there were very sound, very simple reasons for the success of the UK (or Team GB, as we took to calling it, with more pride and less irony, the more successful the athletes became) at the

2012 Games. 104 medals didn't come from nowhere – they were the result of sustained investment, a centralised splurge of money, based on the faith that the talent was there, if we would only, collectively, put the effort into supporting it. For one summer, the script of the state, and what it was capable of, was rewritten: it didn't have to mean a prizes-for-all culture where excellence and exceptionalism were frowned upon, and mediocrity would result as inexorably as enough colours, mixed together, will make a greyish-brown. It didn't have to mean the government spending just enough to squeeze out the private sector, but never enough for anybody to get results. The state has never had to mean these things; it has always been a fallacy that governments stifle innovation and smother brilliance. But this fallacy is proving dispiritingly tenacious, amped up and foregrounded by a political struggle that feels binary and sudden – do we want to pool our resources, and share them? Or does pooling resources merely waste them, and sharing merely weaken our self-reliance?

The fight started low and got dirtier, so that a relatively short time into our current government, the shared discursive space started to feel like a mud wrestle. And into this unedifying atmosphere stepped those athletes – beacons of excellence, self-denial, effort, perfectionism; a credit to themselves, of course, but also to their institution, be it the Royal Yachting Association or British Cycling. Whoever said we were a nation of failures, whose only future lay in clawing back our resources from the hordes of skivers and freeloaders – those people were wrong. In fact, working together, we were unbeatable. It seemed to fill the political lungs with a cleaner air. Everyone was extrapolating a wider triumph from all the medals – it was a triumph for our infrastructure, or for our spirit of volunteering, or for our peerless self-deprecation, which led the rest of the world to think we'd mess it up, only to be even more overwhelmed and impressed when we didn't.

But Will Hutton's conclusions were the boldest: on the day of the closing ceremony, he wrote:

> British sport embraced a new framework of sustained public invest-
> ment and organised purpose, developing a new ecosystem to support
> individual sports with superb coaching at its heart. No stone was left
> unturned to achieve competitive excellence. The lesson is simple. If
> we could do the same for economy and society, rejecting the princi-
> ples that have made us economic also-rans and which the coalition

has put at the centre of its economic policy, Britain could be at the top of the economic league table within 20 years.

It is part of the post-Olympic hangover that we have to figure out exactly how to translate this ethos, and who we have to get rid of before we start. But something important happened last August – optimism was allowed back into the conversation. Once we'd sloughed off the straitjacket of misery for a fortnight, it never fitted properly again.

THE COMRADESHIP OF CYCLING

All the cyclists were at the vanguard of this new mood, not because of the nature of the sport, nor because British Cycling, and Chris Boardman in particular, encapsulated so well the hybridity of comradeship and individualism that spurs champions. Whenever I get too carried away with the timeless equitability of cycling, how honest and immutable the bicycle is, how sustainable and fundamentally socialist is the entire activity, the words 'Lance Armstrong' pop into my head. In the end, if you progress high enough up its ranks, cycling is as corruptible as any sport, with stakes that can turn a genius into a cheat and back again. It's as appealing to the rabid possessive individualist as it is to the national hero, the side-burned Odysseus. The fact that Bradley Wiggins is a champion as well as a fundamentally decent person seems to be pure coincidence, a naturally occurring phenomenon, something like a comet or an eclipse.

He is the classic leftie pin-up, from the beaky, amused face to the ironically rebellious slouch. The sheer unexpectedness of it, a skinny mod with the courage of Che Guevara, the natty threads a fig-leaf for this stringy, heroic physicality; he's like a superhero on his way to a fancy dress party, dressed as London. When he won his gold medal, he cycled out of the Henrecian boulevard of Hampton Court, back onto the street, before returning for the frankly bizarre ceremony of golden thrones and bemused expressions. He wanted to say 'hi' to his wife and kids, and he wanted to say 'hi' to the people who don't get invited into the enclosure. His actions, his whole demeanour, were a powerful reminder of the spirit of the opening ceremony, a parade of achievements brought about through sheer scope of ambition – normality shot with greatness. In the press conference afterwards, five minutes before Wiggins arrived, Chris Froome sat down, having just taken a bronze for the UK in the same time trial event. Somebody's hand shot up, and he took the question: 'Having seen him win the Tour de France, and then win Gold ... exactly how good is Bradley Wiggins?' It was pointless, insultingly pointless. But Froome smiled, understandingly; it was hard to talk about anything other than Bradley Wiggins in 2012. Especially when you were talking about cycling. Once the champion had arrived, a cycle-geek made the observation that to win the Tour de France and the Olympic time trial, when your other medals are for individual pursuit, team pursuit and the madison, was truly unusual, to the point of being bizarre – like winning one medal for rowing, another for sailing and a third for canoeing. At this point, Bradley Wiggins showed some genuine pride; he would take that recognition. He would gladly stand congratulated for his versatility. He has mastered the art of accepting adulation, laughing off the bits that are meaningless, accepting what matters, always with this understated gratitude, never gushing.

'It's the world's favourite fairytale', some journalist said, puffing down from the media stands, into the mud behind: 'Good Bloke Wins Medal'. Everyone claims Wiggins as one of theirs, and I think if he had never once opened his mouth, if all we knew of him was that he won everything and really liked wheat beer, this still would have been enough to make a national hero of him, even though neither victory nor wheat beer would nominate themselves as the defining traits of Englishness.

I wonder if, in a similar manoeuvre, I have claimed him as a left-wing icon by an act of emotional syllogism – that he is great, and the left is great, therefore he is on the left. But there are these persistent bits of evidence: the fact that he always underlines, and takes such obvious pleasure from, cycling being free, even if this means he spent the first decade of his career scouring his furniture for pound coins; and his facial hair, which I can't see as anything but a visual reference to a worldview, an effortless, Weller-ishness, where you could be driven without being disconnected, perfect without being unapproachable, victorious but not alienated. He seems to me to be more than a good bloke, although he is that, of course, and an athlete who is as likeable when he's not winning as when he is (though it seems like a long

time ago since he wasn't winning, and I may be misremembering).
He personifies a different type of extraordinary, a man who draws his
strength not from his own superiority so much as from the crowd that
rejoices in it.

THE MEANING OF MO

David Renton

Going into the London Olympics, Mo Farah was far from being the favourite for either of the events in which he was running. Of the competitors in his first final, the 10,000 metres, Wilson Kiprop and Moses Masai of Kenya had both run the distance in 27 minutes earlier in the year, while the 2004 and 2008 Olympic champion Kenenisa Bekele, as well as his younger brother Tariku (both running for Ethiopia), had times of under 27:05. Mo's best time for the year was a relatively mediocre 29 minutes and 21 seconds. Andy Bull of the *Guardian* tipped Bekele for a third 10,000-metre gold: 'From the mountain top he occupies, Farah is a figure somewhere in the foot-hills, a man only just beginning to prove himself capable of competing at the highest level'.[1] In the 5000 metres, Mo had run a decent 12:56.98. But at just one race in July 2012, the Diamond League in Paris, ten Kenyan or Ethiopian runners had finished faster than this. And the winner of the Paris 5000 metres, Ethiopia's Dejen Gebremeskel, was focusing on just this one distance at London 2012. Mo, by contrast, would face a punishing schedule of two finals and two heats in not much more than a week.

As a home nation athlete at these Games Mo faced closer scrutiny than his rivals. In June, at the Olympic Trials, he had warmed up by racing in the 1500 metres heats. Anthony Whiteman, who had run a four-minute mile earlier that summer (and was the first forty-year old ever to have done so outdoors), accused Farah of showboating after he gave his 'Mobot' victory sign 50 metres from the end. 'Was in 2nd coming off the bend when @Mo_Farah pulled out the F'ing Mo-Bot', Whiteman tweeted, '#notcricket#ifonlyiwas15yearsyounger'. The feeling that Mo was losing his focus was only accentuated when the press revealed that he had skipped the 1500 metres final, and had not warned other athletes before doing so, thus depriving the next-fastest finisher Ricky Stevenson of the chance to race for an Olympic place.[2]

As a black British athlete Mo was also forced to carry further burdens. Weeks before the Games, an anonymous article in the *Daily Mail* complained that there were 61 'plastic Brits' in the Olympic squad.[3] The article gave examples of nationality-swappers such as a formerly Ukrainian wrestler Olga Butkevych, who had been granted a UK passport only in 2012 at the age of 26. The figure of 61 'plastic Brits' had been gathered by counting every UK Olympic competitor to have been born (like Mo) outside Britain. Its journalists illustrated the piece with a photograph not of (white) Olga Butkevych nor of (white) Bradley Wiggins (born in Belgium to an English mother and Australian father), but of Yamile Aldama, a black triple jumper who had been born in Cuba.

To emerge, as Mo did, doubly victorious, attests to something extraordinary in his character. His victory, and his exuberance on winning, touched off a moment of genuine popular euphoria. There was an unmissable spark of recognition between the millions watching him and Mo Farah. Mo, a dozen lifestyle pieces told us, had been educated at a comprehensive and then an FE college, had lived with his partner for years before marrying her, and had worked in pizza restaurants before he was an athlete. He was, briefly, the perfect poster boy for twenty-first century Britain.

LONDON: THE RUNNING CITADEL

Team GB did relatively poorly at London 2012 in athletics. This was especially true of the other middle- and long-distance runners. In 2012, not a single Briton made it to the men's 1500 metres final. Just one British athlete made it to the men's 800 metres final; in which Andrew Osagie broke his personal best by two seconds but finished in last place.[4] Lisa Dobriskey was a best-placed tenth in the women's 1500 metres, while in the women's 800 metres the sole British athlete competing, Lynsey Sharp, out-performed expectations but could only reach the semi-finals.

To decry the performances of these middle-distance runners representing Britain at the London Olympics makes sense only in terms of a comparison with previous moments of British athletic dominance at these distances. The starting point is Roger Bannister's four-minute mile in 1954, and the subsequent success of his pacemaker Chris Brasher, gold medallist in the 3000 metres steeplechase at the 1956

Olympics. Gordon Pirie was a silver medallist over 5000 metres at the same games. Ian Stewart came first in the 5000 metres at the 1969 European championships. Tony Simmons won the silver medal in the 10,000 metres at the 1974 Europeans. Dave Bedford held the men's 10,000 metre world record from 1973 to 1977. And this is without mentioning the women Olympians – Ann Packer, who won gold over 800 metres at the Tokyo Games in 1964, Liz McColgan, silver medallist in the 10,000 at the 1988 Seoul Games, gold medallist at the 1991 World Championships for the same distance, and of course Kelly Holmes, with her gold medal double in the 800 metres and 1500 metres at the Athens Games in 2004.

Between 1978 and 1990 British men won thirteen middle-distance golds at major championships. One effect of London 2012 was to constrict this history, and to reduce a group of four runners (Seb Coe, Steve Ovett, Steve Cram and Peter Elliot) to one. Seb's pre-eminence within this generation was earned not by his championship record of three golds – on a par with Steve Ovett's and less than Steve Cram's – but by the nine world records he broke, above all his 1981 world record of 1.41.73 for 800 metres, which lasted for sixteen years. A useful comparator here would be Calvin Smith's 100 metre record of 9.95 seconds set in 1983: since then Usain Bolt has shaved off 4/10 of a second, thereby reducing the record by 4 per cent. In thirty years, athletes have reduced the 800 metres world record by just 1 per cent from Coe's 1981 world best.

The hegemony of the British within international middle-distance coincided with an amateur running boom. This began in 1978, the year that Coe and Ovett first challenged each other for a major championship gold, although unsuccessfully, with both being out-kicked in the 800 metre final by the East German Olaf Beyer.[5] That year the *Sunday Times* sponsored a 'National Fun Run', for which 12,000 people signed up. The following year John Disley and Chris Brasher entered the 1979 New York Marathon, and then in autumn 1979 they announced plans for a London Marathon.[6]

The running boom was a complex phenomenon fuelled by different social causes. It was neither American nor British but international, and was driven by new global leisure companies, who were adept at new kinds of brand marketing. The value of Nike's worldwide sales was in the process of increasing by an extraordinary 70-fold, from $14 million in 1976 to $1 billion ten years later.

With Coe and Ovett battling it out on the track for supremacy, Britain could boast the top two middle-distance runners in the world. And their contest over 800 metres and 1500 metres came to symbolise other dimensions to social change during the Thatcherite 1980s. The press built up the career of the supposed 'toff' Seb Coe, at the expense of the 'monster' Steve Ovett. Sociologically, they were much more similar than different. Both were products of different fragments of the lower middle classes: Ovett's parents were market traders in Brighton, while Coe's father was an industrial manager who moved from London to Sheffield for work, and was unable to afford a private education for his children. Ovett attended grammar school while Coe failed his 11-plus and attended a comprehensive school. Both obtained good enough grades to attend university, Coe at Loughborough, the sports college, while Ovett drifted away from higher education to concentrate on athletics. The press built Ovett up as the running equivalent of Britain's trade unionists – spiky and confrontational. Coe was the establishment man, the goody-two-shoes. Ovett's world records were won racing in an old red Soviet running vest. Coe almost always pictured in his official GB kit.[7]

Steve Cram and Peter Elliott, meanwhile, were the products of a different, more proletarian, Britain. Born in the decaying ship town of Jarrow, Cram has remained based in the North East ever since, unlike Coe, who left Sheffield in his teens and has mainly lived in London. Peter Elliott was born in Rotherham, and was working as a welder for British Steel when he was initially selected for the Los Angeles Olympics, ahead of Coe. Peter Elliott fitted into a long tradition of proletarian runners that includes Colin Smith, the hero of Alan Sillitoe's 1959 short story, *The Loneliness of the Long Distance Runner*, who throws a race with public school rivals in order to demonstrate his refusal to comply with the rules of the borstal into which he has been placed.[8] And, before Colin Smith there was the cartoon hero Alf Tupper. First appearing in the *Rover* comic in 1949, and surviving in one media or another until 1992, Alf was a perennial underdog, who ran short of sleep from a night's work as a welder (like Elliott), and hitch-hiked everywhere. His main rivals were pampered athletes like – in one story – Harold Pilkington, the boss's son.[9] Colin Smith and Alf Tupper appealed to a running and reading milieu which was as young and working-class as they were.

In the early 1970s, the largest occupational sectors in Britain were manufacturing, distribution and public sector employment, with the former accounting for 35 per cent of all employment.[10] Manufacturing now accounts for around 10 per cent of UK employment and since the early 1980s the demographic re-making of Britain has intensified. There are fewer members of the traditional working class, more older people, and more comparatively well-off and healthy older people. And one change has been in how we make use of our leisure time: today around one million people in Britain have run at least one marathon in their lives. But running is no longer a young people's sport. The average age of those competing in the London Marathon is 49.[11] Running has now acquired an apparatus of magazines that sell accessories such as GPS watches capable of tracking a runner's route and uploading it to a home computer (£250-£350); running tops made of merino wool (£75); running sunglasses (£125-£200); energy gels (£36 for three boxes) – and so on.[12] Joining a running club and competing as a club athlete remains considerably cheaper than watching football, but, like football, the scene feels older and more middle-class than it once did.

GB ATHLETICS IN DECLINE

The Coe-Ovett days are history. No male or female Briton has run the world's fastest 800 metres time in a season since Peter Elliott did in 1990. Between 1945 and January 1984, of the 25 world record holders at the men's marathon, eight were British. Since then there have been ten world record holders at the distance, but not one of them has been British.

Part of the reason that Britain is less of a world running power today is that sports science, nutrition and technique have been globally dispersed, creating a broader competitive space, which is correspondingly harder to dominate. A quick check of the London 2012 medal table will show where the new centres of middle-distance running can be found. Looking at the five men's and five women's events between 800 metres and 10,000 metres, and temporarily excluding Farah's double gold, of the remaining eight gold medals five were won by African athletes, two by Russians and one by a member of the Turkish team.

In 2010-11 *Guardian* journalist and contributor to *Runner's World* Adharanand Finn attempted to unpick the puzzle of Kenyan athletic success. In the excellent book he wrote about this, *Running with the Kenyans*, he describes travelling to Iten in Kenya, a village which has produced many world-class athletes. There he found a rich running culture, which began early in a runner's life, in which running to a high standard was seen as a straight path out of poverty. Attempting to absorb the local running culture, Finn changed his running style, from a heel to a front-foot strike, and experimented with light running shoes. He ate the carbohydrate-rich local diet, shedding 5 kg. He trained with local runners, sharing the local fartlek-style programme. In taking all this on board he reduced his personal bests by about 5 per cent. This was a noteworthy improvement for someone in their mid-late thirties who had already been running consistently for more than 10 years.[13]

At one stage in Finn's book he considered the part played in Kenyan running success by genes. He noted that, even within Kenya, a disproportionate number of runners came from a few villages, and from one particular ethnic group (the Kalenjins).[14] He acknowledged that biology must play some part: men run faster than women on average; a top runner often has a particular build, an above-average lung-capacity, etc. He interviewed biologists who had tried to find ethnic markers of running talent, and paid particular care to a study of Kenyan migrants to America. All were academically talented students rather than young athletes; yet around one in five took up running in the US. Why did they blossom as runners in particular? Finn considered race as a potential explanation, before settling on another: the athletes all spent their childhoods in Kenya. They had had active childhoods, no doubt running to and from school. To the age of eighteen they had had carbohydrate-rich, low-fat diets. They arrived in America with what he terms 'a strong inbuilt endurance base'.[15] It is not too fanciful to see the same processes at work in another running story.

FROM PERIPHERY TO CORE

Born in Mogadishu in Somalia, Mo Farah left the country two years into the civil war that began with the fall of the Barre dictatorship in 1991. In 1993, on his arrival in London, he barely spoke English. It was hardly an auspicious year to settle in Britain: in September the British National Party won a seat on Tower Hamlets council, securing its first ever electoral breakthrough. At secondary school Mo first took up football, but his PE teacher encouraged him to start cross-country running, at which he was already showing considerable talent. During his first year of track running, at the age of 14, Mo's personal best was 4:06.41 for the 1500 metres. Neither Coe nor Ovett, both of them prodigious schoolboy athletes, had run faster before their seventeenth birthdays.[16]

In 2006 Mo won silver at the European Championships over 5000 metres, but came only ninth at the same distance in the Commonwealth Games. In 2007, he was sixth in the 5000 metres at the World Championships and fifth over 3000 metres at the European Indoor Championships. At Beijing he failed even to make the final of the 5000 metres. Two years later, at the 2010 European Athletics Championship, Mo did the double of winning the 5000 metres and 10,000 metres for the first time, but this was with none of his African rivals present, and in anything but a world-class field.

Without much doubt, the moment that changed Mo from a successful Team GB athlete into a world-beater was his decision in early 2011 to relocate to Portland, Oregon in the United States, to work with a new coach, Alberto Salazar. Here Farah trained with the American athlete Galen Rupp, and Salazar refocused their training regimes to reduce their sprinting times over the very shortest distances. A part of their training included 100 metre repetitions in around 11 seconds. This is dramatically faster than the normal regime of a middle- to long-distance runner, where the emphasis is more often on accumulating miles, as suits the typical runner's physique of predominantly slow-twitch muscle. The impact was almost immediate. At the 2011 World Championship Mo won silver in the 10,000 metres and Gold in the 5000.

At London 2012 Farah's first event was the 10,000 metres. Here, despite Mo's medals at the Worlds the year before, as we have noted, most seasoned observers predicted a Kenyan victory. Kenenisa Bekele of Ethiopia was clearly the most gifted athlete in the field; he was a world record holder as well as the Olympic champion. But he had been injured, and there remained doubts over whether his recovery was sufficient for a major championship. Mo had the kick that could win him a slow race, but lacked the stamina for a fast one. If the race had been run hard from the outset it is unlikely that Mo would have been in contention for any kind of medal. At the start Bekele made his way straight to the front, with Farah in second. Yet far from stretching the pack, Bekele slowed the race, going through 400 metres in 65 seconds. The pace then slowed further, so that when Zersenay Tadese of Eritrea hit the front, after six laps, his average time was 76 seconds, or about 13 seconds per lap outside world record pace. Tadese, the world record holder for the half-marathon, might have been expected to hit the front hard and sustain a fast pace, yet, having briefly opened a gap, he raced hard for just one lap (in 61 seconds); after this Farah went down to twelfth, and seemed to be losing touch with the leaders; but then Tadese allowed the race to settle again into a pace of 64-65 seconds per lap, allowing 'sprinters' such as Farah and Rupp to narrow the gap on the leaders. After Tadese's abortive kick there was a series of ineffective breakaways: Muchiri of Kenya, and Tadese again battled for the lead, before each leader, on hitting the front promptly slowed the overall pace. In effect, Farah's rivals lacked the bravery to put in a properly blistering mid-race stint.

At this stage three countries still had teams of athletes in contention: Kenya had two runners (Kiprop having pulled out after losing his shoe mid-race), Ethiopia had three, and Eritrea also had three. Victory for these teams would have required only a first runner in the team to set a fast enough pace, and a second (or third) to stick with them. But athletes hate running like a team; at the elite level athletics is a fiercely individualistic sport, nobody wants to be the 'hare' who sets a hard pace, knowing they will not sustain it and will have to drop out, while someone else will benefit from their pacing. But the refusal of the Kenyan, Ethiopian and Eritrean athletes to run collectively gifted the race to those known for their fast finishes.

With two laps to go, a leading pack of twelve athletes was led by Tariku Bekele from Farah and Rupp, followed by Muchiri, Masai and Kenenisa Bekele. Farah was around half a metre ahead of Tariku Bekele at the bell. From there he pulled ahead, with Bekele trying to kick back at him over 200 metres but lacking the legs to do so. Rupp caught Bekele 40 metres from the line, for silver.

Mo Farah's race-winning time was slow: outside the top twenty times run in 2012; half a minute down on the best Kenyan times for 2012, 45 seconds outside his own personal best, and 75 seconds outside the world record. Yet one part of the race, above all, was impressive: Farah's last lap was run in just 53 seconds, a shattering 9 seconds faster than any other lap he ran throughout the race. The race produced a poor result for the African nations; it was the first time that only one African nation athlete had made the podium in the men's 10000 metres since the (partially-boycotted) 1984 Olympics in Los Angeles. But it was a great result for British athletics – the country's first Olympic gold at the distance.

Rupp has said since the Games that if only he had started his kick a little sooner, 'you know I probably would have had a chance'.[17] This in turn raises the question of why he didn't do what now seems obvious. At the very top level of athletics, very little is down solely to natural talent. Fitness is important, but only negatively: the days when a runner could guarantee success by simply training twice as hard as any of their rivals belong to the distant past. What distinguished Farah is that he had the determination to stick to his race plan, while other athletes ran passively, and could not impose themselves on the race. For every successful runner that sense of purpose has a different underlying origin. To take just one source: in athletics, as in every other area of sporting activity, being on home ground is an advantage. Spain, having won just four medals at the 1988 Olympics, gained 22 as hosts at Barcelona in 1992. China jumped from 63 medals in 2004 to 100 in Beijing in 2008.[18] Being the focus of a cheering crowd can strengthen an athlete's belief that she or he has an entitlement to win. Of course, home advantage also brings greater expectation, which in turn can raise or wilt an athlete. Here, it emboldened Mo Farah and discouraged his rivals.

The final of the men's 5000 metres followed the same script as the 10,000 metres, with a series of athletes coming to the front briefly before slowing immediately on reaching the head of the race. Mo was one of barely a handful of runners who were 'doubling up' by running in two events (David Rupp was another; while Abdalaati Iguider of Morocco combined the 5000 metres with the 1500 metres, in which he came third). This time, to a far greater extent than in the 10,000 metres, Mo had to fight to impose himself on the race. Into the last lap, he was leading from only two to three metres, from a group of runners that included Iguider and Bernard Lagat of America, a former Olympic silver medallist over 1500 metres, both of whom could have been expected to have a faster kick.

A sign of how much better Mo ran in the 5000 metres than he had in his first final was the position of his training partner Rupp in the two races: Rupp was second in the 10,000 metres but only seventh in the 5000 metres. Of course, Rupp is a fantastic athlete in his own right. For eighteen months he had followed the same training programme as his partner Farah. The only relevant difference between him and Mo was the British athlete's greater desire to win.

Mo's winning time was again very slow: 64 seconds outside the world record, well outside the top 20 times run in the year. At 13 minutes 41 seconds, Mo was more than 15 seconds slower than the slowest time that any of the runners had run in qualifying for the final. Once again Mo's victory was down to his finishing sprint. As in the 10,000 metres he ran the last lap in 53 seconds. By way of comparison, at the same Games, David Rudisha of Kenya ran laps of 50 and 51 seconds in the 800 metres final, and in doing so shattered the world record. Farah was only two seconds slower over his last lap, having run six times as far.

BEYOND BIGGLES

'Racism', Dave Widgery of Rock Against Racism once wrote (in 1977), 'is as British as Biggles and Baked Beans. You grow up anti-black, with the golliwogs in the jam, the Black and White Minstrel Show on TV and CSE dumb history at schools. Racism is about Jubilee mugs and Rule Britannia and how we won the War'. This was evident in the visible racism of the National Front – active on Britain's streets at the time – but Widgery also turned his fire on what we would today describe as the 'institutional racism' of the police, courts and immigration system:

> Outwardly respectable but inside fired with the same mentality and the same fears, the bigger danger is the racist magistrates with the cold sneering authority, the immigration men who mock an Asian mother as she gives birth to a dead child on their office floor, policemen for whom answering back is a crime and every black kid is a challenge.[19]

Yet anti-racism is a British tradition too, and it has taken many forms in popular culture, sporting as well as musical. Many football fans will be familiar with the story of how John Barnes, on signing for Liverpool in 1987, became only the second black player for the club, and initially faced racist abuse both from away supporters and

Liverpool's own fans, before winning over the Anfield crowd by his brilliance on the pitch. It is a story that is encompassed in a famous photograph of Barnes back-heeling away a banana that had been thrown onto the field.[20] Most football clubs in Britain have something like their own 'John Barnes' story, and most sports have their 'John Barnes' moments too. National sporting teams play a part in this story; with anti-racists promoting their multiracial character as a rebuke to the racism of the Far Right.[21]

Mo Farah's victory generated a moment of near-universal national celebration. 'Mo-mentous' was the verdict of the *Mail on Sunday*, and other papers were no less effusive: 'Mo-ment of history' (*Sunday Mirror*), 'MoJestic!' (*Daily Star Sunday*), 'Greatest Mo on earth' (*Sun on Sunday*), and 'Slow, slow, quick quick Mo' (*Metro*). The iconic image of the Games was the sight of Farah swapping his 'Mobot' celebration with 100-metre champion Usain Bolt's 'lightning Bolt'. Former Children's Laureate Michael Rosen tweeted, 'Nick Griffin just choked on his dinner when Mo Farah won. Been rushed to hospital. An Asian doctor is treating him'. Oliver Holt wrote in the *Mirror*: 'Mo Farah's famous victories in the 10,000m and 5,000m seemed like a validation of British society's inclusivity and openness. They felt like a victory for tolerance and acceptance, a thumb in the eye to the BNP and bigots everywhere'.[22]

Since the mid-1990s, and post 9/11 in particular, there has been a sustained increase in racism, encouraged by politicians from each of the main parties but finding an unwelcome resonance in popular attitudes. It began with new Labour's relabelling of refugees as 'bogus asylum seekers', continued with press attacks on Muslims during the hot days of the War on Terror, and was helped along by the easy ride given by the same papers to the anti-immigrant 'think tank' Migration Watch; while in the build-up to the Games, David Cameron courted the hard right in his party and beyond by denouncing multiculturalism.

The old racism of the 1970s looked ridiculous in the bright glare of the Mo-moment; and the 'new racism' was temporarily silenced by the victory of this Muslim former child refugee. After twenty years of defeats, the Mo Farah moment articulated anti-racism in a highly visual and immediate form, requiring little or no 'cultural translation'. This was one of those instants when a commonsense anti-racism becomes almost dominant. The challenge, however, is to convert the kind of enthusiasm for a multicultural Britain that this inspired into the energy campaigning requires to oppose the racism that continues to affect so many lives: against ethnic profiling by police officers, against deportations, against racial bias in sentencing. 'Only connect' is what we need – an anti-racist idiom that joins up the sports fan with the protester against deaths in custody; the blogger with the athlete; the radical artist with the hundreds of thousands who grasp that racism is a poison and are open to the activist's question – 'so what do we do about it?' For a moment, Mo reminded millions of us of the essential sameness of our lives whatever our country, race or religion (or none), and of the brutality of the racism which treats the same experience so differently. His victory was a step to advance the great strides that are still to come.

NOTES

1. Andy Bull, 'London 2012: Kenenisa Bekele targets historic 10,000m Olympic treble', *Guardian*, 11 May 2012.
2. See *Athletics Weekly*, 23 June 2012.
3. 'Team GB have 61 "plastic Brits" taking part in the London Olympics', *Daily Mail*, 11 July 2012.
4. Andrew Osagie's times, along with those of other elite and club athletes, can be accessed at www.thepowerof10.info.
5. Ovett subsequently came first in the 1500 metres, with Coe not racing.
6. See Mark Perryman, 'The Running Boom', *Marxism Today*, October 1984.
7. Their rivalry is a theme of David Renton, *Lives Running*, Zero Books 2012.
8. Alan Sillitoe, *The Loneliness of the Long Distance Runner*, W. H. Allen 1959.
9. Morris Heggie (ed), *Victor, The Best of Alf Tupper the Tough of the Track*, London 2012.
10. Ken Coutts et al, 'Structural change under New Labour', *Cambridge Journal of Economics*, 31.5.07.
11. Sophie Goodchild, 'Marathon men run into a real mid-life crisis', *Evening Standard*, 12 April 2011.
12. These examples are based on miscellaneous articles in the May 2012 issue of *Running Free* magazine.
13. Adharanand Finn, *Running with the Kenyans*, Faber, 2011, p170.
14. Not all Kenyan runners come from this group. David Rudisha, for example, is a Masai.
15. Finn, op cit, p203.
16. Melvyn Watman, *The Coe and Ovett File, Athletics Weekly* 1982, pp156-7.

17. See www.flotrack.org, interview with Galen Rupp, 20 August 2012.
18. Jennifer Mahony, 'London 2012 Olympics: do host nations benefit from home advantage in medal table?', *Daily Telegraph*, 23 July 2012.
19. David Widgery, 'What is Racism?', *Temporary Hoarding* 1, 1977.
20. The image is used on the front cover of the second edition of Dave Hill's *Out Of His Skin: The John Barnes Phenomenon*, When Saturday Comes 2001.
21. See, for example, 'Why the England team is a victory for racial harmony', *Daily Mirror*, 5 May 2010.
22. Oliver Holt, 'The Games made Britain feel like a better place – how long that feeling lasts is up to us', *Daily Mirror*, 10 September 2012.

A UTOPIAN MOMENT OF BEAUTY
AND BECOMING

Suzanne Moore

As someone once said of that Great Briton Bez, of Happy Mondays fame, 'Bez is not on drugs. Bez *is* drugs'. I felt the same about the Olympics. Not being a sports fan I had never really understood the fuss about doping and wondered why we couldn't have an Olympics with drugs. These people are a different species, after all. Some of them bear as much relationship to me physically as dolphins. But I now see the error of my ways. The Olympics don't need drugs. They are drugs.

I was not an Olympics naysayer: I loved going to see the torch *and* I got to hold one, something that I have hardly even mentioned to everyone I have ever met. It was clear from the opening ceremony that we had already won at everything that matters – music, mayhem, the NHS, making Mary Poppins drones, pagan drumming and beautiful cauldrons. It wasn't just me at this rave; you could feel the whole country coming up.

The boring bit of the ceremony was when the athletes trailed around, but then something amazing happened: the sports started and we were really good at some. I say 'we' but I excelled myself. I stopped cooking, reading, looking after the children. 'There must be stuff in the freezer, surely?' was my Olympian *cri de coeur*. They were a little shocked because up until the London Games the only sport I had shown any interest in was boxing, and that's because it was my mum's favourite.

But thanks to the Olympics, though, I know what a pommel horse is! I see male grooming is omnisexual. I am not so keen on cycling (it looks like a pinball machine) and the horse dancing is most peculiar. But after all the effort of competing, you get these lovely people, sweating and being respectful.

It was a wonderful combination of equal opportunity, ogling, admiration and, aaaw shucks, another medal! It's wasn't just the taking part, it was the winning.

All of this was about more than simply catching a reflection of ourselves that we like. It was more like a giant mirrorball glinting back at us, showing us fragments of humanity that are beautiful and which give thanks when they lose and thanks when they win. The Olympics made professional footballers look like the nasty, egotistical bankers of sport, for here instead were glowing people full of dreams and spirit. Yes, it was a collective dream, and one from which by now we've all woken up – but it was significant none the less.

Sometimes these moments occur, and one of the ways we know that they matter is because the official culture tries desperately to appropriate or to deny them. The mourning of the death of Diana was dismissed as hysterical and mad. It wasn't, it was simply a marker of a shift in culture, a recognition that things had changed. The Tories were gone, we hoped for something new, that thing called 'society', to be acknowledged. Diana, disruptive and flawed, had reached out – and people responded. Of course she was not a republican. She wanted her son to be king. But she symbolised a break with a narrative that she would not go along with. She spoke of a way of being and feeling that reached out into the culture at large. Who do we think we are?

Well, the moment Mo Farah wrapped himself in the union flag, we asked this again. An embrace happened. Not tolerance. (I hate the word 'tolerance'. Who wants to be tolerated?) No, this man was celebrated. Likewise, Jessica Ennis's mixed-race parentage is just normal. Athletes running on blades gives meaning to the phrase 'differently abled'. People wanted to see the Paralympics, not out of worthiness but because they were so exciting.

Of course, comedown has happened. The issues around sport and class are not new and remain. The Olympic boroughs are poor, their sporting facilities leave much to be desired. Youth unemployment is as high as it was before the riots. But this mood – well, let's go with it. I would use the term 'structure of feeling', which Raymond Williams coined to describe the rhythms and flux of culture. Williams was a marxist with an acute understanding of how our culture is made of dominant parts, residual parts and emergent parts. Those grumbling about the lack of military history in the opening ceremony were, for instance, clinging on to what is residual in their vision of nationalism.

What is special now is that the dominant culture is being pulled up sharp by what is emerging. This is not a fantasy of imposed multiculturalism, it is a reality of mixed relationships, of a place where your faith is but one part of your identity, not all of it.

Sure, it's not utopia. Day to day we remain in a recession and lots of what emerges is difficult, edgy and contested. It is rare to feel we are one nation under a groove. But we saw ourselves for a while in our best light: glittery and happy, belonging to something bigger than all of us. Joy unconfined when the mirrorball throws back these myriad reflections. Here we were, all in it together, just for a while. The Olympics felt and looked like political correctness gone mad. And guess what? We bloody loved it.

An earlier version of this chapter first appeared in the Guardian, *as 'London 2012 Olympics; a Beautiful, Utopian, Collective Dream, 9 August 2012.*

From podium to park

Barbara Bell

My personal experience of the Olympics goes back to watching grainy black and white images from Tokyo, Mexico and Munich – Mary Rand, Anne Packer and Mary Peters – which meant athletics became my first sporting love. As a schoolgirl I expanded my sporting horizons to any other sports I could get access to. My own sporting career never, despite my early enthusiasm, went beyond the dizzy heights of County and University representation, but it led to a lifelong fascination with sport as a subject. After graduating from a leading sporting university, my professional career subsequently included ten years of working in community sport and thereafter lecturing and researching in sport studies and development. I have been personally and professionally enthralled by the Olympics for most of my life.

It's hard not to align with the overarching message of Olympism, despite any reservations about the IOC, if you believe ultimately that sport is a 'good thing', and can see the power of the sporting mega event to harness the inspirational performances of elite athletes for potential impacts on 'grass roots' sport and beyond. But until the summer of 2012 my assumptions about the role and purpose of sport and its impact, and my beliefs about the Olympic movement, were based on a mediated experience. For the vast majority of the British public, and many British academics like myself, our experience was at arms length, at a remove from the 'reality' of the event. For the majority, our engagement with sport is very detached from the Olympics as an event – apart from those TV images. London hosting the Games in 2012 offered the chance for a much more personal experience of the Olympic 'magic'.

Like tens of thousands of others, I was determined that 2012 was going to offer me the chance, not just to see this event 'first hand' as a once in a lifetime experience, but to become part of it. After having been a volunteer in the Velodrome at the Manchester Commonwealth

Games in 2002, I was determined to be a part of the London Olympics, in whatever way I could. I joined the scramble for tickets and became a local Torch Relay volunteer. I also signed up to 'Sportmakers', and duly completed ten hours of logged activity supporting community sport.[1]

In the five years prior to London 2012 I also carried out research into legacy planning and creation, seeing at first-hand the work in schools, local authorities, clubs and colleges that aimed to maximise the benefits of the Olympic and Paralympic Games to localities across the country. In these different ways, ever since the announcement was made in 2005 that London would host the Olympics, I've embraced the popular enthusiasm for a 'home games', while also being part of a sometimes cynical and always critical academic community – which has both tested and challenged a lot of the rhetoric coming from Government and the London Organising Committee of the Olympic Games.

THE RHETORIC OF SPORTING LEGACY

The expectation that the Olympics would be a catalyst to inspire people to become more active and thus contribute to the health and social objectives of the country was made clear in announcements even before the bid was submitted, as the government justified their investment in supporting the bid.[2] Boosts were expected in grassroots sport and in general fitness and activity levels – despite the DCMS/ Strategy Unit's conclusion in the 2002 report *Game Plan: a strategy for delivering Government's sport and physical activity objectives* that major events were really only useful to health due to the 'feelgood factor' they promoted. This report also suggested that gains in participation and activity would be possible only by concerted efforts across govern- ment, and all sectors of a modernised sporting landscape. However it did also repeat the assumed link between elite success and the growth of sport in the form of a 'trickle-down' effect and a positive feedback loop. This assumed that more successful athletes inspired more participation.

In 2008 the Labour government for the first time set out its Olympic objectives in detail: making the UK a world-leading sporting nation; transforming the heart of East London; inspiring a generation of young people to take part in volunteering, cultural and physical activity; making the Olympic Park a blueprint for sustainable living; and demonstrating that the UK is a creative, inclusive and welcoming place to live in, visit, and for business.

The notional link outlined here, between high levels of investment in elite sport and mass participation, has been shown to be deeply flawed, but it still persists in the rhetoric of government, both in the UK and abroad. Much of the evidence comes from investigations into the 2000 Sydney Games, which found very limited impacts on national sport participation from the Olympics and other major sports events, as highlighted by Tony Veal and colleagues.[4] For evidence at home there was the MORI report into the Manchester 2002 Commonwealth Games, which also concluded there was no major impact on sports participation as a result of hosting the event.[5] The basis of these assumptions of event-led increases in participation have been subject to critique, interrogation and challenge over many years – but a lack of credible evidence has at no time been able to deflect the government from its chosen route, either then or since.

The government tied the success of the Games to two key national surveys of engagement in sport and other 'cultural' activity: Active People and Taking Part; while The Youth Sport Trust also conducted a schools-based survey, designed to capture the impact of government strategy in school sport, the targets for which were linked to 2012 legacy, as set out in the 2008 plans. These surveys address levels of sporting participation, and are linked to the ambitious targets set in 2002, as a result of Game Plan, to increase sport participation by 1 million by 2012. This was later revised to 2 million by 2013, but then dropped as a target entirely in 2010.

The targets represented an attempt to achieve levels of participation to something like those in Scandinavian countries, which enjoy more equal and healthy populations, and an elite success rate that is at least better than that of Australia, a country with a much longer history and deeper commitment to elite investment. But although such extensive and expensive national surveys contribute to the evidence base, they have not addressed the challenge of finding ways to increase participation in what is an arguably marginalised grass-roots sport community – one which was already struggling to increase capacity, and that relied largely on voluntary effort and private or voluntary sports clubs. Yet the rhetoric of sport policy makes clear that, whether sport is for the wider good or for sport's own sake, any benefits to individuals or society will only flow from an increase in the numbers of people more actively engaged in sport.

The legacy of opportunity was to extend post-Games, and was thus central and fundamental to the bid and successful outcomes. This 'inspirational' message was significantly influenced by the perceived success – despite the lack of participation data – of the Commonwealth Games in 2002. The aim was that the legacy, in whatever form, would be 'leveraged' by specific plans and activities, as they had been after Manchester. The role of Sport England and the other non-departmental public bodies was thus to fulfil these ambitious promises.

Finding a way to link any evidence of increased participation in sport to London 2012 was necessary if it was to be possible to claim that any increases were due to its legacy – as opposed to resulting from any longer-term efforts to increase sport participation. But earlier documents identified that efforts to create a legacy would not work in isolation, and there would be a need for 'embedding the Olympic message within the mainstream sport infrastructure'.[6]

The Active People research, which began in 2005, made it possible to identify the extent and context of adult sporting participation; whether or not this took place in the club sector; whether it involved receiving coaching or instruction; and whether it involved volunteering – all within the aegis of the different sport's national governing bodies. These were then to build participation through their 'Whole Sport Plans', and in the lead up to 2012 over £400 million funding for this was made available from Sport England and National Lottery. This was alongside the approximately £1bn of local authority and national government funding that already went into supporting community sport each year. (The Active People survey also captured evidence of other 'activity', and the extent of inactivity in the population. This underlined the disconnect between organised sports – as a clearly national 'activity' – and more individual and informal recreational activity, which might include recreational walking and individual exercise, but does not rely on organised competition.)

But when the evidence of sport participation in the lead-up to 2012 is examined, the results of legacy planning, sport funding to governing bodies and Olympic influences are not at all clear. As the National Audit Office was suggesting in 2010, though plans for the Olympics were on time and on budget, linking these funding streams into community sport outputs and outcomes was difficult.[7] The NAO report raised questions about the delivery of legacy outcomes in sport participation, pointing to static or declining rates in the sports which had received significant amounts of public money for their 'Whole Sport Plans'. These plans were themselves described as over-ambitious – or, as Sue Campbell, the former head of UK Sport and an ex-governmental advisor on sport recently admitted, 'pure fiction'.[8]

The policy rhetoric in the lead-up to the Games was arguing for an inherent 'inspiration' impact from the Games, but this was not clearly tracked, in terms of the specific policies and programmes introduced to build the expected increase in activity. Government-funded agency plans were developed and funds distributed to projects aiming to 'deliver' rises in participation. But plans and evidence were rather belatedly produced, with some still not having been commissioned by 2012 and the change of government in 2010. With the impact of the economic downturn, priorities and targets were once again changed; and local government also came under significant pressure to reduce their budgets after the spending review in 2010, when non-statutory sport services became an obvious target for cuts. These were felt particularly acutely in the metropolitan boroughs in the north, a long way from the Olympic-based developments in the Lower Lea Valley and the host London boroughs.

The Coalition government funded Sport England's £135 million Places People Play strategy, but expected the provision of specific opportunities for extending participation among the non-sporty, and offering better and more satisfying sport to keep people engaged for longer, to be undertaken by the governing bodies and their clubs, the education sector and local authorities. This happened at the same time that the spending review of 2010 forced many local authorities to cut services and facilities for sport at the grass roots level.

But despite this drop in funding, the rhetoric of the Coalition government remained consistent with that of their predecessors, even if they were not supporting the same tactics and or targets: as we have seen, the 1 million more participants target was quietly dropped, while – with rather more public attention – the School Sport partnerships and School Sport Strategies were closed by an announcement by Michael Gove late in 2010.[9] Given the significance of youth in earlier legacy announcements, this showed an almost breath-taking disregard of the work of the education sector and Youth Sport Trust in helping achieve the sport targets, and of the role of youthful sport experience in establishing lifelong sporting participation habits, something that was well established in the literature. After some outcry there was a partial reprieve, when funding was provided for School Games Organisers and limited teacher release. However, when the government's A Sporting Habit For Life was published in early 2012, its emphasis on competitive sports and traditional team games signalled a further disregard for evidence – this time of how to engage the less sporty and in the sorts of recreational activity needed for lifelong activity habits to be established; and it downgraded the priority of inclusion, or 'sport for all'.[10]

REALITY CHECKS

For many the Olympics actually arrived when the flame landed in May 2012, and the Olympic flame set off on its journey across the UK. It arrived in Chester on 29 May and Cheshire East a few days later, to an enthusiastic public response of which I was a tiny part. This was the start of the most incredible sporting summer in the UK, and of our experience of the inspirational impact of the Olympics.

Public enthusiasm for the Games had certainly not been diminished by concerns over access to tickets, security, or whether or not London would be 'ready'. The Torch Relay engaged the British public to such an extent that they were already as 'inspired' as they could ever be. The daily relay routes, continuous torch cam-broadcasting and evening celebrations on national TV meant that even before the start of the Games, many communities had been touched by the Olympic magic dust, and there was rising expectation and excitement about the event itself. By the time of the closing ceremony of the Paralympics, hardly anyone could have claimed that they had not been provided with an inspirational Olympics – they had clearly been a success on every level, regardless of concerns of their long-term legacy.

Unfortunately, as predicted, the immediate impact of high levels of TV, social media and spectator engagement in the Olympics was always unlikely to add to participation or physical activity levels, especially considering the lack of sufficient properly planned and researched investment in grassroots infrastructure. This was certainly true for me – despite my usual intermittent cycling I still didn't achieve the recommended activity levels (150 minutes per week), and I barely reached the three-times-30-minutes activity sessions target either. But then I was hardly alone – this was true of the great majority of the British public in the sporting summer of 2012. BBC coverage via the red button and iPlayer ensured that audiences were engaged with new and compelling Olympic sports via an unprecedented number of digital channels: the level and extent of BBC (free to air) coverage was as ambitious, if not more ambitious, as any legacy efforts. And London 2012 did indeed seem to inspire a new form of engagement with the Olympics. Via social media, people could share their Olympics and follow individual athletes on personal devices even from within the stadium. But what impact all this would have on activity levels is another matter entirely.

The huge response to the Games in the social and broadcast media was clear evidence of the social impact of, and public engagement in, the Olympics, as 'normal life' was suspended so we could watch every available minute of sport. And although it would clearly take some time for any long-term changes in physical participation to show up, the anecdotal evidence suggests that many sports clubs were reporting a decent response and high rates of enquiry. Yet all this evidence has remained at the descriptive or anecdotal level – since no systematic monitoring was in place by local or national sports governing bodies.[11] Some local authorities reported increased use of facilities, but they were not always able to say if these were existing participants returning more often, or people new to activity. The Sport and Recreation Alliance published their survey of clubs just after the Games, and this indicated that economic conditions and the political environment were very difficult for many sports and their clubs, which meant that they had been unable to convert interested newcomers to active participants.[12]

A number of other issues adversely affected the potential for assessing the impact of all this inspiration on participation rates. School sport was in disarray, given that Michael Gove's change of policy had meant that school governing bodies now had the 'freedom' to choose not to provide sporting opportunity and support. This had left a patchwork of surviving partnerships and committed local champions to drive through planned activities, while other schools lost staff, resources and commitment to fulfil legacy promises. The coalition government, however, claimed it had cut the 'box ticking' mentality of the previous regime, by abolishing the need to complete the school sport survey.

The School Games programme that had been brought forward to

replace more extensive school sport strategies was not being evaluated locally: apparently no resources had been made available for monitoring its effectiveness, or for evaluating its impact on young people's activity in the county. This was a £90 million, 4-year programme of investment by government and commercial sponsors, but local deliverers were not expected to provide any information other than a measure of the number of schools taking part. Instead, DCMS statistics reported the number of schools that had access to the School Games – which was 8341 in 2011-12, across all levels, and therefore allegedly represented access for 3.85 million children.[13] This was estimated purely on the basis of the numbers on the school roll, a spurious figure to say the least. Was the DCMS seriously suggesting that every child in a school took part?

The Sport England funded Sportivate programme aimed at 14-25 year olds was meeting its engagement targets. But it was proving more difficult to find data to show that this was resulting in ongoing regular sport participation by this key age group.[14]

Some sports clubs, as reported in the Sport and Recreation Alliance research, and in local research investigations, were not planning for, or had limited interest in, expansion, because of the existing pressures they were experiencing – rising running cost, including the hiring of space, the lack of coaches or leaders, and increasing bureaucratic requirements from their governing bodies.[15] These were all factors that had been pinpointed in the lead up to the Games as potential limits to legacy ambitions. In some sports, however, such as hockey, reports of a buoyant start to 2013 in terms of new members seemed to reflect that the Olympics had both rekindled the enthusiasm of existing members and reinvigorated the clubs who were welcoming new juniors – very much as had been expected by Mike Weed and colleagues.[16]

All of this means that, while LOCOG and the government – the main enthusiasts for the impact of the Olympics on boosting sports participation – were clearly delighted with the Games themselves, it is not going to be easy to disentangle the results for the increased participation objective. As many articles in the press reported, there was genuine concern that the careful work to build a legacy of enthusiasm and motivation, in young people in particular, was being frittered away at precisely the crucial time for leveraging the biggest possible impacts.[17] As a fencing coach reported in one article: 'My concern is that the potential to marshal that enthusiasm has been lost because the programmes that allowed us to work with young people in schools have withered away.'[18]

Many other coaches and PE teachers reported similar 'missed opportunities', and an ebbing way of the impact of the Games due to a lack of capacity, as a sporting infrastructure of already overburdened voluntary clubs and schools was creaking under the weight of expectations from new participants.

GRASS-ROOTS SPORT AFTER 2012

Over and above a resounding confirmation of the power of the 'feel-good' factor, the key successes of the London Olympic and Paralympic Games appear to be in women's sport and disability sport, and in strengthening the Elite/High Performance sport system.

At the base of the national sporting pyramid in sport participation, the Active People data published by Sport England showed only a moderate increase in 2012, as had been the case for the preceding five years. The Taking Part report in late 2012 indicated that 15 per cent of 16-24 year olds who had participated in sports in the last twelve months claimed that the UK's hosting of the 2012 Olympic and Paralympic Games had motivated them to do more sport, compared with just 9.9 per cent of 25-44 year old sports participants.[19]

But in terms of impacts on sport participation data, the initial signs are not too convincing that there will be a surge of participation to come, given that there were already drops expected in both youth and adult sport activity, and the Olympics has had little impact on these. Local government, the Sport and Recreation Alliance and other agencies were already reporting mixed results early in 2013. They did record increased enquiries, and some evidence of an 'inspirational' impact amongst young people, but – tragically – this was matched by a lack of capacity in grass-roots sport, closures of facilities, and some lack of progress in converting those showing interest into new sports club members or regular participants.

Active Women projects, on the other hand, have reported reaching targets for recruitment, but these projects were designed to increase participation in non-sporty women or inactive communities – so their success can hardly have been due to any simple 'Olympic' association. Rather, these results have been due to the specific methods and approaches of the initiative, which have been to target and provide opportunities in new and interesting ways and in clearly defined project areas. But even these will only result in short-term improvement, or pockets of growth, unless they are adopted into mainstream sporting provision in the UK and sustained in the future. We need to see significant increases in the numbers of young women who are more active, and who engage in a wider range of activity and progress in larger numbers to regular lifelong activity over the long term. Arguably, such changes will take seven to ten years to be seen, despite the millions invested in order to demonstrate the level of increases. Far from a rise of 1 million more participants per annum since 2005, there have been only 1.6 million additional participants overall since 2005-6. In the Olympic year, the numbers taking part were 750,000 more people than the previous year, but the shortfall against the target remains considerable. Clearly the multiple and complex motivations for youth to engage with, and for adults to stay with, sport means that we will need to watch carefully in the future to see whether participation will rise as the 'inspired' generation move into adulthood. But any inherent impact on sport participation by a successful Olympics can clearly not be taken for granted; and there is a very limited evidence for attributing increased participation to success at elite level.

The moderately good news, however, is that the gender gap appears to be narrowing – with 31.1 per cent of women meeting the 1X30 target in 2012, compared to 29.8 per cent in 2005-6. Similar gains for those with a disability show small levels of growth, but at least the figures are moving in the right direction – from 17.7 per cent in 2005/6 to 18.3 per cent in 2012. But these are small gains, and levels of activity are still well below widely recognised guidelines for health. Active People shows that the share of the population playing sport or being 'active' is increasing overall, but that this rise is not really based on the sports which received many millions over that period or were most visible in the Olympics. Furthermore, any impact is most likely to affect those already interested in sport, if not particularly active. Overall levels of activity remain stubbornly low, particularly in lower socio-economic groups; levels of sedentary behaviour or physical inactivity, combined with increasing obesity, remain of great concern to the health lobby. So though there are some 'winners' – in sports such as cycling, athletics or swimming – this is because the survey counts all individual, informal and recreational activity in these sports. Most, if not all, of this is unlikely to be influenced by the policies and campaigns of the governing bodies of these sports, nor by the millions of pounds in funding they receive. In the national surveys, many of the more 'club-based' sports, for example golf, football or badminton, have actually either shown no change overall, or declined. The sport of netball has shown an increase of 47,000 participants since 2005-6, buoyed by the success of the imaginative Back to Netball programme, but it isn't even an Olympic sport! However within the adult population women are still likely to be less active, and low physical activity levels by young women in particular remains a major concern.

In 2013, UK Sport effectively concluded that no 'trickle-down' could be seen to thereby justify continued investment in sports like handball, volleyball and basketball in the period up to Rio 2016. Overall, the funds it allocated to elite sport cemented UK Sport's 'no compromise' management philosophy; in effect they make it imperative for sports seeking public funding to demonstrate that they are capable of success internationally. This is because of a desire to demonstrate that GB is a 'world-leading sporting nation', through meeting medal targets. Sport England made similar decisions regarding public funds for participation sports and the sports governing bodies.

London 2012 was particularly important for female elite athletes, given that they formed a major part of the success in securing GB's third position in the Medal table, and this may yet help to boost women's sport through increased media attention and public support or recognition. But the data seems to show that this higher media profile for women's sport is not translating into any real growth in young women's participation in sport. What is perhaps more likely is that women who would otherwise have dropped out of sport by the time they reached adulthood may be retained in recreational activity, and through the more imaginative 'back to...' projects.

Despite all the positive signs of inspirational performances at London 2012, and the reports of resulting increased motivation in young people, I must concur with Marc Keech, who suggested ahead of the Games:

> It seems unlikely that London 2012 will come close to keeping its legacy promise. No amount of political blame and counter-blame will shield the fact that for young people, sadly, London 2012 looks likely to be a missed opportunity, and once the circus has left town, who will be there to clear up the mess after the elephants?[20]

While the Queen Elizabeth Olympic Park may well in fact become home to several large white elephants, it will be five years before we are able to measure the inspirational impact of the Olympics on grass roots sport in the round – provided reliable participation and other relevant data is collected. To fail to do this would be the worst possible way to mark the importance of these Games, founded as they were on the message 'inspire a generation'.

Meanwhile, it remains to be seen whether any useful lessons can be learned on how any legacy in sport has been inherited and who by. Unfortunately the moment to make good any deficiencies is passing, and the 'once in a lifetime opportunity' is moving on to other countries and communities. Essentially, despite the excitement and interest London 2012 generated, delivering an inspirational and successful Olympics/Paralympics was not sufficient on its own to get more people taking part in sport – as many had already predicted. What remains after it is all over, however, are the many at sport's grass-roots who are still committed to ensuring more and better sport, for all. That, at least, we can be certain of.

NOTES

1. Sportmakers was the official sport volunteering project of Sport England, aimed at harnessing Olympic enthusiasm to increase volunteering and leadership in communities.
2. Fred Coalter, 'London Olympics 2012: The Catalyst that Inspires People to Lead More Active Lives?', *Journal for the Royal Society for the Promotion of Public Health* 127(3), 2007.
3. DCMS, *Before During and After: Making the Most of the London 2012 Olympic Games*, DCMS 2008.
4. Tony Veal, Kristine Toohey and Stephen Frawley, 'The Sport Participation Legacy of the Sydney 2000 Olympic Games and Other International Sporting Events Hosted in Australia', *Journal of Policy Research in Tourism, Leisure and Events*, 4:2, 2012.
5. MORI, *The Sports Development Impact of the Commonwealth Games 2002: Final Report*, Research Report MORI 2004.
6. London Bid Committee, *Community Sport Legacy*, Candidate City document 2005, p1.
7. National Audit Office, *Preparations for the London 2012 Olympic and Paralympic Games; Progress Report* HC 298 Session 2009-10 February 2010; and *Increasing participation in Sport*, report 22, session 10-11; reports on legacy plans and Sport England targets, May 2010.

8. Sue Campbell, Speech to Sport and Recreation Alliance Leadership conference, January 2013.

9. Michael Gove, *Ministerial Announcement,* Department for Education, 10 October 2010.

10. DCMS, *Sporting Habit for Life*, London 2012.

11. Local Government Association, *Announcement of increased usage of council-operated facilities and services*: www.local.gov.uk, 8 March 2013.

12. Sport and Recreation Alliance, *Survey of Olympic and Paralympic Legacy in Clubs*, 2012: www.sportandrecreation.org.uk.

13. DCMS, *School Games Statistical Release*, September 2012. A national evaluation by Sport Industries Research Centre had yet to publish their report at time of writing.

14. See Sportivate, *First year summary report*, November 2012: www.sportengland.org

15. See Sport and Recreation Alliance, *Olympic Legacy Survey*, 2013: www.sportandrecreation.org.uk.

16. See Mike Weed, Esther Coren, Jo Fiore et al, *A systematic review of the evidence base for developing a physical activity and health legacy from the London 2012 and Paralympic Games*, SPEAR/Department of Health 2009; also Mike Weed, Esther Coren, Jo Fiore et al, 'Developing a Physical Activity Legacy from the London 2012 Olympic and Paralympic games: A Policy-led Systematic Review', in *Perspectives in Public Health*, 32, 2012.

17. Owen Gibson, 'Headteachers and Athletes Warn against Cut to School Sports Funding', *Guardian*, 6 February 2013.

18. Toby Helm, 'After All the Promises, Where is the Legacy of London 2012', *Guardian*, 26 January 2013.

19. TNS BRMB, *Inspire a Generation: A Taking Part Report on 2012 Olympic and Paralympic Games*, 2012. See also Active People summary Data, available from Sport England.

20. Marc Keech, 'Youth Sport legacy', in John Sugden and Alan Tomlinson (eds), *Watching the Olympics*, Routledge 2012, p94.

CONSUMED BY THE GAMES

Anne Coddington

Major international sporting events are almost always an opportunity to raise the profile of women, either as athletes or as fans. John Williams suggests that women are attracted by the sense of community that is created by World Cups, European Championships and the Olympics. Even women who do not regularly engage with sport become involved during these events.[1]

Football's Euro '96, which was hosted by England, was the first major international sports event I took part in as a fan. It was significant in terms of gender because it was also the first football event to specifically target women fans. The tournament was promoted via a range of magazine advertisements – which included, among others, the slogan 'How can I lie back and think of England when Venables hasn't finalised the squad?'. While some more traditional female fans found that these rather tongue-in-cheek adverts did not fit their idea of fandom, that was the point. The idea was to reach out beyond the already converted.

Football had already seen major changes since the Hillsborough stadium disaster of 1989. The 1990 Taylor Report had demanded clubs clean up inside the stadium, with better facilities and family areas; and in the top two divisions the terraces had been replaced by seating. As Williams noted, these changes coincided with the exceptional popularity of the 1990 World Cup, for which Pavarotti's *Nessun Dorma* provided the soundtrack, and Gazza's tears the emotional backdrop (before the final exit on penalties to Germany). This was football that was softer, more elegant, more emotional than it had ever been before, and it appealed to women. Of course most spectators were still men, but for the first time substantial numbers of women – making up to half of the TV audience for some games – joined in too.

Post Italia '90, with football changing and actively seeking a broader fan base, it seemed that women might be able to take an authentic part in what was and still is the national sport, the people's game. No longer would being a female fan be an oddity – the new marketisation of football, with its cleaned up image and ticket prices to match, was specifically aimed at attracting women and families. And after the publication in 1992 of Nick Hornby's *Fever Pitch*, these structural changes were complemented by the growth of a more cerebral football publishing culture, which projected a softened vision of what a fan might look like – still male but perhaps less dogmatic. Maybe women could now be part of this culture – if not on equal terms, a significant presence nevertheless.

But if the structures of how football was consumed had changed, the majority fan culture had not. As one of the new fans who began attending games back in 1992, I soon found that when I looked behind the adverts, beyond the new stadium and the media hype, the majority of fans sitting awkwardly on those bright new shiny seats had not changed. The dominant motif was that of the suffering fan, there through the wind and rain, unquestioningly following the team home and away. This was a culture passed down from father to son, learned in school playgrounds kicking a ball around, in a game that girls did not play. I, and many other women fans, did not realise just how difficult it would be to feel at home in this culture. You could join in for a period of time, even years – feel comfortable, enjoy the banter like a stranger looking in – but it was very difficult to feel a real sense of belonging or welcome.

The most significant factor was just how impervious football is to adapting or changing. I guess if you have a fandom that is all about refusing to give in, or to let go, and staying loyal whatever the players, the manager, the owners, do to your club – it can be seen as being all about not changing. Refusing to bow down. Being with the same group of mates, singing the same songs and having the same rituals, rejecting anyone who is different. For new fans to belong probably needs a transformation in fan culture in order to incorporate new voices, and many fans – male and female – do not want that. And this creates a barrier to diversity. The stands at almost all grounds bear witness to this. Of course the price and availability of tickets is a factor, but there is a deeper reason for football's failure to change.

Being a female fan in what is still a predominantly male environment – even now just 23 per cent of fans at Premier League games are women – might be described as displaying what Judith Butler calls 'inappropriate embodiments of gender'.[2] This can be playful, an opportunity to question and play with tradition, but playing is a two-way process. Given that the majority of the fans are male, there has to be some desire on the part of at least some of them to play the ball back.

So, looking back, Euro '96, alongside all the other changes there had been in football, was a key moment in the attempt to broaden the fan base for the people's game. With its festivals of culture around the host cities, Skinner and Baddiel's 'football's coming home', the bright English sunshine, and families going to the tournament for a day out, '96 presented for a couple of weeks the idea of a gentler, more open, culture, free of the racism and hooliganism that had previously been associated with all things England. But what it did not do was grow a whole new generation of female fans.

FROM EURO '96 TO LONDON 2012

The 2012 Olympics is for most of us the greatest sporting event we will ever see in Britain. But what kind of alternative ideal of fandom did it offer? With its opening and closing ceremonies that appeal to national pride, the Olympics is a spectacle that draws in larger audiences than might ordinarily be interested in sport, people who have no connection with the routine sports media coverage that usually focuses on the Premier League and not very much else.

Kevin Garside was right when he suggested that the Olympics made manners cool. The Games were – to use a phrase that is treated with derision in football – 'civilised'.[3] Female football fans are often associated with that term. As John Williams suggests, there is an assumption that modern football has become sanitised because women attend – female fans remind the old guard that they should not swear, should not use sexist or racist language and that they can no longer stand up in the terraces.[4] They have to constantly consider their behaviour and effect on others (outsiders). The resistance to our presence is often wrapped in the vocabulary of class, but this is a version of class tradition that serves to exclude women.

If modern football has become sanitised it is not the fault of new fans, including women. It is to do with rising ticket prices, but also the new marketised environment – the tiers of corporate boxes that disturb the naturally raucous atmosphere, the transformation of football's stadiums into event destinations for a substantial part of the crowd, who see the match more as part of a day out than as a journey towards a life of fandom. Women are part of those changes, but don't blame us for them. As Liz Crolley and Cathy Long put it, 'no woman fan goes to football because of improved toilets'.[5] More women started going to football because of the impression that we would be welcomed within the new football, that we could share in its very special atmosphere.

But what the Olympics disturbed much more effectively than football ever has is the idea that being civilised is simply about curtailment and restraint. Garside suggests, more positively, that the Games were a holiday, a breath of fresh air that enabled us (as a nation) to reflect on our usual preoccupation with football – and only one small segment of the game at that: not the women's game, not mass participation at grassroots level, not even the lower leagues, but just the twenty-two clubs in the Premiership.[6] And those clubs have, he suggests, for too long been undeserving of our time, money and loyalty:

> Football represents the worst excesses of sport, too much money, lack of respect for referees, some fans who display poor behaviour in the name of fandom. Olympians work at their sports day in day out, don't get paid huge amounts of money, don't get constant attention, huge audiences yet still perform under pressure.

Or as Geoffrey Wheatcroft argues:

> Could there be one reason we loved the Olympics so much: it wasn't football? We return from the loyalty and fair game of our cyclists, rowers, runners to the vast carnival of cheating, brutality and avarice known as the Premier League. We return from one vision of our country, personified by the decency and charm of Brad and Jessica, Laura and Mo, to that other isle, full of noises made by John Terry, Wayne Rooney and Joey Barton.[7]

Both writers appear to be suggesting that the Olympics offered another model of engaging with sport. One that retained the excitement and intensity of football, but managed to do so in a more open and welcoming – feminised – way. The Games offered us all the opportunity to watch sports with which we are less familiar – given that the mainstream media covers little sport beyond football, rugby, cricket and formula one, with occasional appearances from boxing and tennis. For the period of the Olympics, though, the 26 Olympic sports were treated with genuine interest and respect by the media commentators, and indeed by the audiences in the stadium or watching on TV.

A giant patchwork of spectators came together with various degrees of sporting knowledge and fan-commitment, and somehow that did not matter. No one felt excluded, or that they were spoiling the fun. Watching the bronze medal game of the men's hockey in the Olympic Park, surrounded by British and Australian supporters, it was clear to me that there were serious hockey fans at this game, and for them this was a key sporting moment. There was intense concentration, cheers, boos, flag-waving and chanting – though without the self importance or arrogance associated with top flight football. But the less committed and well-informed amongst us were involved too, we felt just as much part of it, and able to ask about the rules without fear of ridicule – indeed the hockey fans were eager to encourage this interest.

During the Olympics, Julie Nerney, a longstanding football fan who follows Aston Villa and England, was the Head of London 2012's Transport Integration.[8] She was thus able to observe the crowds both in and out of the various venues throughout the tournament. She noticed that the atmosphere was much gentler, far less tribal than the typical football crowd she was more used to. 'But then you had a very different set of social influences,' she says. 'Lots of people, male and female, came to watch the Games who were not followers of any sport. They came to see the Olympic Park, have a drink or picnic with the family and part of that experience featured sport'.

These fans didn't come with a set of preconceptions about how to behave at a sporting event; but rather than diluting the atmosphere with the oft derided (and largely mythological) polite clapping, they contributed to the creation of a vibrant sporting utopia. Despite the fact that many members of the audience hadn't got tickets for their first choice events, they threw themselves into the various sports with gusto. Water polo, handball, taekwondo – even the most avid sports fans were unfamiliar with some of these sport's rules and conventions – but the feeling was bring it on, whatever the sport and who ever was competing, let's just celebrate.

COMMUNITIES OF CONSUMPTION

London 2012 challenged the idea that the much fabled atmosphere of live events can only be created by the long-standing serious fans who care the most. Sports fandom, which has generally been analysed in terms of football culture, is associated with belonging – what Garry Crawford describes as 'following and supporting a common cause'.[9] Typically this communality emerges from a feeling of being part of an 'imagined community', acknowledging that we share rituals and beliefs as a group. According to this model, fandom comes from identifying with the 'we' of the crowd – hence the roots of tribalism and rivalry. Because you care so much you are allowed to be emotional, shout abuse at the referee, criticise the players, your own as well as theirs, and scream whatever you want at the opposing fans. Any bad behaviour can be blamed on the emotions of the moment, being part of the 'we', which means that the group is clearly blameless. And the 'we' depends on an assumption that we are all the same.

Of course this is why it is so difficult for new fans to find a way in, because this reasoning assumes that either you are part of the group or you are not. It skips over a more messy reality, which is that fandom is a continuum. All fans – male and female – have to start somewhere, firstly with a loose connection that then grows over time. It also ignores the children who gradually come to learn that sport is meaningful, and completely blanks out the newer fans, who don't simply slot seamlessly into the 'we', because we are different – in particular women, families, and people of black and ethnic minority origin.

Garry Crawford suggests that we need to create a new typology of fandom that breaks away from the romantic 'us and them' categories of the past, including the traditional/masculine fan versus the new sports consumers who are often feminine.[10] All fans are to some extent consumers – 'be that attending a live sport event, watching it on television, buying a team's replica jersey, or observing displays and performances of other fans'. Garry puts forward a more flexible ideal, one that moves 'towards an understanding of how sport is located and experienced in everyday life and social interactions'.

SOME SPORTS ARE MORE EQUAL THAN OTHERS

The Olympics showed that sport can engage with this more complex and diverse idea of fandom while still being exciting and vital. Or, as

Julie Nerney puts it, 'there was a sense of belonging at the Olympics, but the glue that bound one to the other was not tribalism but the celebration of sporting success'.[11] This more complex form of fandom can accommodate aspirations of national identity – yes, we wanted our Team GB athletes to win – but at the same time can incorporate a broader internationalist perspective. The majority British crowd moved effortlessly between the 'we' of the nation rooting for our home-grown heroes and acknowledging with awe and affection the outstanding array of other talented athletes – Usain Bolt, Missy Franklin, Marianne Vos – even when they were beating our own. As Team GB supporters we enjoyed the 'we', what Cornell Sandvoss calls the way 'fans articulate their image of themselves', and we projected it onto the sports stars as we rooted for our own athletes.[12] But we were also able to step out of our particular fan identity and enjoy being hosts, as well as enjoying the successes of other nations' teams.

Many had never realised before that there was such a range of sports to enjoy. Sharon Olawale, a sports journalism student and volunteer during the Games typifies this sentiment:

I wasn't into sport when I decided to volunteer. I did it because I'm from Stratford and I wanted to meet people and give a good impression of East London. But my eyes were opened to what sport can be, so many women taking part, so many sports I'd never heard of, and these fantastic athletes that suddenly appeared from nowhere. I'm like, wow this is interesting, maybe there's something for me here.[13]

What Sharon had realised is that sport can be about more than what is covered in the mainstream media. A 2011 report, the International Sports Press Survey, found that 90 per cent of articles written in the print media are by men, and that over half – up to 85 per cent – in Europe are on men's football alone.[14] A similar 2011 survey by the Women's Sport and Fitness Foundation found that outside the Olympics only 5 per cent of media coverage is given over to women's sport – and most of that is for tennis.[15]

So it is no wonder that many people during major tournaments and the Olympics in particular feel like they have discovered sport, in a broader sense, for the first time. In Britain at least, it is easy to feel locked out of mainstream sport by the absolute hegemony of football. Media coverage of football speaks to those already established on their path to fandom, with commentary and opinions that privilege ex- professional players and serve to reinforce a commonsense understanding that you really have to have played the game to understand it.

In their comparison of Team GB gold-medal winners with premiership footballers, Geoffrey Wheatcroft and Kevin Garside hint at a class differential that might suggest that Olympians are more articulate in connecting sport to a broader audience. And it is true that competitors at an elite level in some of our most successful Olympic sports – rowing, equestrianism and yachting in particular – draw on an almost exclusively middle and upper class base. But those same social advantages of access don't apply to boxing, the martial arts, many of the athletics events or cycling, at which Team GB also excelled. The social construction of sport is vital to its understanding, but a simple class analysis, often expressed via media snobbery or a conservative and masculine fan culture, doesn't provide the full picture. As Matthew Syed and others have argued, a complex range of factors provide the conditions for becoming an elite athlete.[16] But there's a broader point too. No footballer in an England shirt has won a major trophy since 1966, or even reached a semi-final since those heady days of Euro '96 or Italia '90. No Scottish, Welsh or Northern Irish international football team has ever won a trophy. Yet at London 2012 Team GB won gold, silver and bronze, often with world record performances. And many of those victors were women, whose achievements were never overshadowed by their male counterparts – in fact sometimes the reverse was the case. This was both a different level from what international football has been able to provide, and a different version of success. If the footballers seem a bit grumpy and mono-syllabic in their post-match interviews following yet another early exit from a World Cup or Euro, maybe it's because they're upset at realising they're not very good?

AFTER THE FINAL WHISTLE

As the host Olympics nation, we had a gradual and lengthy media build up that showcased a range of sports and gave equal coverage to women athletes in almost all of them. For four weeks we could imagine what it might be like if all sports were treated the same in terms of respect, funding and media coverage. That is a point that silver medal cyclist Lizzie Armistead, a fierce critic of the differential funding given to women athletes, makes: 'the positive side for me is that the Olympics is the biggest platform there is, and there's total equality across all sports. I'm at the games and I'm getting equal media exposure and support as any other athlete, male or female'.[17] It would be hard to argue that Laura Trott enjoys less of a media profile than her team-mate and partner Jason Kenny. Was Jess Ennis's part in 'Super Saturday' overshadowed by Mo Farah's on the same night? Whose boxing gold was celebrated the most, Nicola Adams's or Anthony Joshua's? In each case there was a rare sporting equality.

This was surely aided by the style of the Olympics media coverage, which was more accessible than what we have become accustomed to, precisely because of the numerous sports being covered. In order to attract viewers with a range of sporting knowledge and levels of interest, the sports had to be explained and presented in a more accessible, consumer-friendly way. This created space for a broader range of presenters – 8 out of 25 presenters on the BBC were female. And four – Gabby Logan, Clare Balding, Sue Barker and Hazel Irvine – were part of the main hosting team. Yes, female sports journalists might still be in the minority – the International Sports Survey notes no growth in numbers since 2005 – but at the Olympics women reporters and presenters were asked to take centre stage to bring sport into the living rooms of millions of British families.[18]

There was a sense that these women would appeal to audiences beyond established sports fans. But it also meant that, freed from the long-established conventions of how to cover sport, new thinking was permissible. Gabby Logan makes the following point: 'The Olympics were deemed suitable for women presenters because of a residual resistance to them covering football'.[19] A she adds: 'And it's funny because so many of the Olympic sports are far more technical. You would think men would be more suspicious about women talking about these sports, whereas football is everywhere and actually not that hard to understand'.

Indeed no one did more to make the 2012 events accessible than Clare Balding, whose knowledge across a vast range of sports and consummate professionalism has led to her being hailed as a national treasure. For Belinda Wheaton, Senior Researcher in Sport at the University of Brighton, a growing respect for Balding is an important marker in terms of women's impact on the sports media at least. 'Clare Balding does not fit the typical female sports media stereotype. She is an out lesbian, and doesn't try to be overly glamorous, yet she has crossed over into the mainstream and gained the respect of men and women sports fans'.[20]

But it is very important that we do not romanticise the Olympics, and assume four weeks of seeing lots of women taking part in, and reporting on, sport will lead to fundamental change. Indeed the 1996 Olympics in Atlanta, were, like London 2012, dubbed the gender games, because for the first time in the history of the Games, NBC, the designated media channel, presented equal coverage of male and female sports. But as Alina Bernstein notes, 'given the media's treatment of the 1996 Olympics as a pivotal event for women's sports, the extent to which coverage of women athletes and women's sport failed to grow is astonishing'.[21]

The rules, conventions and culture of modern sport were created and shaped by men back in the late nineteenth century; hence the unspoken assumption that sport is masculine, and that women who do participate are weaker, lesser – unnatural even. Katharina Lindner points out that women who play contact sports like football, rugby or basketball, with their connotations of strength, power, aggression and muscularity, are perceived as endangering their femininity.[22] And when women do play sport, they are often encouraged to take up those activities that encourage feminine – and graceful – behaviour, gymnastics being the most obvious example.

These preconceptions are reinforced in the modern day context by a lack of media coverage of women in sport outside of the Olympics. If the media is seen as covering what is important, the lack of attention given to women's sport (beyond the occasional gender appropriate activity) suggests that it has little value. Alina Bernstein suggests this leads to a vicious circle. 'Since the growth in sport is hindered by lack of funds which comes primarily from sponsorship, sponsors are interested in teams and athletes that feature prominently on television, where women's sports do not feature'.[23] Indeed a 2011 report by the Women's Sport and Fitness Foundation shows that women's sport accounts for just 0.5 per cent of all sports sponsorship in the UK.[24]

But if gender inequalities in sport are to be dismantled, we need to look beyond media coverage. Girl-specific coaching initiatives in schools, imaginative campaigns to encourage women's participation in sport of the sort launched ahead of the Games by *Stylist* magazine, and affording equal funding and profile elite to women athletes will all play a part. But most of all what is required is a shift in British sporting culture. Until the masculine hegemony of football faces a serious challenge from the more gender-equitable sports, any advances made at London 2012 will be over before we've even had a chance to forget them in all their feminine sporting glory.

NOTES

1. See John Williams, in Anne Coddington, *One of the Lads: Women Who Follow Football*, HarperCollins 1997.
2. 'Premier League set to pass 250 million fans': www.premierleague.com, 27 November 2012; Judith Butler, 'Athletic genders: hyperbolic instance and/or the overcoming of sexual binarism', in *Stanford Humanities Review*, vol 6, no 2, 1998.
3. Kevin Garside (2013) 'After the Olympics football returns-to the Stone Age' in the *Independent*, 16 January
4. John Williams, op cit.
5. Liz Crolley and Cathy Long, 'Sitting Pretty? Women and football in Liverpool', in John Williams (ed), *Passing Rhythms: Liverpool FC and the Transformation of Football*, Berg 2001.
6. Kevin Garside, op cit.
7. Geoffrey Wheatcroft, 'From Jessica Ennis to Joey Barton. Could a contrast by more ghastly?', *Guardian*, 16 August 2012.
8. Julie Nerney, personal interview.
9. See Garry Crawford, *Consuming Sport: Fans, Sport and Culture*, Routledge 2004.
10. Garry Crawford, op cit, p34.
11. Julie Nerney, personal interview.
12. Cornell Sandvoss, *A Game of Two Halves: Football, Television and Globalisation*, Routledge 2003, p37.
13. Sharon Olewale, personal interview.
14. Thomas Horky and Jorg-Uwe Nieland, *First Results of the International Sports Press Survey 2011*, German Sport University, Cologne 2011.
15. The Commission on the Future of Women's Sport, *Big Deal? The case for commercial investment in Women's Sport*, Women's Sport and Fitness Foundation 2011.
16. See Matthew Syed, *Bounce: The Myth of Talent and the Power of Practice*, Fourth Estate 2011; and Rasmus Ankersen, *The Goldmine Effect: Crack The Secrets of High Performance*, Icon Books 2012.
17. Emine Saner, 'Saturday interview: Lizzie Armitstead, Olympic cycling silver medallist', *Guardian*, 4 August 2012.
18. Thomas Horky and Jorg-Uwe Nieland, op cit.
19. Vanessa Thorpe, 'Gabby Logan: "The Olympics was positive for female

presenters – we got the chance to show what we could do"', *Observer*, 30
September 2012.

20. Belinda Wheaton, personal interview

21. Alina Bernstein, 'Women in Sports Media: Time for a Victory Lap?
Changes in Media Coverage of Women in Sport', *International Review for
the Sociology of Sport*, Sage 2002, p417.

22. Katharina Lindner, 'Women's Boxing at the 2012 Olympics: Gender
Trouble' in *Feminist Media Studies* Vol 12 No 3, 2012.

23. Bernstein, op cit, p417.

24. Commission on the Future of Women's Sport, op cit.

We have nothing to lose
but our medals

Gareth Edwards

On 5 August 2012 Usain Bolt crossed the finish line with a cursory dip, to claim the men's 100 metre Olympic title. It was the second fastest time ever recorded, and one of three gold medals he would win at the Games, as well a being the first time in history an athlete had successfully defended their sprint title. Here was an athlete who transcended his sport; a truly global superstar who had confirmed his entry into the pantheon of Olympic legends. In front of 80,000 live spectators (the lucky ones of the one million people who had applied for tickets to this Olympics blue-ribbon event), and an estimated 20 million people in the UK watching on the BBC, Bolt raised his index finger to indicate he remained number one. Stopping in front of the assembled media he posed for the cameras, and the unmistakable image of the 'Lightning Bolt' was beamed to track and field fans around the world. As the adrenalin ebbed away Bolt's face lit up with a broad infectious smile, reflecting the joys of achievement and triumph. He took pleasure not from the act of running but from his execution of the race. His satisfaction stemmed not only from his victory but, unavoidably, from the defeat of others.

Two months later I stood watching a mass of runners stream past the window of my girlfriend's ninth floor council flat as they took part in the Great South Run. Stephen Mokoka and Jo Pavey, winners of the men's and women's races respectively, had long since finished. The 25,000 people below were the amateurs, the occasional joggers and those running to raise money for charity. They were an assortment of tired, heavy limbs, grimaces, silly hats and fancy dress. Ligaments and sinews stretched, lungs heaved greedily, lactic-acid-burned calf muscles reducing some to little more than the pace of a Sunday morning amble. No doubt there were friends and colleagues competing against each

189

other, with the winner claiming a year's worth of bragging rights. But most did not race their fellow runners; instead they competed against themselves, against the clock, and against those ten miles.

Whether for fun or for Olympic glory, the physical act of running remains much the same. Of course techniques and abilities vary, but it is also obvious that Usain Bolt and the man who completed the Great South Run dressed as Elmo from Sesame Street are engaged in the same activity. Yet at the same time we also recognise that they occupy completely separate worlds. Sport at an elite level is concerned with victory; its structures and competitions are designed to produce winners and champions, and its inevitable by-product is the crushing disappointment of defeat. For Mhairi Spence, the British modern pentathlete who entered the 2012 Games as World Champion and favourite for the Gold Medal, the Olympics were catastrophic. Following four years preparation and a single day of intense competition, Spence finished in twenty-first place. 'For me, it was a disaster', she said. 'I can't describe it in any other way. I felt it destroyed part of me'.[1] But elite sport is not simply reducible to stories of success and failure, as though it were hermetically sealed from the rest of society. Sport is big business, in which professional athletes and administrators can make fortunes; while politicians use sport as a barometer of national success, measuring the relative strength of countries in gold, silver and bronze.

Nowhere is the idea of elite sport more visible than in the Olympic Games, where, as Mike Marqusee argues, the 'podium is a symbolic package: individual excellence at the service of the nation-state under the overlordship of multi-national capital'.[2] The injunction to strive for physical excellence contained within Baron Pierre de Coubertin's Olympic motto *citius, altius, fortius,* was long ago appropriated by the marketing department of the International Olympic Committee. In their hands it has become the mantra employed to reinforce the idea that the Olympics represent the very pinnacle of sporting excellence.[3] But the Olympics is also the epitome of the corporatised sports world. The IOC, which Jules Boykoff describes as being 'somewhere between multinational corporation and global institution', heads an 'Olympic Movement' whose power and influence stretch far beyond the confines of the sporting world.[4] This singularly unaccountable body owes its power in no small part to their immense financial resources.[5] Numerous companies pay exorbitant sums in sponsorship to associate themselves the ideals of the Olympics. The Games are not simply a festival of sport: they are an idea, a product and a brand.

OLYMPIC PROTEST

Protest is part and parcel of Olympic history – much to the annoyance of the IOC, which would prefer to maintain the façade that the Games are an apolitical event. Broadly speaking, four distinct types of Olympic protest can be identified, although these inevitably overlap on occasion.

First there is the use of the Olympics by nation states as a proxy for wider geo-political disagreements, for example the tit-for-tat Cold War boycotts in the early 1980s.

Second, athletes have used the Olympics as a platform in which to stage political protests. These are often an expression of wider social struggle, the intensity of which has risen to such a level as to permeate the insularity of the sporting world. Witness the way in which the iconic clenched fist salutes of Tommie Smith and John Carlos were a reflection of the civil rights movement in the United States during the 1960s. Another example is when Cathy Freedman wrapped an Aboriginal flag around her shoulders following her victory in the 400 metres at the 2000 Sydney Olympics.

Third, political activists have used the heightened media coverage of the Games to highlight a particular political injustice, for example the demonstrations of workers and students in Mexico 1968, or the campaigns to exclude Apartheid South Africa from the Olympic movement.

Fourth, there have been localised campaigns protesting against the impact that staging the Games has on a host city.

Of this list the localised campaigns have been the least visible; but they have also been the most prevalent over the past two decades. Notwithstanding specific host city issues, the protests have raised broadly similar concerns: the costs incurred in staging the Games; the impact on local communities and green spaces; and the records of Olympic sponsors on issues of environmental and workers' rights. Ahead of London 2012 the Counter Olympics Network brought together the diverse groups and individuals concerned with these and other issues. As I wrote at the time, there was plenty to protest about:

Against a backdrop of austerity-driven public spending cuts, thousands of athletes from more than 200 countries will contest 26 events, 'competing in the true spirit of sportsmanship, for the glory of sport and the honour of our teams'. Awash with brands and corporate logos, the Olympics have become the quintessential mega-event; a global, neo-liberal, five-ring circus. Those five rings of the Olympic symbol adorn everything from soft drinks cans to aircraft, the product of billion dollar sponsorship deals. To protect the Games the UK government is deploying 13,500 troops, locating surface to air missiles on the rooftops of residential housing, and stationing the HMS Ocean on the River Thames.[6]

Two things were noticeable about the campaign by the Counter Olympics Network. Firstly, the organised left and trade union movement were conspicuous by their absence. Secondly, amongst the protesters, while there was much talk of the social cost and disruption that accompanied the Olympics, there was very little talk about the sports themselves. Both of these points are symptomatic of the fact that much of the left remains hostile to sport, and ambivalent about the idea that it may represent an arena of struggle.

LEFT BEHIND AT THE START

The left has, on occasion, attempted to utilise sports in an attempt to highlight questions of oppression and exploitation. For example, the Fair Play campaign, backed by the TUC, used the London Olympics as an opportunity to focus attention on the working conditions of those working for the largest sportswear manufacturers. And the Anti-Nazi League actively sought the support of footballers, managers and fans in the fight against a rising tide of racism and fascism in the late 1970s and early 1980s. Yet very rarely is sport confronted as a phenomenon in its own right. Aside from some notable exceptions, renowned, celebrated and influential leftist writers have been almost universally condemnatory when passing judgement on sport.[7] Consider, for instance, this quotation from Theodor Adorno:

Sport is ambiguous. On the one hand, it can have an anti-barbaric and anti-sadistic effect by means of fair play, a spirit of chivalry, and consideration for the weak. On the other hand, in many of its varieties and practices it can promote aggression, brutality, and sadism, above all in people who do not expose themselves to the exertion and discipline required by sports but instead merely watch: that is, those who regularly shout from the sidelines.[8]

The presence of nuance and caveats do not detract from the essential thrust of Adorno's argument. For Adorno sports are, on balance, harmful social phenomena, and although their worst aspects may be offset by certain conventions, they damage the players and debase the spectators. And the context in which these words appear is fascinating. They are taken from *Education after Auschwitz*, an essay exploring how a repeat of the Holocaust might be avoided. The fact that Adorno, in the middle of a discussion of the worst atrocity in human history, takes time for such an aside reveals much about his attitude to sport.

There is, however, still much to commend in the left critique, not least the analysis of the relationship between elite sport and capitalism. Jean-Marie Brohm, a marxist whose works have become something of a touchstone for left-wing writers on sport, wrote in the 1970s that the 'tendency for international sport to be directly subordinated to big capital has in fact increased steadily'.[9] Today that process has reached its logical conclusion, and sports are awash with brands and logos, sponsored by multinational businesses, and run by transnational organisations that have the power and wealth to rival the largest corporations.[10]

A consequence of this relationship is that sport has become 'structurally analogous' to work under capitalism.[11] The activities of athletes have succumbed to the logic of capitalist rationalisation, with sports subject to 'a high degree of specialisation and standardisation, bureaucratised and hierarchical administration, long term planning, increased reliance on science and technology, a drive for maximum productivity and, above all, the alienation of both producer and consumer'.[12] The human body is transformed into a machine, and at their most brutal modern sports can leave their superstars broken and wretched – evidenced in the most heart-rending fashion by the appearance of Muhammad Ali at the 2012 Opening Ceremony.

However, there are two key areas in which existing marxist criticisms of sport remain unsatisfactory and deficient.

Firstly, there is little, if any, attempt to distinguish between elite sport as represented by the Olympics and the activities that the rest of us may engage in on a recreational basis at evenings and weekends. In the case of Brohm such a distinction is met with outright rejection: 'the distinction between top-level sport and mass sport is not a valid one, in that both are fundamentally based on the principle of maximum output'.[13]

Secondly there is sometimes a suggestion that sport has come to play the role of a transmission belt for bourgeois ideology. The Russian revolutionary Trotsky went so far as to suggest that sport was one of a number of superstructural impediments to class consciousness:

> The revolution will inevitably awaken in the English working class the most unusual passions, which have been hitherto been so artificially held down and turned aside, with the aid of social training, the church, the press, in the artificial channels of boxing, football, racing and other sports.

Of course such a claim should not be entirely dismissed. Professional sports – competitive, aggressive and so often seen in a national (and indeed nationalistic) context – are ideally suited to function as a transmission belt for the dominant norms and values of society.[14] But there is an overwhelming tendency to overstate the hegemonic nature of modern sports. Such is the case with the recent work of Marc Perelman, a French intellectual writing in the shadow of Jean-Marie Brohm.[15] Whatever valid insights Perelman may have about capitalism's pernicious effects on sport are off-set by the patronising tone he adopts when describing working class people who watch sport. We are, according to Perelman, under the influence of a new 'opiate of the masses', leaving us as 'people who can never live fulfilling lives, being in the grip of that enslaving power known as sport'.[16] This is a crass and one-dimensional approach, a theory in which the very idea of working-class agency is entirely absent.

TAKING PLAY SERIOUSLY

What then could trigger the left's critical engagement with the world of sport? Above all else, a materialist analysis of the left's historical relationship to sport will note that it is tied to the vicissitudes of the class struggle. It is no accident that the workers' sport movement in the 1920s and 1930s should have occurred at the point in the twentieth century when the European left was at its height; and nor should it come as a surprise that there was a renewed interest in the left's approach to sport in the period following the May events and others of 1968.[17] At these historical junctures, when the working class has been politically strong, there has been a history of building sporting alternatives.

Today, with millions of working-class people playing and watching sport, the left may still be compelled to engage, but the class struggle is at its lowest ebb; political parties (and their intellectuals) cut away such extraneous questions, and shun heterodoxy in favour of ideological purity.

In these unfavourable conditions, to generate any sort of engagement between left politics and sport requires that we must first of all answer the question: what is the relationship between play and sport? Answers to this question have historically fallen into one of two camps. One, exemplified by the liberal-idealist Allen Guttmann, sees sport as being a distinct subset of play, marked by its physicality, its competitiveness and its rules.[18] In summary, Guttman and his co-thinkers argue that, while not all play can be considered sport, all sport is necessarily play. The opposing argument, and one that characterises much of what passes for sports theory on the left, is the complete rejection of a link between play and sport, as typified by the work of Brohm, who claims that: 'a child who practices sport is no longer playing but is taking his place in a world of serious matters'.[19] The problem with this latter position is that the theory of play offered is so lacklustre. Instead of theorising play in any meaningful way, this approach amounts to little more than simply listing a set of characteristics that describe – rather than define – play. These characteristics include spontaneity, a certain sense of freedom, fun, a separation from everyday life and make-believe, although this is by no means an exhaustive list. And in the absence of any more serious working definition, nearly all the critical writers on this topic fall back on the same four words: play is not work. Or, to give it a sophisticated feel, they talk of play as being a non-productive or non-utilitarian activity. And when they're feeling particularly wordy, they describe play as being autotelic, i.e. an activity performed for its own sake.

This commonsense dichotomy between work and play might seem to be a fair approximation to reality, but it is fraught with problems; and it is possible to arrive at a far more satisfying and insightful

definition of play by using marxist concepts. I would argue that play is
the *unalienated, simultaneous production and consumption of use value*.
Defining play as a use value is to recognise it as fulfilling a human need.
As Trotsky notes in *The Problems of Everyday Life*: 'The longing for
amusement, diversion and fun is the most legitimate desire of human
nature'.[20] Whether this need for play is an innate biological drive or
socially and historically conditioned is unimportant; the fact is that
the desire for pleasure and excitement exists. That this creative drive
should manifest itself in so many forms is an indicator of humanity's
ingenuity and inventiveness. It is, therefore, possible to see how play is
the creation of use value. As Marx suggests:

> Whoever directly satisfies his wants with the produce of his own
> labour, creates, indeed, use values, but not commodities. In order to
> produce the latter, he must not only produce use values, but use
> values for others, social use values.[21]

By stating that play is an unalienated activity – and here I use the
term 'alienation' in Marx's original conception, namely that alienation is the loss of control over one's own creative process[22] – we are
able to both incorporate and transcend the quality of freedom But
rather than limiting the question of freedom to whether we choose to
play or not, such an analysis also encompasses the freedom of the
players to create and control their play environment. Whether individually or collectively, people choose how they play; there are no
structures delimiting play's potentiality; and nor are managers and
supervisors issuing instructions as to the players' conduct.
Furthermore, the separation of producer from product, a key feature
of alienation, is missing, as play belongs immediately and irrevocably
to the players. In similar fashion, the notion of the simultaneous
production and consumption of use values allows us to overcome the
limitations of the autotelic model. Play is still seen as an end in itself,
but this definition avoids getting caught in the theoretical trap of
trying to guess the players' intentions. Equally, it renders redundant
the notion that play is an essentially non-instrumental activity.
Instead play differentiates itself from other spheres of human activity
not so much through what is (or is not) produced, but in the way it is
consumed. Here, the very act of production *is* the act of consumption. In a dialectical sense they occupy the same moment. Labour

produces use values that may be consumed at some indeterminate point in the future, but in play, production and consumption occur simultaneously. The very act of playing is the satisfaction of the need to play.

TOWARDS A NEW VERSION OF SPORT

How then does this relate to sport? The key to our understanding is, as Richard Gruneau has written, the fact that 'the structuring of sport has become increasingly systematised, formalised, and removed from the direct control of the individual players'.[23] Governing bodies exercise control over sports across the globe, setting rules and issuing directives. In sport the players are not free to participate, instead they are faced with a series of gatekeepers – managers, coaches, selectors. Some of these people then exercise control over the way in which players play. Tactics are prescribed, plans and set-pieces become part and parcel of the contemporary sporting world; and as they increasingly predominate, they not only affect how a match or a race is conducted, but also regiment training routines.

At the heart of sport there is a constant tension between play and competition. As the importance of the contest – and the financial stakes involved – increases, so playfulness gives way to 'playing the percentages', 'playing it safe' and 'stopping the other team from playing'. This means that for those of us who participate in sport for fun, the further we are from the insanity of the corporatised sports world, the more likely it is that the playful can assume dominance over the competitive. Anyone who plays sport is, by definition, engaging in a competitive activity, but for most of us, most of the time, the contest is but one aspect of our participation. Sport is also an opportunity to spend time with our friends and family, a chance to exercise, or simply to experience the joys of movement, accomplishment and completion. As Mark Perryman has written of his own experience of running:

> I can see myself as part of a popular movement of people who enjoy sport purely for fun and therefore are the antithesis of all that the Olympics has come to represent. I run free, for free. No rules, no sponsors, no entry fee, no national pride, nobody's stopwatch to calibrate the results except my own. I run because I can.[24]

But it would be wrong, I think, to say that there is no element of play apparent in professional sports. When commentators talk of an inspired move or a piece of ingenuity, it is often the case that the playful, the unpredictable, is reasserting itself in the face of the demands of competition. It should come as no surprise that those sportspeople who acquire iconic status – Lionel Messi would be a contemporary example – are the ones who look as though they are genuinely 'playing', even in the most serious and competitive of situations. The nature of the sporting contest, with its unfolding drama and the need for instantaneous individual and collective decision-making, means that individuality and personality can never be wholly removed from a game.

The world of elite sport is thus not best understood either as existing in the realm of pure play, or as being its total negation. If we use Marx's criteria, and look at 'the relation of labour to the act of production in the labour process', professional sports can be seen as involving the alienation of play. Equally, the use values produced by those playing sports no longer belong to them. Play is now mediated through the prism of capitalist relations – reconfigured as a spectacle, and placed on the market as a commodity. In elite sport, use values do not present the fulfilment of the need of the player; they satisfy the demands of capital, where spectators are the consumers of a product. The sporting spectacle is no longer the by-product of play; it is the product, deliberately cultivated: it is now play which is incidental. As Gideon Haigh laments of one sport, 'cricket must be sold in order to be played'[25] – an ugly maxim that could be applied to almost all modern sports.

As 'work' is the contemporary manifestation of labour, so sport is a historically conditioned form of play. We may still point to its physicality, its competitive nature and the development of physical and intellectual skills as defining characteristics. But when defining the relationship between sport and play these alone are insufficient. Instead, professional sport is commodified, alienated play. We should perhaps adapt the famous aphorism of Marx and declare, 'Players play, but not in the conditions of their own choosing'. The more we begin to understand the link between play and sport, the more we safeguard against writing sports fans off as mere dupes in front of capitalist ideology; and the better prepared we become to contribute to sport's struggles, and to expose all its contradictions, whether they take place on the pitch, in the stands or in the boardroom. As the American radical sports writer Dave Zirin has argued:

> I think a big problem is that often the left in general is so dismissive of sports as an avenue of struggle that the effort isn't made to try and articulate what these sporting events actually represent – an opportunity for corporations and governments to carry out their neo-liberal agendas even more aggressively.[26]

Dave Zirin here raises an important point: the commercialisation and commodification of sport is far from being inevitable. Rather, sport is a contested cultural space.[27] Throughout 2012, politicians constructed narratives around Team GB's sporting endeavours in order to score political points. Across all the major sports fans battle multinational capitalism for real or symbolic ownership of their clubs and game. Players can and do take industrial action. An effective, popular left should not be absent from these struggles; instead we should be at the heart of each and every one of them.

NOTES

1. Tom Fordyce, 'Modern pentathlete Mhairi Spence: Olympic Failure Destroyed Me', 25 January 2013: www.bbc.co.uk/sport.
2. Mike Marqusee, 'A Critical Perspective on the Olympic Enterprise', 10 August 2012: www.redpepper.org.uk.
3. In the 1980s and 1990s the IOC consciously harnessed the rituals and symbols of Olympism in order to cultivate a strong brand known the world over. For a surprisingly honest appraisal of this period see Chapter 5 of Michael Payne' *Olympic Turnaround*, Business Press 2005. Payne was the marketing guru at the centre of this process, and oversaw the marketing of 15 separate Winter and Summer Olympic Games.
4. Jules Boykoff, 'Anti Olympics', *New Left Review*, 67, 2011.
5. One World Trust, *Global Accountability Report 2008*.
6. Gareth Edwards, 'Faster, Higher, Stronger: A Critical Analysis of the Olympics', *Irish Marxist Review*, 2012, p73.
7. The exceptions include CLR James, *Beyond a Boundary*, Duke University Press 1983; Mike Marqusee, *Anyone But England: Cricket and the National Malaise*, Verso 1994; Dave Zirin, *Welcome to the Terrordome: The Pain, Politics and Promise of Sports*, Haymarket Books 2007.
8. See Theodor Adorno, 'Education after Auschwitz', in Rolf Tiedemann (ed), *Can One Live After Auschwitz: A Philosophical Reader*, Stanford University Press 2003.

9. Jean-Marie Brohm, *Sport, A Prison of Measure Time*, Ink Links 1978, p121.

10. See Paul Hoch, *Rip Off the Big Game: The Exploitation of Sports by the Power Elite*, Anchor Books 1972; Vyv Simson & Andrew Jennings, *The Lord of the Rings: Power, Money and Drugs in the Modern Olympics*, Simon & Schuster 1992; David Yallop, *How They Stole the Game*, Poetic Publishing 1999.

11. See Bero Rigauer, *Sport and Work*, Columbia University Press 1981.

12. John Hargreaves, *Sport, Power and Ideology*, Routledge 1982, p41.

13 Jean-Marie Brohm, *Sport, A Prison of Measure Time*, Ink Links 1978, London, p69. I can assure readers that my participation in sport most certainly cannot be characterised by the 'principle of maximum output'.

14. Derek Birley, *Sport and the Making of the British*, Manchester University Press 1993, p340. I agree with his conclusion that sport 'is essentially a conservative influence', even if I dispute his reasoning.

15. Marc Perelman, *Brutal Sport: A Global Plague,* Verso 2012.

16. Ibid, pp39, 69.

17. See Arnd Kruger and Jim Riordan (eds), *The Story of Worker Sport*, Human Kinetics 1996.

18. Allen Guttmann, *From Ritual to Record: The Nature of Modern Sports*, Columbia University Press 1978, pp6-9.

19. Jean-Marie Brohm, op cit, p41.

20. Quoted in Jim Riordan, 'Worker Sport Within a Worker State: The Soviet Union', in Arnd Kruger & Jim Riordan, op cit, p57.

21. Karl Marx, *Capital Volume 1*, Penguin Books 1990, p131.

22. Karl Marx, *Economic and Philosophic Manuscripts of 1844*, Lawrence & Wishart 1977, pp65-66.

23. Richard Gruneau, *Class, Sports and Structural Development*, University of Massachusetts Press 1983, p34.

24. Mark Perryman, *Why The Olympics Aren't Good For Us, And How They Can Be*, OR Books, London 2012, p131.

25. Gideon Haigh, *Sphere of Influence: Writings on Cricket and its Discontents*, Simon & Schuster 2010, p372.

26. Dave Zirin and Gareth Edwards, 'Resistance: The Best Olympic Spirit', in *International Socialism Journal*, Vol 135, 2012, p90.

27. See Pierre Bourdieu, 'Sport and Social Class', in *Social Science Information*, 17(6), 1978, pp819-40.

OF SPECTACLE AND SPECIES

Bob Gilbert

It is not often that I find my thoughts turning to the Crimean War –
even though my children would have you believe that I fought in it.
Nonetheless, it was a famous quote from the Crimean War that came
to mind when I visited the Olympic site at the height of the Games.
'It's magnificent', General Pierre Bosquet had said (albeit in French),
whilst observing the mad gallantry of the charge of the Light Brigade.
'But it isn't war'. There in the park, surrounding the scattered stadiums,
were the acres of lawns and ponds and planting, the yellow-blossomed
'ribbon of gold', the great swathes of flowers, and the clever conjuring
that had persuaded them to all to come into bloom at the same time.
It was a remarkable horticultural achievement. The greening of the
250-hectare Olympic site had included the planting of 4000 trees and
150,000 perennials. It had involved the introduction of 300,000
wetland plants and the creation of 15,000 square metres of lawn. An
area the size of ten football pitches had been sown as 'wild' flower
meadows. It was undoubtedly magnificent. And yet, and yet. Was it
really what it was supposed to be?

This, remember, was to be the greenest Olympics ever. And
so, the horticulturalists said, the planting would provide not just
'an outstanding aesthetic experience', it would also be 'driven by
biodiversity and sustainability objectives'. Alongside those ubiquitous
recycling bins there would be bird boxes, bat boxes and 'created
habitats'. The Olympic press releases held out a vision of a reed
warbler 'singing from her nest' in the shadow of the stadium. It
seemed almost churlish of Peter Marren to point out in his column
in *British Wildlife* that no self-respecting female warbler would sing
from its nest, either here or anywhere else: if it did it would attract
predators from far and wide.

The planting schemes designed to achieve these objectives were in
a style described as naturalistic. Gardening, like every other aspect

of life, is governed by fashion, and the regimented precision of the once beloved bedding display, even the 3D sculpting of the carefully structured herbaceous border, are now virtually things of the past – as is the generation of gardeners that was trained to tend them. Instead we have the more informal approach; plantings or sowings in drifts or swathes, massed groupings, perhaps intermixed with grass, which bear at least a superficial resemblance to our lost floristic meadows. So while on the one hand they represent the height of horticultural modernity, they are also a nostalgic look back to a lost agricultural past. Rather like parts of the opening ceremony in fact. It is as valid as any other approach to gardening, and more attractive than many, but while it may be described as 'naturalistic', this should certainly not be confused with being natural. Though it may be described as 'wildlife gardening', one thing it certainly isn't is 'wild'. So how valid are those breathless claims of enhanced biodiversity? They depend in no little measure on how we understand what was actually there before the Olympics came.

AGAINST THE TIDE

Without wanting to become too anthropomorphic, there seem to be some interesting parallels between what happened to the human communities of the old Stratford Marsh and what became of the existing natural habitats. This was a group of people, and a location, that was persistently portrayed as virtually worthless. As Ken Worpole, writing in *Spaces*, the newsletter of the Hackney Society, pointed out, there was a 'frequent misrepresentation of the (Olympic) site and the people who lived and worked there as being in a state of near derelic-tion'. Here was a vibrant and anarchic area of depots, warehouses, car workshops and breakers yards; of small enterprises, community endeavours and allotments. But to justify the suspension of routine planning policies, the huge scale of the compulsory purchase orders, the wholesale displacement of personal livelihoods and the removal of a whole community, the area was increasingly described as a sort of post-apocalyptic wasteland – a suitable setting for a zombie film. Unsurprisingly, the same sort of judgements were applied to the natural value of the site. It was nothing but a toxic and sterile waste-land of stinking mud, burning tyres and abandoned supermarket trolleys. Could this really be the same place as I had walked and written about in the 1990s, with its 'factory yards covered with a thick growth of shrubs and wild flowers; campions, melilots, spurges, toad-flax, bird-sown sunflowers and three different types of rose'; the same place where I had found angelica on old lock gates, a pheasant strolling across an urban allotment, a skylark singing in the shadow of electricity pylons and sandpipers in flight up the Bow Back Rivers?

To be precise about it, this part of the Lea valley already contained two valuable natural habitats of its own, both of which had to be obliterated to enable the Olympic 'vision' to be realised. The first and oldest of them was formed by the tidal nature of the river itself. Here, just a few miles from its confluence with the Thames, the River Lea fans out into a complicated network of channels, criss-crossing the broad shallow valley of the Stratford marshlands. For most of their history the channels were tidal, and for at least 900 years they served dozens of tidal mills, two of which still survive just south of the main site. It is a general rule in ecology that the margins between habitats support the greatest biodiversity; that the edges of a wood, for example, are ecologically richer than its centre. Tidal estuaries, the shifting, uneasy edges between land and water, the covering and uncovering of mud banks, the mixing of river and sea, are one of the great illustrations of this fact. The daily revealed – and often reviled – tidal banks support a wealth of burrowing worms and molluscs and other invertebrate life, which in turn provide food for visiting birds. The rising and falling channels, carrying their varying mix of fresh and salt waters, support a distinctive fish community of their own, fed on by the herons that stand seemingly frozen on their edges, or by the increasing numbers of London cormorants. All this was to change in 2009, however, with the start of the construction of the Olympic Park. The main channel was dammed just above Three Mills, whilst on the nearby Prescott Channel the little wooden Prescott Lock was replaced by a massive new concrete construction to contain and regulate the river's flow. From that moment, the upstream Lea ceased to be tidal.

The stated purpose of this ugly piece of engineering, unsoftened by its new name of the Three Mills Lock, was to admit the massive barges that would carry construction materials to and from the Olympic site. For this was part of another of the major claims for the sustainable Olympics – a switch to water-borne transport: barges would carry 250,000 tonnes of construction materials, and 25 per cent of all the aggregates, onto the site, and transport the excavated and polluted soil away from it again. Such at least was the stated plan, but the first heavy barges grounded as soon as they cleared the lock, and suddenly the money for the additional dredging became unavailable. The anticipated 12,000 tonnes a week dwindled to an overall total of 1000 in six months. But it wasn't just the barges that couldn't get up the river; it was also the fish. Despite the fact that the new lock had been helpfully fitted with a 'fish gate', the newsletter of the *London Natural History Society* reported that early surveying was already showing a decline in estuarine fish species. And what was replacing them? Take a walk along the Olympic riverside today and you will very probably catch sight of the massive bulk of a crucian or mirror carp; exotic, introduced, 'leisure' species, which will pretty much do away with any other form of wildlife that cares to hang on in the waterway.

If it wasn't contributing to sustainable transport or to biodiversity, just what was the purpose of that new £21.5 million lock on the Bow Back Rivers? Local people were never in any doubt. It was to impound the river, to conceal the unsightly banks, to create a static pool of 'clean' and permanent water that would add millions to the value of adjacent properties and enable the creation of upmarket marinas. And that, of course, is just what has happened. Since the area already supported up to 200 resident boat owners, the creation of more, and better serviced, permanent moorings could have provided a local benefit – were it not for the fact that the cost of those moorings rose from £600 to £7000 a year. The boat people regarded it as social cleansing; or, as Sally Ash, Head of Boating at what was then British Waterways, helpfully told *The Guardian*, 'we have to send the message that in future, living on the river will not be such a cheap lifestyle option'.

BULLDOZING THE BROWNFIELD

If tidal estuaries are routinely underestimated as a natural resource, how much more can this be said for that other classic Stratford habitat, the brownfield site? Brownfield is the new term for the backland, the urban wasteland, the abandoned industrial site. It is hardly less pejorative, but in environmental circles at least there is an increasing recognition that such sites constitute a unique, and threatened, habitat type of their own, and one with an extraordinary richness. The irony is that this is happening at the same time as the more valued 'greenfield' sites are becoming chemically-drenched ecological deserts. The unused, or underused, urban spaces, the weedy factory yards, the railway embankments, the walls and edges, can, by contrast, become an unrestrained riot of species, of goat's rue, common and purple toadflax, white and yellow melilot, lucerne, tansy and the everlasting pea. They can be dynamic and evolving natural systems, and ones which, according to an *English Nature* report, support some 15 per cent of all our scarcest insect species – as well as the black redstart, one of our rarest birds. The brownfield sites of the Stratford Marsh even had their own speciality – the danewort, a species otherwise scarce in London, but which seemed to love it here. Danewort is a relative of the elder, but, unlike its larger woody relative, it is herbaceous, dying back each winter to produce a new crop of its tall leafy spikes in the spring. It is sometimes a relic of mediaeval herbal usage, and it may even have had a connection with the ancient abbey of Stratford Langthorne that once stood here, on the river's east bank. According to English legend, it sprang up from the blood of slaughtered Danes as they were driven back by King Alfred, but there is a different, and more likely, explanation for the name. The danewort bears profuse, but poisonous, black berries. A dose of them induces severe diarrhoea or, to use the old name for it, of the 'danes'. It seems appropriate that such a plant once grew abundantly on the embankments of the North London sewage system that bisects the Olympic site.

In reality, the attempt to argue the ecological value of a brownfield site, or the suggestion that we could tailor design to enhance not eliminate such sites, has never made much mileage – not even in the world of nature conservation. I have several times been involved in successful campaigns to save urban sites, only to see them subsequently bulldozed by conservationists so that they can 'create' a nature reserve: a managed site with planted trees, butyl-lined ponds and sown meadows, replacing the unrestrained naturalness of what was there already. A space for 'wildness' is OK, it seems, as long as there is nothing really wild about it. Nature clearly needs careful human management, and the real mystery is how it has survived for several million years without an organising committee.

THE LOSS OF THE LOCAL

If the claim that the Olympic site represents the enhancement of biodiversity requires examination, so too does the suggestion that these new planting schemes are genuinely sustainable. They were not, of course, created by a couple of wandering farm workers in smocks, scattering seed from a wicker basket. They were the result of intensive management, plant plugs brought on in nurseries and then transferred to the site, seed mixes carefully sourced and calibrated, a highly managed watering regime, and even a 'Chelsea cut'. This is the practice, developed by exhibitors at the Chelsea Flower Show, of cutting off the tops of plants at an earlier stage of growth in order to delay their flowering for a previously determined date. Just as with the Chelsea Flower Show, what we were seeing here was an exhibit, and a very successful one. But what we saw is not what we will get. Is there really any possibility that the new park site will have this level of expensive and labour-intensive site maintenance on a permanent basis? Scattered everywhere across the country are parks that have benefited from previous capital injections, with millions spent on makeovers and upgrades and improved infrastructure, but which then lack the year-on-year funding – or the skilled workforce – necessary to maintain the improvement, and so simply slide back into a cycle of decline.

I am aware of the danger that my arguments can be read as a defence for doing nothing; a plea for appreciating the aesthetics of dereliction or a suggestion that we should, so to speak, let dying dogs sleep. But it is not. It is the suggestion, instead, that for human communities and natural habitats alike, real regeneration can only begin from an appreciation of what is already there – and then by building on it, not building over it. How else can we have renewal that is not complete replacement, or enhancement that does not entail elimination? The bulldozing of the danewort, in order to allow for a managed scheme of 'biodiversity', becomes a sort of icon for both the natural and the human communities that were, and continue to be, displaced in Stratford and its environs. As affordable local dwellings disappear under the family-unfriendly tower blocks and the high-rise professional apartments, as high-priced marinas and luxury waterside dwellings proliferate, both local communities and the genuinely 'wild' are driven increasingly to the margins. Whilst the grand vision of the Olympics was of a global spectacle bestowing local benefits, what it actually brought was the same model of globalisation as we have seen in the market place, the standardisation – and the sterilisation – of locality, where the site is the spectacle and where the new forms arising

– both physical and natural – are the same as in any other similar city in the world.

In Stratford, and elsewhere, we are witnessing the loss of the local and, in ecological terms, this cannot help but represent a decline in diversity. And this matters, for a declining biodiversity – now continuing globally at an alarming rate – represents a rapid reduction in the strength and resilience of the natural system as a whole; a system on which, however much we try to deny it, we ultimately depend. There was, it turned out, a little more to General Bosquet's Crimean quote than I had remembered; a few more words I came across only after I had researched it for this essay. 'C'est magnifique, mais ce n'est pas la guerre', he had said – and then added 'c'est de la folie'.

OLYMPIAN READING
AND RESOURCES

Books and films, websites, blogs, twitter feeds and campaigns to help inform an understanding of the politics of sport

For an introduction read the 2008 updated edition of Garry Whannel's *Blowing The Whistle: Culture, Politics and Sport*; and, for a variety of viewpoints from the left, *Marxism, Cultural Studies and Sport*, edited by Ben Carrington and Ian McDonald. A more journalistic approach is provided by *The Meaning of Sport*, by Simon Barnes, or Ed Smith's *What Sport Tells Us About Life*.

The best critical writer on sport I've come across is Dave Zirin; his latest book is *Game Over: How Politics Has Turned The Sports World Upside Down*. Dave also has an excellent website: www.edgeofsports.com.

To keep updated on the latest academic research into sport follow the University of Brighton Centre for Sport Research twitter feed: @sport_research.

The Olympic Studies Centre at the Autonomous University of Barcelona provides excellent materials on past, present and future Games: http://olympicstudies.uab.es.

On London 2012 two books were published ahead of the Games which are both well worth a read. My own *Why The Olympics Aren't Good For Us And How They Can Be*, and a collection of essays edited by Alan Tomlinson and John Sugden, *Watching The Olympics: Politics, Power and Representation*. The inside story on London's bid is provided by Mike Lee's *The Race for the Olympics*.

Martin Polley's *The British Olympics 1612-2012* provides an invaluable historical dimension on the British Olympic tradition, all the way back to the Much Wenlock Games. *The First London Olympics,* by Rebecca Jenkins, is a fascinating account of the 1908 Games, while on the 1948 London Games, Janie Hampton's *The Austerity Olympics* is superb. To explore the parallels between the 1948 and 2012 Games, read Matt and Martin Rogan's *Britain and the Olympic Games: Past, Present and Legacy*. A very good history of the modern Olympic movement is *The Olympic Games Explained* by Vassil Girginov. *National Identity and Global Sports Events: Culture, Politics and Spectacle in the Olympics and the Football World Cup*, edited by Alan Tomlinson and Christopher Young, provides a range of case studies, including chapters on a number of previous summer Olympics. Christopher Young, with co-writer Kay Schiller, also provides a superlative example of how an academic account of an Olympic Games can provide a richness of detail and insight yet at the same time be highly readable. Their book, *The 1972 Munich Olympics and the Making of Modern Germany*, of course covers the Israeli athletes' hostage-taking, but also much else besides. On the current and future state of the Olympic Movement read *Post-Olympism: Questioning Sport in the Twenty-First Century*, edited by John Bale and Mette Krogh Christensen.

A huge variety of scholarly research was published in the build-up to London 2012 – and continues to be published. One source for these is the Routledge Online Studies on the Olympic and Paralympic Games (ROSO), see www.routledgeonlinestudies.com.

The website www.gamesmonitor.org.uk provides a rich resource of material relevant to the social and economic impact of London 2012.

Race, Sport and Politics: The Sporting Black Diaspora, by Ben Carrington, locates sport's role in the formation of nations and identities. The story of the 1968 Olympics Black Power protest remains one of the most epic moments in the history of resistance through sport, and it is retold by one of the participants, John Carlos, in *The John Carlos Story*.

An insight into how the 2016 Games is affecting local communities in Rio is provided by the website www.rioonwatch.org. A superb critical account of the 2012 Games' impact on East London is provided by Phil Cohen's *Wrong Side of the Tracks? East London and the Post Olympics*, written, like this book, in the twelve months following the Games.

The film *Murderball* is a quite extraordinary documentary about the Paralympic sport of wheelchair rugby. P. David Howe's *The Cultural Politics of the Paralympic Movement: Through the Anthropological Lens* is the definitive text on Paralympism.

Track and road cycling has been one of the success stories of British sport in recent years. Two books by Richard Moore, *Heroes, Villains and Velodromes* plus *Sky's The Limit* go a long way towards chronicling the reasons why. The autobiographies of Victoria Pendleton – *Between The Lines* – and Bradley Wiggins – *My Time* – are far, far better than the tell-nothing ghosted versions usually produced. For a grassroots view of what the sport of cycling means to enthusiastic club cyclists, Matt Seaton's *The Escape Artist* is a hugely enjoyable read. For the more leisurely commuter or recreational side of cycling read Bella Bathurst's *The Bicycle Book* or *Cyclebabble*, edited by James Randerson and Peter Walker. For current or aspiring cyclists, online follow the Bike Blog at www.guardian.co.uk.

David Renton's *Lives; Running* is both an excellent insight into why we run and a sharply argued dissection of the Coe-Ovett years of Team GB dominating the 800 metres and 1500 metres. *Running With The Pack* by Mark Rowlands is a philosophical explanation of the intrinsic appeal of running, while Alexandra Heminsley's *Running Like a Girl* puts the case for why running appeals to women. Adharanand Finn's *Running With The Kenyans* seeks to explain Kenya's rise as an athletics superpower. *Running: A Global History*, by Thor Gotaas, is an account of the sport's social construction. For those who believe the best running is free, and wild, read Boff Whalley's *Running Wild* and Richard Askwith's *Feet in the Clouds*. Online the *Guardian* again provides an excellent blog, this time for current or aspiring runners, the Running Blog at wwww.guardian.co.uk.

There are some very good running films. *Chariots of Fire* is the best known of course, but also check out *Without Limits*, and *The Jericho Mile*.

An excellent resource for films and other visual material from the Olympic Games see the IOC's Official Olympic Channel: www.youtube.com/user/olympic.

Not many novels have an Olympics theme. One which was inspired by London 2012 is Chris Cleave's *Gold*, built around track cycling.

Academic studies of the consumption of sport include Garry Crawford's *Consuming Sport: Fans, Sport and Culture*. In *Fans: The Mirror of Consumption*, Cornell Sandvoss looks at the diverse ways in which we become constructed as fans, including sport.

For an understanding of how gender impacts on the representation, practices and consumption of sport visit the excellent website of the Women's Sport and Fitness Foundation: www.wsff.org.uk. A very good source of reports on issues around access and equality in sport is the website www.playthegame.org. Mike Weed, Director of the Centre for Sport, Physical Education and Activity Research, has a very good blog providing invaluable information on participation and other post-legacy issues, see www.profmikeweed.wordpress.com.

Pre-1989 vintage but of considerable interest for those seeking alternative models to organise sport, Jim Riordan's *Sport Under Communism* remains a classic. For a more cultural studies approach to the function of sport read Andrew Blake's *Body Language*. A newly published collection edited by Michael Lavalette, *Capitalism and Sport: Politics, Protest, People and Play*, explores the actuality and potential of sport from a left-wing point of view.

Bob Gilbert's *Green London Way* includes a walk around the Olympic Park and through the Olympic boroughs too. Bob also has a website, see www.greenlondonway.com. *The Stadium* by Tim Abrahams is a very well written critique of the Olympic Stadium, its function, purpose and design. *The Art of Dissent: Adventures in London's Olympic State*, edited by Hilary Powell and Isaac Marrero-Guillamon, is both hugely radical and beautifully written, detailing how the Olympic Park changed an existing lived environment, and not, as always assumed, necessarily for the better. China Mieville provides a superbly written dystopian account of 2012-era London in *London's Overthrow*.

Anna Minton's *Ground Control: Fear And Happiness in the Twenty-First Century City* has an excellent opening chapter on the Olympic Park and the spurious claims of socio-economic regeneration, while the rest of the book is an extremely useful insight into the ways in which modern urban living is being transformed, for the worse, by corporate power. Other good reads which help us to understand the broader context in which London 2012 took place and the aftermath of its failed legacy I would recommend include Eliane Glaser's *Get*

Real: How to See through the Hype, Spin and Lies of Modern Life; Andrew Simms *Cancel The Apocalypse: The New Path to Prosperity*; and, from Stephen Graham, *Cities Under Siege: The New Military Urbanism*.

London 2012 How Was It For Us consists of a variety of viewpoints and experiences framed by the Olympics. It doesn't claim to be a social history of that glorious summer of sport. That is a book that is still to be written, and indeed should be written. The best book I have ever read on any Games is *Rome 1960* by David Maraniss. As an author he captures not simply the sporting action of an Olympics but the ways in which 1960 was shaped by the beginnings of both the Cold War and the Civil Rights Movement in the USA. If anybody takes on the task of writing something similar for London 2012, combining the sport with the social, economic, cultural and political context, and reaches the standard of engagingly imaginative writing David Maraniss has set with his superb book, that will certainly be something worth reading.

NOTES ON CONTRIBUTORS

Mark Perryman is the author of *Why The Olympics Aren't Good For Us And How They Can Be*. A regular media commentator on the politics of the Games throughout London 2012, Mark is a Research Fellow in Sport and Leisure Culture at the University of Brighton. Prior to the Olympics Mark wrote primarily about football, Englishness and national identity including *Ingerland: Travels With A Football Nation*, and, more recently, on England and the break-up of Britain, including *Imagined Nation: England after Britain*, and *Breaking Up Britain: Four Nations after a Union*. A former competitive road runner he is now a 50 plus-mile-a-week long-distance runner who runs for pleasure not to race. In 1994 Mark co-founded the self-styled 'sporting outfitters of intellectual distinction', aka Philosophy Football. Keep updated with Mark's writings on sport via the University of Brighton Centre for Sport Research twitter feed **@sport_research**.

Billy Bragg is a singer-songwriter and political activist. His latest album is *Tooth & Nail*. Apart from his music Billy is also the author of the book *The Progressive Patriot: A Search For Belonging*. Billy blogs at www.billybragg.co.uk and can be followed on twitter **@billybragg**.

Alan Tomlinson is Professor of Leisure Studies at the University of Brighton. In 1984, ahead of the Los Angeles Games, he co-edited one of the first critiques of the Olympic Movement, *Five Ring Circus*. 28 years later, ahead of London 2012, he co-edited with John Sugden *Watching The Olympics: Politics, Power and Representation*. Alan is recognised as one of the world's leading academic experts on Olympism.

Eliane Glaser writes about polemic, ideology, vested interests and hidden agendas for the *Guardian* and other publications, including the *London Review of Books*. The author of *Get Real: How to See Through the Hype, Spin and Lies of Modern Life*, Eliane is also a radio producer, and Associate Research Fellow at Birkbeck, University of London. She can be followed on twitter **@elianeglaser**.

Kate Hughes has worked in sport for over 30 years, including playing golf for England at international level. In 2011 Kate was awarded a Graduate Fellowship at the Australian Olympic Centre, University of Technology, Sydney. Kate helped develop Podium – the Further and Higher Education Unit for the London 2012 Games. In 2013, after completing her PhD at Leeds Metropolitan University on Sport, Mega Events and Participation, she set up a Community Interest Company to help disadvantaged young people access sport and physical activity.

Yasmin Alibhai-Brown writes a weekly column for the *Independent* as well as being a regular commentator on a wide variety of radio and television programmes. The author of *Who Do We Think We Are: Imagining the New Britain*, Yasmin has also written reports on multiculturalism, race and national identity for a range of think-tanks, including the Institute for Public Policy Research and the Foreign Policy Centre. Yasmin's writings and updates can be found at her website: www.alibhai-brown.com.

Andrew Simms has been described by *New Scientist* magazine as 'a master at joined-up progressive thinking'. An architect of the Green New Deal, he invented the term 'Clone Towns' to describe what is happening to Britain's High Streets, and, with his best selling book *Tescopoly*, was one of the first to expose the pernicious influence of the big supermarkets. Andrew's latest book is *Cancel The Apocalypse: The New Path To Prosperity*. A Fellow at the New Economics Foundation, Andrew can be followed on twitter **@AndrewSimms_UK**.

Ben Carrington teaches sociology at the University of Texas at Austin and is a Carnegie Research Fellow at Leeds Metropolitan University. Ben's most recent book is *Race, Sport and Politics: The Sporting Black Diaspora*. He is also the co-editor of the collections *Marxism, Cultural Studies and Sport* and *'Race', Sport and British Society*. Ben is widely regarded as one the world's leading scholars on the sociology of race, especially in relation to sports culture. Ben can be followed on twitter **@BenHCarrington**.

Gavin Poynter chairs the London East Research Institute as well as being Professor in Social Sciences at the University of East London. He has published widely on urban regeneration in East London. His most recent book, edited with Iain MacRury and Andrew Calcutt, is *London After Recession: A Fictitious Capital*. Gavin also edited with Iain MacRury *Olympic Cities, 2012 and the Remaking of London*.

Mark Steel is a stand-up comedian, writer and political activist. He writes a weekly column for the *Independent* and presents an award-winning Radio 4 series 'Mark Steel's In Town'. The author of a number of painfully honest yet richly amusing political memoirs, including *Reasons to be Cheerful* and *What's Going On?*, Mark's twitter feed reveals a parallel life as a sports obsessive, follow Mark **@mrmarksteel**.

P. David Howe represented Canada at four Paralympics, including winning a Bronze Medal at the 1988 Games in the 5000 metres and a Silver Medal at the same event in the 1992 Games. Senior Lecturer in the Anthropology of Sport in the School of Sport, Exercise and Health Sciences at Loughborough University, he is currently also the Vice President of the International Federation of Adapted Physical Activity (IFAPA). David is author of *The Cultural Politics of the Paralympic Movement*.

Zoe Williams writes features, a column and comment pieces for the *Guardian*, as well as being the restaurant reviewer for the *Sunday Telegraph* Stella magazine. In between she is to be seen about London riding a bicycle ducking and diving her way through the capital's notorious traffic. Follow Zoe on twitter **@zoesqwilliams**.

David Renton is the author of a sporting memoir *Lives; Running*, as well as books on subjects as diverse as a history of the Anti-Nazi League, CLR James, and Employment Law. Now working as a barrister, he has previously been an academic historian in the UK and South Africa. Between the ages of 13 and 18 David was a county standard schoolboy middle distance runner, recording a time of 1.59 for the 800 metres when aged just 16. David's blog is at www.livesrunning.wordpress.com and he can be followed on twitter **@dkrenton**.

Suzanne Moore writes a weekly column for the *Guardian*. She has previously written for the *Mail on Sunday*, the *New Statesman* and *Marxism Today*. After having lived in the Olympic borough of Hackney for 20 years, at the 2010 General Election she contested the Stoke Newington and Hackney North seat as an independent candidate. Follow Suzanne on twitter **@suzanne_moore**.

Barbara Bell is a Senior Lecturer in Sport Development at Manchester Metropolitan University. Her research has focused on youth sport and sport development, and more recently on women's and girl's football, sports events and their participation outcomes. As a member of the Institute for Performance Research at Manchester Metropolitan University, Barbara is currently contributing to various strands of Olympic legacy related research concerned with the 'soft legacy', including youth and school sport, community sports clubs, and pre-Games Training Camps and their social capital.

Anne Coddington is Senior Lecturer in Sport Journalism at the London College of Communications, University of the Arts London. She is the author of *One of the Lads: Women Who Follow Football*. Her critical approach to sport culture builds on a background in political journalism, including as editor of the *New Times* newspaper and deputy editor of *Marxism Today*.

Gareth Edwards writes on the politics of sport for a range of publications including the *International Socialism Journal* and the *Irish Marxist Review*. He also contributes to the sports websites *Some People on the Pitch* and *Left Hook*. Gareth's own blog is www.inside-left.blogspot.co.uk and he can followed on twitter at **@potski1917**.

Bob Gilbert has enjoyed a varied career, from three years as a stand-up comedian to Director of Sustainability at a London local authority. He is also a long-standing campaigner for the protection of urban open spaces and for public access. Bob's most recent book, *The Green London Way*, is a 110-mile walking route encircling the Capital to explore the city's wildlife and history.

INDEX